Like Clockwork

Like Clockwork

Run Your Business with Swiss Army Precision

Sam Goodner

LIONCREST
PUBLISHING

LIKE CLOCKWORK
Run Your Business with Swiss Army Precision

FIRST EDITION

ISBN	978-1-5445-4861-6	*Hardcover*
	978-1-5445-4860-9	*Paperback*
	978-1-5445-4859-3	*Ebook*

To my two amazing children, Sam Jackson and Catherine

Contents

"*Imagine that you met a remarkable person who could look at the sun or the stars and, amazingly, state the exact time and date. Wouldn't it be even more amazing still if, instead of telling the time, that person built a clock that could tell the time forever, even after he or she were dead and gone?*

Having a great idea or being a charismatic visionary leader is 'time telling'; building a company that can prosper far beyond the tenure of any single leader and through multiple product life cycles is 'clock building.' Those who build visionary companies tend to be clock builders. Their primary accomplishment is not the implementation of a great idea, the expression of a charismatic personality, or the accumulation of wealth. It is the company itself and what it stands for."

—JIM COLLINS, *BUILT TO LAST*

"*You do not rise to the level of your goals. You fall to the level of your systems.*"

—JAMES CLEAR, *ATOMIC HABITS*

Introduction

When people find out I served as an officer in the Swiss Army, they always ask me two questions:

"Did they give you a Swiss Army knife?" (Yes, although it's not the same one you buy in shops.)

And, "Wait a minute, I thought Switzerland was neutral. Why do they even need an army?"

That requires a more complicated answer.

You see, neutrality does not mean defenselessness—at least not to the Swiss. Switzerland has long been considered the "crossroads of Europe." Despite being known primarily for beautiful Alpine views, delicious chocolate, and luxury timepieces, its position in Europe is surprisingly strategic. Geographically, the country falls smack in the middle of the two primary axes running through the continent. If a belligerent force wants to go north-south or east-west, the fastest route is through Switzerland. For centuries, everyone has wanted to control those strategic crossroads, and for centuries we Swiss have focused on making that very difficult for them.

Long ago, Switzerland learned that being neutral on paper means nothing. Of the five countries that declared neutrality in World War

II, for example, four were invaded. The only one that avoided this fate was the one that mobilized four hundred thousand soldiers along its border—the same country ready and able to blow up all its infrastructure should anyone think to cross into its territory.

Essentially, Switzerland is neutral in the same way a porcupine is harmless. It has no interest in attacking anyone, but just try and eat one.

Now, here's the thing about a country maniacally focused on executing at an elite level for its very survival: there's a lot you can learn from that approach. Whether it's how you train people to perform, how you organize your operations so everyone knows what's expected of them, or how you share the necessary intelligence in real time to enable decision-making, the Swiss military has a lot to teach entrepreneurs and business leaders.

In fact, I've come to realize that most of the lessons I've learned in business I initially encountered during my time as a special forces officer in the Swiss Army. Those same lessons can allow you to execute in your own business, whatever your industry.

SWISS AMERICAN

Perhaps I've been able to see these lessons so clearly because I've always been a bit of an outsider. I grew up in Switzerland. I served in the Swiss military. But I was born in Houston, Texas—to two parents from Texas. When I was a year old, my parents moved our family to Europe. Two years later, my father started his own company, and my parents decided to raise their family in Switzerland. We moved to a small farming village just outside of Fribourg with a population of six hundred. Needless to say, throughout my entire childhood, my sister, Melanie, and I were the only American kids in the area. I grew up speaking English at home and French at school.

After graduating from high school and after a year training to be a Mountain Grenadier—the elite Swiss Army special forces—I went back across the Atlantic for college. Since I was born in Texas,

I applied to the three largest state universities and ended up at Texas A&M.

One of the great benefits of my time at A&M was the friendship I forged with David Jacobson. David and I enjoyed training for triathlons together and discussing our big plans to start a tech company someday. I didn't jump into entrepreneurship right after college, though. Instead, I finished my military training in Switzerland and then flew back to America, where I landed my first job at Service Systems International (SSI), a small software company in Kansas City. Incredibly, the company hired me so they could send me across the Atlantic *again*, this time to London to help open their European sales and support office.

David, in the meantime, had started working as a programmer at Lockheed Martin in Austin. We met up a year later and decided if we were ever going to start that business we always talked about in college, we needed to live in the same place.

Austin just seemed the better fit for a new tech company, so off I moved again, with my two duffle bags carrying all of my worldly possessions. I initially found a job as a software developer with Dell Computer Corporation. Eighteen months later, we launched Catapult Systems, an IT services firm. The year was 1993, and we had $17,000 in the bank—the sum total of our collective savings.

Using many of the very lessons in this book, we bootstrapped Catapult and, over the next twenty years, turned it into the number one Microsoft systems integrator in the world. In 1996, with the addition of our third founding partner, Jim Martin, we branched into software product development, creating Inquisite, the leading online survey tool at that time.

Eventually, Inquisite grew large enough that we spun it off into its own company. After successfully selling Catapult to a public company in 2013, I retired for the first time and traveled around the world for a year with my family. When I returned home to Austin, I started looking for another company to scale. I evaluated over one hundred startups, and eventually landed on FlashParking, a technology company in the parking industry. Over the next few years, we built the company up from twelve employees to an industry leader with over $100 million in revenue and a $1 billion valuation at our last round of funding.

SWISS PRECISION

Since then, I've stepped away again, enjoying my second temporary retirement. When I reflect back on my thirty-year career running three successful technology companies, I keep coming back to the same observation. Though I may not have realized it at the time, I first encountered almost every principle I used to run my businesses during my days in the Swiss military.

When it comes to executing a mission, the Swiss military understands all the principles to get it done. And it turns out, those are the same principles required to execute in a business.

Along the way, I've read hundreds of business books. I've read books on strategy, marketing, management, and sales. I've read inspirational and aspirational books that make you want to become a better leader. I've read books on innovation and customer experience, finance and corporate culture.

This book isn't like any of those.

The truth is, when I pick up a business book of any kind, I always look for one idea—just one executable idea—that I can walk away with and implement in my own business. So I decided to put as many practical, executable ideas as I possibly could in one place.

That's my natural wheelhouse anyway. Entrepreneurs and business leaders don't call me in to refine their strategy. They call me in to help them execute. I'm very Swiss in that way. Growing up in the land of great timepieces and extreme punctuality, I'm naturally good at building companies and machines that run efficiently without me at the helm every day.

My goal in this book is to share with you the principles I've learned across my two careers: as a Swiss Army officer and tech entrepreneur.

In each chapter, I'll tell you a story from my time in the Swiss Army with one principle at its heart. I'll then show you how each concept can be implemented in your business. Each chapter also contains a case study from another entrepreneur or CEO, showing how they implemented that same concept in their company.

While some of these principles may initially feel modest in scope, they build on one another, and their value compounds over time. Any one of these ideas may not radically transform your business overnight, but the more you implement and sustain them, the more profound the impact.

There's no need to read this book in order. While there's a loose organization to these chapters, the book is designed to allow you to jump in wherever and grab the lessons most relevant to you right now. To make it easier to dive in based on your current needs, I've included a reading guide in Appendix 4 outlining which chapters are most relevant for certain common business challenges.

Whether you read cover to cover or jump in as needed, you will gain the most from this book if your business is in the right place. This is a book for entrepreneurs who have done more than dream about running a company—they're doing it. They have a product or service, they have a team, and they have established there's value in their ideas. It's also for leaders who run a business unit—those who have the authority, courage, and motivation to take big swings and try new ideas.

Chapter 1

First Day

I will never forget my first day of basic training in the Swiss Army. I'd left my hometown of Fribourg very early in the morning, taking a six-hour train ride to Cadenazzo in canton Ticino in southern Switzerland. From Cadenazzo, I took a thirty-minute bus ride up the mountains to our military base in Isone.

For the traveling tourist, the trip would have been a pleasant one. All along the way were those famous mountains in the distance and beautiful ancient towns. On that day, though, I had no time to enjoy the scenery. I was nervous the entire way—and I wasn't alone. Everyone on the bus was coming from different parts of the country, all heading to the same destination. We all had that same look of anxiety and anticipation on our face. I don't think anyone said a single word on the ride.

It was a bus full of nineteen-year-old young men, and no one had any real idea what was ahead of us.

As our bus got closer to the base, we caught our first sight of what life would look like for the next five months. We could see hordes of young men running in formation and others doing push-ups and sit-ups. As soon as the bus stopped, a drill instructor jumped on board and started yelling. Every moment from then on was nonstop. In an instant, a whole team of instructors was getting our names, sending us off to various groups, and putting us into formation. There was no time to catch our breath. As soon as we were done with one task, we were on to the next. We filled out paperwork, we picked up our uniforms, and we ran to get equipment and helmets. No sooner did we have the new equipment in hand than we were whisked away to our barracks. No rest there either. Instead, we spent the time learning to make our beds the military way. All the time, we were being yelled at and put in formation.

That was just our initial introduction. The instructors at the camp were only getting started. Marching out of our barracks, we went to get a physical assessment. We did push-ups, pull-ups, sprints, and climbed poles. We ran up and down the side of a mountain—all in the clothes we arrived in. I was lucky enough to be wearing comfortable tennis shoes. Some of my fellow recruits were racing up the rocky incline in their best dress shoes.

In the midst of all this movement, it felt like chaos. Everyone seemed to be running in a different direction, heading for a different task. Yet, somehow, as evening began to descend, every new recruit was maneuvered into one giant parking lot at the same moment. In an amazing example of Swiss coordination, no sooner were we all in place than the base commander, Colonel Hess, walked over. Wearing a green beret with mirrored sunglasses and a cigar in his mouth, he looked like the very definition of a cool, tough military commander. He stood on a hill against the sunset, scanned his new set of raw recruits, and began welcoming us to special forces boot camp—in three languages.

I'll never forget his final message. "My wish for you," he shouted over the parking lot, "is that the next five months be the most difficult of your life—and in that process you find out who you really are."

It was a speech worthy of concluding a Hollywood training

montage, but the day still wasn't over. After Colonel Hess departed, we had more running to do, then chow time, and then still more running.

We ended the day cleaning our boots before finally getting the call for lights out at midnight.

It was a tough day, but one that left a powerful impression. In fact, I still feel that no day could have more effectively shown me where I was and what was expected of me. By the time I closed my eyes that night, I already felt like I was on my way to becoming a Mountain Grenadier.

FIRST DAY FAILURE

I remember everything about that first day—what the sun looked like as it set, the smells in the air, the taste of the food when I finally got to eat.

By contrast, I'm not even sure whether I'm recalling my first day at Dell Computer Corporation correctly now—after sitting down in an effort to fully remember it. The best I can reconfigure it, the day started when I walked up to the receptionist. In that bright, generic tone receptionists often employ, she asked, "Hi, how may I help you?"

I told her who I was and that it was my first day. For some reason, this perplexed her.

"Do you know who your manager is?" she asked.

I didn't. No one had shared that information with me yet.

"Hmm… Let me see what I can do."

She directed me to a chair where I sat for about thirty minutes. Eventually, someone came to find me. That person was not my manager. My manager, it turned out, wasn't there. HR wasn't even sure if I was supposed to be in that building. After some more waiting, someone else arrived and gave me a pile of paperwork. No one knew what to do with me, so once the paperwork was filled out, they sent me home.

That was my first impression of my new employer.

Dell might have done a particularly bad job in that case, but when it comes to first days, most companies are closer to Dell than the Mountain Grenadiers. First days are an afterthought, if they're thought of at all. That crucial first shift is used to fill out paperwork and maybe show someone where their desk will be. It's common for employees to be sent home early because there's nothing else for them to do.

The problem with this process is that most new employees—particularly young ones—are nervous, just as I had been on my way to Isone. They don't know what to expect. Have they made the right decision taking this job? Will they like the work and the team?

When a company isn't ready for them, that leaves a lasting impression. And this is the period when regret first settles in. It's the time when their former employer may call and ask, "Are you sure you wouldn't be happier coming back?"

In other words, first days can determine how well a new person starts in your company, how well they settle in, and whether they stick around or not. This new employee might someday turn out to be an all-star, but that first day could set them on course to leave your company as soon as they find a better opportunity.

CONSTRUCTING A GREAT FIRST DAY

At Catapult Systems, I was determined to avoid the mistakes I experienced at Dell. So I made sure we did the opposite of what I saw on my first day there. To begin with, we made it very clear that we were expecting our new team member. We printed out a big banner that said, "Welcome, John Smith" and hung it in the entryway. It was the first thing the new employee saw when they walked in. At the same time, the person at the front desk was always told who was starting and who their manager was. That way, the first person the new recruit spoke to knew who they were and what was supposed to happen next.

From that first moment on, we designed the day around keeping our new employee busy and engaged. Their manager would come right out and take them to their office, where they would spend the next hour explaining everything about the company and their position.

They would then show the new person around and informally introduce them to the team they'd be working with. At their desk, they'd find balloons and a laptop already configured for them, with their login password on a sticky note.

That quick tour concluded, their manager would take them out to lunch before sending them an email with all the paperwork they had to complete online. They'd be introduced formally at a team meeting to everyone, and crucially, they would receive their first assignment on that day. It's incredibly important to give people a sense of what work is going to look like on their first day—the same way the Swiss special forces gave a taste of basic training right up front. Even if it's nothing more than reviewing progress on a project they'll jump into later, they should have something to do.

That's not to say that everything was about getting right to work. We also celebrated their arrival at Catapult. Along with the banner, the balloons, and the free lunch, they'd also receive an office bag filled with a bunch of Catapult swag. The HR manager would later give them a link to a $150 credit to buy even more company merch. And for those new employees with family at home, we'd send a big tin can full of freshly baked cookies with the Catapult logo on it, as well as a personal note from their manager about how excited we were for their spouse to join us. Every note ended with an invitation to the next Catapult family event.

THE FIRST WEEK

We reinforced that positive first impression throughout the rest of the first week. Over that entire period, we made sure our new team member had no idle time. Our focus was on making them feel productive and part of the team—leaving no time to question their choice or feel any regret. By the end of their first week, they were fully integrated into the team and doing something of value.

That sense of place was further reinforced when I personally took them out to lunch later in the week. In their second week, the whole team would take them out to lunch all over again. It's impossible to overvalue the importance of breaking bread with someone. From ancient times, connections have been forged over a good meal. By the end of that second week, a new employee would have spent at least three meals building those new social bonds, making Catapult feel more like the place they really belonged.

KEY TAKEAWAYS

- New employees are nervous. Their first day can significantly impact their sense of belonging at your company. Ensuring a structured, welcoming first day helps new hires feel valued and integrated from the start.
- Keep new employees busy and engaged on their first day and week. When possible, assign them a real project immediately.
- Recognizing a new hire's arrival through a welcome banner, company swag, and family outreach creates a positive emotional connection with both the employee and their family. This helps the employee feel appreciated.
- Make sure you have all of your new employee's equipment and system access ready on day one.
- Have the new employee's manager take them out to lunch on their first day and have their entire team take them out to lunch later that week.

PRO TIPS

- Pair new hires with a "buddy" or mentor who can help them navigate their first few weeks. This adds an informal support system and accelerates their adjustment. We'll discuss mentorship further in Chapter 27.
- Before the new employee starts, brief the team about their role and background so they are ready to welcome and engage with the new hire more effectively.

- Send the new employee a checklist of what to expect before their first day. Include things like what they should bring, their first assignment, and a schedule for the day. We'll cover checklists in Chapter 11.
- Schedule a follow-up one-on-one meeting during the first month to address any questions, provide feedback, and ensure the new hire is settling in well.
- Other than taking the new employee out to eat, all of these recommendations can be implemented for remote workers just as easily as in-person employees.

CASE STUDY

Building a Positive First Impression at TicketCity

Randy Cohen, the founder of TicketCity, began his journey into the ticket-selling business while still in college at the University of Texas. In 1986, he took his life savings of $1,200 and bought tickets for a Texas vs. Arkansas game, reselling them at a profit after the game sold out. A few years later, he launched TicketCity full-time.

TicketCity specializes in selling tickets for sporting events, concerts, and theater performances worldwide, both through owned inventory and as a secondary ticket marketplace. From its inception, Randy recognized the importance of creating a company culture centered around fun and engagement, which he believed was crucial for retaining employees and maintaining high morale.

Understanding the significance of an employee's first day and first week, Randy implemented a unique and engaging onboarding process at TicketCity. New employees were welcomed with a confetti-filled party, creating an immediate sense of excitement and belonging. Upon arrival, new hires would run past their new colleagues, "high-fiving" everyone along the way like a star basketball player running onto the court.

This high-energy start was followed by pairing the new employee with different seasoned coworkers in two-day increments, whom they would shadow in order to learn the ropes of their new role. Thanks to this hands-on training, which started on day one, new hires quickly immersed themselves in the company's operations and culture.

Additionally, during their first week, employees met with every manager, including Randy himself, who would take them out to lunch to ensure they felt connected to leadership and understood the company's open-door policy. Randy took this opportunity to introduce them to his LAER model—Listen, Acknowledge, Explore, Respond—emphasizing the importance of effective communication in the office and with customers.

Randy's commitment to a strong onboarding experience had a profound impact on TicketCity's work environment. The emphasis on making a positive first impression not only helped new employees feel valued and motivated, it also reinforced the company's core values. By so effectively integrating new hires into the team, Randy successfully created a workplace where employees were eager to contribute and grow. TicketCity has maintained high morale and low turnover rates—with an average employee tenure of over twenty years.

Chapter 2

Boot Camp

DIFFICULTY: 3/5

I was a good athlete growing up. I played basketball through high school—perhaps not that surprising for a Swiss kid with American parents. As a teenager, you think your body can do anything. Then one morning, at the age of eighteen, mine couldn't. I woke up and couldn't move. I was in so much pain, my father had to carry me to the hospital. Once I got in front of a doctor, though, he was as confused as we were. Doctor after doctor—hospital after hospital—we went looking for an answer, but no one could figure out what was going on. In total, I spent ten days in the hospital and three months on crutches. The only thing that could relieve the pain was massive doses of aspirin.

Eventually, I was diagnosed with an autoimmune disease called ankylosing spondylitis. The doctors told me I'd be lucky to walk again, let alone run. That was the end of my basketball career. It was also supposed to be the end of my military career. After delivering the bad news, the medical team gave me the paperwork I'd need to explain to the Swiss military doctors why I couldn't join. Every other male my age would be going to basic training soon. I was apparently too sick.

I refused to accept that diagnosis. Going against the doctor's orders, I began training my body. Within months, I was walking again, then I was running. By nineteen, I felt ready to join the military. To prove to myself I'd overcome my illness, I signed up for the most rigorous branch of the Swiss Army, the Mountain Grenadiers special forces.

I felt if I could survive that boot camp, I could do anything. Basic training for the Swiss Mountain Grenadiers is about as intense as you can imagine. Like every other special forces division in the world, it is long and grueling. We train in everything you'd expect—hand-to-hand combat, survival skills, reconnaissance, demolition, and marksmanship—with an additional focus on fighting in the cold, snowy Alps. We develop elite rock-climbing skills, learn to rappel down a mountain with a rifle, and practice surviving in sub-zero temperatures. We ski and snowshoe; we learn to shoot at high altitude. We develop the skills to read the weather and forecast. We conduct patrols from the mountain peaks down to the villages below.

Over five months, my body and mind were tested and my skills enhanced. In the end, the Mountain Grenadier boot camp gave me exactly what I needed. It didn't just prove I could overcome my illness. It gave me a new sense of self: who I really was, what I was capable of, and where I belonged.

THE VALUE OF BOOT CAMP

When I entered the workforce, I found that most companies avoided initial training programs entirely. There were a few that offered extensive training for new graduates—like Andersen Consulting (now called Accenture), who were renowned for their three-month boot camp up in Chicago—but that was definitely the exception. It was so rare, Andersen could use it as a key part of their recruitment.

In my time, Dell very much followed the standard trend in the tech industry. The typical practice was to just throw you in. When I started working there—after that unimpressive first day I recounted in Chapter 1—I had no sense of the purpose behind my work. No one spelled out a bigger picture. What made our company different? What were we trying to do here? Where did I fit in? No one showed any interest in answering those questions.

This determined my overall sense of place in the company. I was just a cog in a vast machine. My job was to just keep ticking along.

It was the exact opposite of how things had worked at SSI, my first job out of college. There, the founder of the small software firm took me aside over lunch and laid out the company's history and their plans for me. It felt so personal. I felt like I understood the company and the part I would play in its success.

I don't know whether this was part of a standardized process for them or not—I may have just been lucky and caught the owner on the right day—but it made a real impression. Like the Mountain Grenadiers, I felt I belonged. At Dell, I felt replaceable.

By the time I started Catapult, I knew which model I wanted to emulate. We couldn't afford the lavish three-month boot camp of Andersen Consulting, but that didn't mean we couldn't offer something scaled down that fit our business.

We landed on a two-to-four-day boot camp—with the length determined by the new recruit's department. This always took place within their first thirty to forty-five days. Once we had around ten to fifteen people to train, enough to justify the flights and time out from our own schedules, we'd bring everyone together in Austin into a new "class."

No matter their department or responsibilities, everyone experienced the same day one. That first day was particularly crucial because it served two purposes:

- Indoctrinate new employees into our company so they felt like they were really part of something.
- Set clear expectations of how they should work within the company and with our customers.

Because this was the main event of our boot camp, the moment when we really laid out what the company was all about, I personally led training for the entire first day. To reinforce the boot camp theme and make the day even more memorable for new employees, I wore camo pants, combat boots, a black Catapult T-shirt, and a red military beret.

The other days were department specific and closer to the sort of training many companies do these days. But that first day cemented a clear impression of Catapult and what each new person would bring to the company.

THE RECIPE FOR A GOOD BOOT CAMP

Because everything after day one is closer to the on-the-job training already featured at many companies, I'll leave that out of this book. After all, you probably already know how to train your new people on your internal systems and already have a set of reading materials about the practical tools they'll need to get them up to speed with the rest of the team. Instead, I'll focus on the most impactful day of boot camp: the first one.

On that day, we made a point of hitting some very important targets. We had to explain to every new employee, all of the following:

- Who we are
- What we believe in
- Where we are going
- What we do
- Elements of our culture
- How we work with our clients

To be part of anything, you have to understand it on a deeper level: its history, its purpose, and its ambitions. That's what we aimed to do with the first day of boot camp. We organized it to feel like a class—one where you get to know everyone else. If you do this right, that first day creates a bond between colleagues—and with the company—that can last for years.

THE MORNING

First things first, day one should be taught by the founder or CEO. This is why I always took the lead on that first day. Don't delegate this. It's one day a month at most for the CEO, depending on how many people you're hiring. Connecting to your people and making an impression is worth the time investment.

You can start making that impression by setting standards and expectations right away. We had one firm, uncompromising rule for boot camp: don't be late. First impressions matter. This was one of the "golden rules" of our best practices (which I'll dig into in Chapter 4). And one of the keys to a good first impression is punctuality.

Whether in the morning or after lunch, if a new recruit was late to class, there were consequences: doing push-ups with me. It didn't matter if the tardy individual could do fifty or barely manage one on their knees, they had to do as many as they could with me keeping up right beside them.

Assuming everyone was on time, we began the day with introductions. Where are you from? Where did you grow up? Where did you go to school? What was your career before Catapult? What's your family situation? What do you do for fun? These are the basic building blocks to create relationships. To get to know each other, we had a deck of cards with ice breaker questions. Everyone drew a different card and answered whatever question they drew.

We continued to draw cards and return to those questions throughout the day.

After our initial round of introductions, I'd transition to Catapult's history. I'd explain how we came up with the idea, the scuba diving trip in Hawaii where David and I really developed it, and the events that led us to become a consulting company (we'd initially planned to be a software products company).

Next, I'd introduce the leadership team. Instead of just putting each person's résumé up next to a stock photo, though, we made sure to dig a little deeper and share more interesting details about our lives. We'd mention if someone loved hiking or played D1 basketball in college. As with the introductory questions, the point was to give everyone a sense of the real person.

The executive team introduced, I then led the new recruits through our org structure. So many companies feel this isn't a priority to share, or in the case of smaller businesses, even put in place. But as I'll explain in Chapter 8, employees want to know where they fit, who runs each department, and how it all fits together. It helps them feel like they aren't just a cog, they're an important part of a complex organization.

To further explain what our company was, I'd next review key elements of our culture. Here, I focused on our core ideology—a concept I borrowed from Jim Collins's book *Built to Last*. I'll walk you through all of these details in Chapter 3, but briefly, according to Collins, a core ideology includes core values plus core purpose. And when you combine core ideology with an "envisioned future" (in Collins's words, "what we aspire to become, to achieve, to create"), you get a company's vision.

At this point, we were well into the morning, but we weren't done yet. We still had to cover what Catapult actually did—how we worked with our clients. I'd lay out all our service offerings and show how those overlaid with our regional offices. I also included an elevator pitch that everyone was required to memorize: "Catapult Systems is a Microsoft technology consulting company that provides a broad range of services from application development to creative services. We build business-critical IT systems for large and midsize organizations in the private and public sector."

This section of boot camp also included a discussion of our unfair advantage (covered further in Chapter 5). This was our overall corporate strategy: the way we were going to win. At Catapult, that included an overview of our strategy to focus on Microsoft and become the number one Microsoft partner worldwide. We even had a Microsoft Manifesto and a Cloud Manifesto that further explained our aims.

The first half of that first day ended with a review of our brand promise and the covenant we made with every customer (also covered further in Chapter 3). For Catapult, this covenant had three principles:

- We always deliver.
- We're easy to work with.
- We bring the whole team.

Finally, to pull it all together, I would review our one-page strategic plan for the year (which we developed using Verne Harnish's *Scaling Up*). With that final piece covered, we were ready to break for lunch.

THE AFTERNOON

The afternoon had fewer items to get through, but it was just as important. Along with continuing to get to know one another, we focused on those Golden Rules of Customer Service that I mentioned before (these were best practices we'd assembled, as I'll relate in Chapter 4).

This was essentially story time. Each lesson included a real story that showed the value of the rule we were discussing. Over the afternoon, I'd relate thirty-five of our sixty best practices.

That way, by the end of the day, every new person knew who we were, what we were doing, the way we worked, and a little bit about a number of people working at the company. In other words, they spent a full day connecting to this new workplace and finding their place in it.

KEY TAKEAWAYS

- All companies should have an onboarding program to give new hires a sense of purpose and belonging. This ensures that new employees understand what the company does, what you believe in, why you exist, and how they fit into the bigger picture.
- The CEO should personally lead the cultural indoctrination portion of your new employee onboarding program. This hands-on approach will signal the importance of the onboarding process and help employees feel valued. It will also ensure that the company's vision is effectively communicated.

- Use real, relatable stories during onboarding to demonstrate the company's culture and best practices. This helps new hires connect more directly with the values and processes being discussed, making the training memorable.
- By integrating personal introductions, ice breakers, and multiple touchpoints with team members, you will create an onboarding experience that builds strong relationships among new employees. This increases loyalty and engagement.

PRO TIPS

- If possible, have your new employee onboarding program in person at headquarters. It's worth the investment.
- Ensure that company executives are actively involved in the onboarding process, especially on the first day. Have them introduce their department in person or virtually.
- One of my favorite questions to ask each new employee is: "Tell us something unique about yourself—something that is not likely to be shared by anyone else in this room. It can be something you can do, somewhere you've been, an experience you've had, anything that only you have done or experienced." This helps cut through the obvious answers people share about themselves, allowing everyone to really get to know them.

FURTHER READING

Built to Last: Successful Habits of Visionary Companies by Jim Collins and Jerry I. Porras

Scaling Up: How a Few Companies Make It...and Why the Rest Don't by Verne Harnish

CASE STUDY

The Scooter Store and the Power of New
Employee Onboarding Programs

Doug Harrison's journey began with a desire to make a difference. He and his wife were frustrated by the lack of mobility options for his grandmother, who was confined to a nursing home. Taking inspiration from the passing of the Americans with Disabilities Act in 1991, they opened The Scooter Store in New Braunfels, Texas, where they focused on selling scooters for the elderly.

Initially, the business struggled to be profitable and grow, but after attending a business program led by Verne Harnish, Doug acquired the knowledge and tools necessary to start expanding nationally in 1999. The company grew rapidly from there, reaching over $100 million in revenue in the next four years and nearly $1 billion over the next ten, with seventy-two locations across the country, 3,500 employees, and a strong online presence.

Along the way, Doug became a big fan of Jim Collins and his research on core ideology in *Built to Last*. With those lessons in mind, he noticed how a local Mexican restaurant he frequented had printed its mission statement on the back of its menu, challenging customers to ask any employee to recite it verbatim. Customers were promised a free dessert if they failed. Despite several efforts, Doug was never able to get that free dessert.

Doug decided to ensure that every employee at The Scooter Store deeply understood the company's mission and core ideology. This led to the development of a comprehensive one-week new employee orientation (NEO) program that became a cornerstone of The Scooter Store's success.

The program, which was held once or twice a month with approximately fifty students, ensured that all new employees learned why the company existed and what it stood for. To reinforce the company's core values, Doug invited different vice presidents to participate in the NEO program, with each one teaching a company core value through storytelling. This personalized approach allowed employees to connect with the company's values in a meaningful way. Doug himself dedicated the last two hours of the final day of NEO class to sharing his favorite genesis story about what the company did. It focused on an elderly lady whose life, after losing her mobility and will to live, was transformed by The Scooter Store's products. This story not only illustrated the company's mission of "providing freedom and independence to people with limited mobility" but also left a lasting impact on new employees, helping them understand the profound impact their work could have.

Doug fundamentally believes that every employee has the potential to be an all-star performer if given the right training, tools, and a clear "why" they can believe in. This belief was ingrained in every aspect of the onboarding process, ensuring that new hires felt a sense of ownership and purpose from day one. To solidify that sense of ownership, all new employees were granted the opportunity to join the company's employee stock ownership plan upon completing the onboarding program. As a result, The Scooter Store was able to cultivate a workforce that was well-informed and deeply invested in the company's mission and values.

Chapter 3

Core Ideology

Halfway through my time in the Swiss infantry officer candidate program, we were out on maneuvers, practicing different combat and leadership skills. We were in the region around Lucerne, a beautiful medieval city nestled between lake and mountains. Our movements circled around the left bank of the lake, leading us eventually to the top of a hill overlooking a peaceful meadow below.

Amazingly, every company arrived at the same time. As we enjoyed a moment's rest and took in the view, one of the senior officers stepped forward.

"Gentlemen, I don't know if you realize this or not, but this is hallowed ground."

For those of us who hadn't yet caught on, he explained that we were standing on Mount Rütli—the birthplace of Switzerland. This was the place where the three original Swiss cantons chose to defy the Hapsburgs and be a free people. This is where Switzerland began, where all our ideals came from.

Over the next forty-five minutes, the officer walked us through our seven-hundred-year history, recounting what defense and neutrality had meant to our ancestors and what it meant to us now. He described how our safety was ensured through both World Wars thanks to people just like us. We were part of a long line of Swiss who would keep the country safe, no matter what happened.

Standing on that hill, it reminded all of us how important what we were doing was. It was impossible not to feel a sense of patriotism. Suddenly, everything clicked into place. We knew what we were doing and why we were doing it.

FINDING YOUR CORE

The reason that exercise resonated so deeply with all of us was because it spoke to something that we recognized as profoundly true. When the officer walking us through our history mentioned the values that we shared as Swiss citizens, it struck a chord because we had seen these values in our lives growing up; we recognized them in our communities and in ourselves.

So often, companies assume concepts like core values or core purpose are easy to develop because it's all a matter of crafting some nice sounding language to print out and post on some office walls. It's just another piece of marketing material. At most, these values are seen as aspirational.

These assumptions are why core values and core purpose so often fall flat in organizations. Core values should reflect what you believe in and what you stand for now and forever. Your core purpose should speak to why your company exists beyond just making money. If something is a real core value, it shouldn't just sound nice. It shouldn't be an aim in the future. It should be reflected in how your employees behave every day; it should influence who you hire, who you reward, who gets promoted, and who gets let go. A real core purpose is not a slogan; it explains why a company really exists and why we are all here.

In other words, your core values and core purpose aren't about producing good marketing: they have to speak to something deeply true within your company that your people and your customers recognize when they hear it.

To assemble these ideas at Catapult, I turned to Jim Collins and his book *Built to Last*. There, he lays out how to build what he terms your "core ideology": the combination of core values and core purpose. In this equation, your core values represent what your company believes in fundamentally, while your core purpose explains why your company exists.

Collins also suggests your company should have a "BHAG"—or Big Hairy Audacious Goal. This is your moonshot, the ultimate goal of your company. Finally, every company needs a brand promise that clearly articulates what customers can expect from you.

If you feel you can fill these concepts in off the top of your head right now, don't. Each requires time, thought, and collaboration—because together, they should *truly* describe your company from every angle.

HOW TO UNCOVER YOUR CORE

Your journey to unearthing these concepts starts with core values. Which leads to an obvious question: if you can't just write down what sounds good, how exactly do you create core values?

To begin with, you don't create them. Core values are core values because they already exist in your company. These are the values that your people display when you aren't around. It's the behaviors and beliefs that your company already values—you just haven't made them explicit.

To discover these values, then, you don't need the founder or the executive team to draft a list of aspirations; you need the people working in the trenches right now. They're the ones living these values every day. Once you know that, all you need is a process to bring these values to the surface. In my experience, the best process once again comes from Jim Collins—this time in his *Harvard Business Review* article "Building Your Company's Vision."

You can find the whole process detailed by Collins online in this article—including the questions he uses for prompts. Briefly, though, it involves splitting your employees into two groups with the task of identifying two fellow employees who represent the best qualities in your company on a mission to Mars. To run this exercise, you need at least twenty employees. If you have fewer than eighty, all of them can take part. If you have more, choose between sixty and eighty people at random across the whole organization.

Each group is then assigned the task of choosing two employees who best represent the values of the company. Crucially, neither person they choose can be in the room or be one of the founders. Once the two employees are identified, each person writes down the qualities they most value in those employees using sticky notes.

The sticky notes are then grouped on a white board into general categories until you have between five and eight clear themes. When the exercise is over, everyone goes to happy hour and compares the results of the two groups. In my experience, even though these people were in different rooms without any communication, the themes almost always overlap about 80 percent.

When we conducted this exercise at FlashParking, the whole process took about two hours, and in the end, we landed on six core values that we later wordsmithed into:

- **Whatever it takes:** We are committed to customer success and go above and beyond to get the job done.
- **Know your stuff:** We come prepared for every situation. We are innovative problem solvers and are determined to find the answers we need.
- **I got this:** We are unwavering in keeping our commitments to our customers and to one another.
- **Here to help:** We are always willing to assist others and have a passion for customer service.
- **With a smile:** We go out of our way to be friendly and to maintain an insanely positive attitude in all situations.

- **Cool under pressure:** We love a good challenge and pride ourselves in remaining calm, cool, and collected at all times.

•

Once you have a set of core values, you have to live by them. Core values only mean something if you use them. They aren't just words on a wall; they should influence everything. If a highly qualified candidate lacks one or more values, they shouldn't be hired. If an otherwise successful employee lacks your values, you should remove them.

In our monthly company meetings, we would give out awards to those who exemplified our core values (more on this in Chapter 16). We'd cover them in employee reviews. They were ever-present and ever-influential—because they were core to how we operated.

CORE PURPOSE AND BHAG

If you look to your people for core values, you have to look to your executive team for your core purpose and BHAG. Once again, for clarity, your core purpose speaks to what you are now: this is why you exist as a company beyond just making money. Your BHAG, on the other hand, is that big, almost unattainable goal you're aiming for at all times. It may take you twenty years, but that's where you're directing the company.

These are big ideas, so once again, don't just accept the first words that come to mind when your executive team is spitballing. You have to put time aside to iterate on these concepts. You aren't going to uncover them in an afternoon. You want to think about them over multiple quarters.

I recommend scheduling an hour at your quarterly offsite meetings to brainstorm ideas on your core purpose and BHAG. Debate the merits of those ideas over dinner. Continually explore and refine these ideas until you have them right.

In my experience, if you make these concepts a priority, each should take about a year to perfect. They can be developed simultaneously, but only if you prioritize them equally and set aside the time for both.

BRAND PROMISE

Initially defined by Verne Harnish in his book *Start to Scale*, a brand promise is a clear, compelling statement that articulates what customers can expect from your company. Your brand promise should highlight what makes your company unique to your customers. How do they feel your business stands out from its competitors?

In other words, this is the customer's view of your company—how they experience those latent core values that have always been there—and for that reason, you need to consult with them to discover the promise you've been making.

To get truthful, complete answers, it's best not to ask for this information yourself. Instead, hire a third-party organization or individual that can call all of your top customers and ask them two questions:

- Why did they select your company in the first place?
- Why do they keep doing business with your company?

Those questions are purposely open ended. You want to solicit real answers, not constrain your customers for your own purposes. Your job is to listen. Once you have a set of answers, you should group them by theme until a pattern appears. Most companies will end up with three dominant themes. As with your core values, once you have that raw material, you can enlist the help of your marketing team to wordsmith them into your company's brand promise.

Our Catapult brand promise was:

- We always deliver.
- We're easy to work with.
- We bring the whole team.

At FlashParking, we really struggled with this for some time. Eventually, though, we landed on:

- We will provide you with a proposal within a half day of your request.
- Your system will be fully installed and operational within three weeks of your signed agreement.
- We will respond to any support request within the hour.

These are more concrete and measurable compared to Catapult's brand promise, but they really spoke to what we tried to offer every single customer. They kept us honest, and they showed every customer the kind of service we always gave.

KEY TAKEAWAYS

- Your employees will be more engaged if they understand what your company believes in (core values), why you exist (core purpose), where you are going (BHAG), and what your customers can expect from you (brand promise).
- Core values are inherent to the company rather than aspirational. They reflect the genuine beliefs and behaviors demonstrated by employees every day, rather than ideas crafted to look good on a wall or website.
- Core values should be discovered through the input of the broader employee base, not dictated by the executive team. Employees are the ones who embody these values on a day-to-day basis.
- Core values are effective only if they are consistently used and reinforced in the company culture—from hiring to promotions and everyday interactions. They should guide who gets hired, rewarded, or let go.
- Developing a core purpose and BHAG should not be rushed. Allocate dedicated time in strategy meetings to iterate on these concepts over several quarters, allowing the ideas to mature into clear, inspiring goals.
- Your brand promise should be derived from customer feedback,

reflecting what makes the business unique in the eyes of the customers.

- To craft a meaningful brand promise, use an external party to conduct interviews with your top customers. This approach helps in getting honest feedback, free from bias, to uncover the genuine reasons customers value your business.

PRO TIPS

- Come up with a unique icon/image and color for each core value. This will make them more memorable.
- At FlashParking, we created a set of six poker chips, one for each core value. We gave them to our core value award recipients during our monthly company meetings.

FURTHER READING

"Building Your Company's Vision" by Jim Collins and Jerry I. Porras, *Harvard Business Review*, September–October, 1996

Built to Last: Successful Habits of Visionary Companies by Jim Collins and Jerry I. Porras

Start to Scale: Secrets to Starting and Scaling Any Size Organization by Verne Harnish

CASE STUDY

Uncovering Falcon Storage's Core Purpose

Stephen Shang's entrepreneurial path began after working for McKinsey and several venture-capital-backed startups in Silicon Valley. Despite these stimulating experiences, Stephen felt unfulfilled, realizing he was constantly "swinging for the fences" without a real sense of purpose. He returned to Austin, where he had attended college, and cofounded Falcon Storage in 2003 with his friend Brian Dieringer. The company initially repurposed used shipping containers and rented them as storage units for industries such as agriculture, construction, and retail. Over time, Falcon Storage expanded its offerings, building military training facilities, urban farms, remote workforce housing, and food and beverage parks out of shipping containers, demonstrating an innovative approach to sustainable construction.

Falcon Storage proved a formidable competitor in its space, but Stephen felt something was still missing. In 2009, he attended a learning conference with other entrepreneurs where he observed that the most successful companies had one thing in common: organizational alignment around a core purpose. This revelation led him to question his own company's "why"—why did Falcon Storage exist beyond just making money?

Fortuitously, at the same conference, Stephen met an up-and-coming author, Simon Sinek, with a leadership philosophy centered around answering that question by "starting with why." Simon agreed to meet Stephen in Houston a few months later to help him uncover Falcon Storage's core purpose.

During their meeting, Stephen offered generic potential purposes, such as "help people with change" and "simplify operations." Simon called him out for these superficial statements. To help Stephen dig deeper, he asked him to recall a cherished childhood memory. Stephen shared a story about building a fort with his best friend, Thor, while growing up in South Carolina. That fort made him feel safe, Stephen said, which sparked an epiphany for Simon. Perhaps the feeling of safety could be the key to understanding Falcon Storage's deeper purpose.

Simon sent Stephen home with some homework: to ask his closest friends and employees why they were drawn to him personally. To Stephen's astonishment, almost everyone responded that he made them feel *safe*. To further explore this idea, Stephen spoke with some of his customers, asking them why they chose to do business with Falcon Storage. The response was consistent: they trusted the company because Falcon Storage made them feel secure and protected in their business dealings.

This feedback resonated deeply with Stephen, leading him to recognize that Falcon Storage's core purpose was "to create a safe place for others." This insight not only reshaped Falcon Storage's organizational mission but also provided clarity to its growth strategy, aligning the company's operations, culture, and long-term vision around its newly discovered "why." With the help of this newfound clarity, Falcon Storage made the Inc. 5000 list of fastest growing companies in the country five years in a row.

Chapter 4

Codify Your Best Practices

DIFFICULTY: 4/5

After months in officer candidate school, I had more than a few manuals lying around. The military is extremely precise and loves documenting everything—and all of that goes into manuals. By the time I was ready to graduate as an infantry officer, I had manuals on: Leadership and Command, Infantry Tactics, Mountain Warfare, Urban Warfare, Winter Warfare, Climbing and Rappelling, Survival, Weapons Handling and Maintenance, Hand to Hand Combat, Explosives and Demolitions, Logistics and Supply, Medical and First Aid, Communication and Coordination, Joint Operations…and more.

I had enough manuals to fill a trunk. Yet, when I graduated, I received one final manual: a single, forty-five-page, laminated booklet. It was about four inches by six, very durable, and fit perfectly in the pocket of my military fatigues. It didn't go into complete, exhaustive detail of everything in those other manuals, but it included all the most important points I needed to know in the field.

It reminded me how to call in an artillery strike, the shapes of all NATO and Russian tanks, and the capabilities of most infantry weapons. In a combat situation, those were the details that would most impact my effectiveness as a leader.

In short, it was essentially a book of "best practices" for a Swiss infantry officer. It was so useful, when training my own nineteen-year-old fresh recruits, I made sure to always have it in my leg pocket.

SIXTY PRINCIPLES IN YOUR BACK POCKET

I didn't start out with any best practices at Catapult. For years, we did what most startups do: we brought in new employees, threw them at the work, and corrected mistakes as they made them.

The idea of doing things differently only came up when I was sitting around with the rest of the leadership team, talking about how all our new people kept making the same mistakes we did when we started out.

Why weren't we heading this off—providing the knowledge we already had so they could avoid those pitfalls?

That same afternoon, I thought of as many lessons as I could based on my own experience. I had quite a list, but I also knew that I wasn't the expert on every side of the company. So I went to all the smartest people across the whole organization. I asked my senior people—my architects, my project managers, and my VPs—to imagine they were sitting their own child down to train them to be the very best at their position in the business. What lessons would they want to impart?

I took that raw material, refined it, and six months later, we had our Sixty Golden Rules of Customer Service (included in Appendix 1). Each "rule" could be distilled down to a tagline and short paragraph, and each also came with a story to help the lesson stick.

For instance, Golden Rule 22 was: "First impressions count: Your first meeting, the first hours, and the first day are what form the client's first impression of you. Believe it or not, it sticks. Be on your best behavior, dress well, act prepared, and project professionalism in those first encounters."

This was a rule about the value of projecting professionalism in your first encounter with a customer. It can make all the difference. To drive this point home, I would tell a story from the late '90s. I had a good relationship with John, a VP of Strategic Alliances at one of our partners. When John left for another company, he contacted me about continuing to work together.

To do this, John told me we'd need to get two of our consultants certified in his new company's platform. Dutifully, I sent two of our top guys. They passed the certification, and then…nothing. We didn't hear a word.

Catapult was so busy back then, I hardly noticed—until a few months later when John called me in a panic.

"Listen, I'm in a real bind," he told me. "One of my other partners dropped the ball. Could you possibly send one of your certified consultants to help out over the next month?"

As luck would have it, one of them was available. He went up and resolved all of John's problems well ahead of the deadline. Afterward, I received a call from John. As he mentioned how grateful he was, I couldn't help noticing how surprised he seemed.

I dug into the reasons why and found out what had happened over that initial certification process. The training began on a Monday up in Dallas—a three-hour drive from Austin. My two consultants decided they'd rather drive up early Monday morning than on Sunday and spend an extra night away from home.

On the way, though, it was rainy, and they got a flat tire. Changing that tire, they got soaked—which wouldn't have normally been a problem. They were wearing casual outfits because they had anticipated having plenty of time to check into their hotel and change ahead of the training. The tire took so long, though, they had to go straight to class.

Now, guess which day John and his CEO decided to show up and meet the new consultants?

The rest of the week, my guys were probably the best dressed and best performing consultants in that class, but it didn't matter. They'd failed to provide a good first impression. And if not for that emergency, we never would have gotten any business from John again.

I made a point of sharing stories like this with my team—in boot camp, as I mentioned in Chapter 2, and in other circumstances. Like my manual from officer candidate school, we also shrank the rule book down to about three inches by six, so employees could carry it with them.

SALES PLAYBOOK

A manual of best practices should include tips that cover functions across the entire organization, but of all the best practices you can codify, the most important—the ones you must not neglect—are sales best practices.

At Catapult, we called this our "sales playbook." A sales playbook is a comprehensive guide that provides your sales teams with a standardized approach to engaging with prospects, overcoming objections, and closing deals. This consistency not only enhances the performance of your existing sales representatives but also helps streamline onboarding for new sales personnel, reducing the learning curve and enabling them to contribute to the team more quickly.

A sales playbook should contain a wealth of information to support your sales teams in their day-to-day operations, with all the strategies, tactics, and best practices necessary to achieve sales success. It typically includes detailed profiles of the target customer segments, complete with demographics, pain points, and buying behaviors. This information helps sales representatives tailor their approaches and engage more meaningfully with potential clients.

The playbook should also outline the sales process steps, from lead generation to closing, providing specific guidelines and techniques for each stage. It should have scripts for common sales scenarios, objection handling techniques, and examples of successful pitches. At Catapult, for example, we had standard, pre-rehearsed answers to as many possible customer objections as we could think of. When our salespeople heard that a customer never outsourced their IT work, already had a preferred IT consulting partner, or sent all of their IT work offshore, we already had a standard, well-tested counterargument at hand to keep the conversation moving forward.

By providing a clear framework for navigating the sales cycle, a playbook empowers sales teams to work more efficiently and effectively, leading to improved conversion rates and increased revenue.

KEY TAKEAWAYS

- Your employees will likely make the same mistakes over and over again until you codify your best practices and train them.
- When developing your best practices, involve your leadership team and your most experienced employees. This collaboration leads to more robust guidelines.
- This is an iterative process and should involve several rounds of input and editing to ensure you've truly distilled the company's best practices. The process often takes six months.
- Creating a pocket-sized guide of key best practices provides employees with a quick and portable reference that can be useful in everyday scenarios.
- Sharing specific stories behind each best practice helps embed the lessons in the minds of employees, making the guidance more relatable and memorable.
- Of all your best practices, codifying your "sales playbook" is the most important.

PRO TIPS

- Emphasize the use of a comprehensive sales playbook when hiring for sales positions. It demonstrates that your organization is committed to equipping its salespeople for success, making it attractive to high performers.
- Find creative ways of reminding your employees of your best

practices. At Catapult, we had a rotating "Best Practice of the Day" highlighted on our company intranet.

- Regularly revisit and update the documented best practices as the company evolves. This ensures the guidance remains relevant and effective in changing business environments.

FURTHER READING

The Sales Playbook for Hyper Sales Growth by Jack Daly

CASE STUDY

Clayton Christopher's Best Practices in Building Authentic Brands

Clayton Christopher's path to success began with a decision to chart his own course. After taking a few credit hours in college, he chose adventure over academia, traveling the world by bicycle and train, before eventually working as a charter boat captain in the Florida Keys and the Bahamas. During his time on the sea, Clayton realized the importance of self-reliance and resourcefulness, and that "it's better to own the boat than to work on it." This epiphany led him back home to Texas, where he cofounded Sweet Leaf Tea in 1998 with his childhood best friend, David Smith. Clayton's determination and innovative approach to creating an authentic, high-quality iced tea brand resulted in a successful exit to Nestlé fourteen years later.

Eager to apply the lessons learned from Sweet Leaf Tea, Clayton set his sights on an industry with higher margins and a distribution model he understood well: premium spirits. In 2011, he launched Deep Eddy Vodka with cofounder Chad Auller, combining his knowledge of authentic branding with Chad's distilling expertise. They introduced a sweet tea vodka to the Texas market. Within fifteen months, they became the number one sweet tea vodka in Texas, a success they attributed to their commitment to natural ingredients, premium packaging, and a consistent brand story.

To fuel the growth of Deep Eddy Vodka, Clayton developed a unique marketing strategy centered around experiential engagement. A significant component of this strategy was getting "liquid to lips"—letting consumers experience the product firsthand through tastings at music festivals, bars, and restaurants. By focusing on high-impact venues that attracted their target demographic, Clayton ensured that consumers not only tasted Deep Eddy but also engaged with the brand's story. This approach fostered a deep connection with their audience, creating brand loyalty and turning consumers into advocates.

This strategy required the company to invest in full-time and part-time brand ambassadors who embodied the brand's image. To ensure that each representative told the company's story in a genuine and consistent way, they were carefully trained through a detailed booklet or "playbook," which covered everything the ambassadors needed to know about the company's best practices, from the brand's origin to the importance of using natural ingredients, their unique distilling process, and key insights into representing the brand authentically. The level of detail in the playbook even extended to how ambassadors should dress, style their hair, and interact with customers, ensuring a consistent experience that reinforced Deep Eddy's brand.

Following the introduction of these best practices, along with their best-selling flavor, ruby red grapefruit, Deep Eddy grew exponentially and expanded distribution to all fifty states in less than two years. The company's success ultimately led to a $400 million exit to Heaven Hill.

Chapter 5

Your Unfair Advantage

DIFFICULTY: 4/5

Any country as maniacally focused on defense as Switzerland will give significant thought to its strategic advantages. These "unfair" advantages start with its natural terrain. The country's landscape is dominated by the Alps—Europe's highest and most expansive mountain range—which provides natural fortifications. The rugged terrain makes it difficult for large armies to maneuver and establish supply lines. Key mountain passes, such as the narrow Gotthard Pass, are strategic choke points.

The Swiss have augmented these natural advantages with extensive manmade fortifications, including a series of bunkers and fortresses designed to offer a formidable defense against any incursion. Hidden in the rock are modern cannons trained on key infrastructure targets. Every bridge, tunnel, highway, and railroad in Switzerland is already filled with explosives, lacking only the detonators to blow them up.

This same philosophy of unfair advantage continues into the military itself. Each unit within the Swiss Army has a specific role and purpose—a specialization in an area of warfare that an invading army could not easily replicate. From our air force squadrons, armored brigades, artillery groups, infantry battalions, to our logistics and engineering companies, each unit has a specific purpose and mission for which they train tirelessly.

As a Mountain Grenadier, all we do is train for guerilla warfare in the mountains. We are experts at infiltrating behind enemy lines in impossible to defend mountainous terrain to gain intel or ambush a convoy. We train to survive at high altitudes through harsh winter conditions. We learn to rock climb, rappel down mountains, ski, recon, sabotage, and rescue hostages.

Because Switzerland's military is entirely defensively focused, the mountains provide us with the ultimate home court advantage. I obviously wouldn't want to take on a Navy SEAL on a beachfront or at sea, and they probably wouldn't want to fight a Mountain Grenadier in the Alps. That's where we have an unfair advantage.

DON'T WAIT TO FIND YOUR UNIQUE STRENGTH

When I speak to first-time entrepreneurs, I always ask them the same question: "How is your company different from everyone else in your industry?" Sometimes, I rephrase it: "What are you best in the world at?" Or, "What is your unfair advantage over your competition?" These are all variations on the same idea: how does their company stand out from the crowd?

This concept is integral to the growth and success of any business, yet most do not have a clear answer.

A lack of clarity around this idea is often the reason these companies are stuck at a certain size. I've seen so many promising small businesses invest their time, resources, and money only to ultimately squander their lead in a given market by prematurely attempting to branch out into other product/service lines, customer segments, or geographies without a real sense of what makes them unique. In trying to do a little of everything for everyone, they never become the best at anything for anyone. Failing to focus on their unfair advantage leaves them at a permanent disadvantage.

To be clear, it's okay to take a shotgun approach when you're getting started. In the beginning, you don't know what you're good at yet or who your most profitable target audience is. But it's the job of the CEO to figure out what your company can someday do better than everyone else.

Once you have an answer, the key to greater success is very straightforward: focus. Direct your company toward its new destination as quickly as possible. Don't get distracted by the next shiny object. Don't waste time on the latest idea you've heard about. Don't divert attention toward a new product/service you think might eventually become a success. Draw a line toward your unfair advantage and drive toward it at full speed.

When you're still growing, this can feel like a secondary concern at most. After all, revenue is still increasing, profits remain high—why spend time redefining yourself if what you're doing is already working? It's an understandable impulse, but there's a real risk in realizing too late that your company lacks an unfair advantage—that it's just like everyone else's. That was my own experience at Catapult.

In the '90s, I had none of the discipline I recommend to entrepreneurs today. At Catapult, we did everything for everyone. Any project that came our way, we'd take. We'd work with any technology platform, with any industry, with companies of any size. And we were successful. There was so much demand back then. With the transition from host-based computing to client/server computing, the rise of the internet, and Y2K remediation, business was so good, I never stopped to even think about an unfair advantage. Who needed one in that market?

Then the market changed. The dot-com bubble burst—and it hit us hard. We lost half our revenue in six months. Companies everywhere were looking to cut costs, and we looked like every other vendor out there. There was nothing we did better than everyone else. Nothing made us indispensable. At our low point, I wasn't sure we would even survive.

If we were going to pull through somehow, I knew I couldn't let this happen again. We needed to look in the mirror and ask some tough questions.

I knew we had to be the best at *something*. Initially, we looked at various verticals. Why not specialize in one industry? But other than government, no other vertical seemed recession-proof or capable of supporting a company of our size. We also lacked the expertise to pivot convincingly in that direction. So we looked horizontally. We would invest in one technology provider and be the top partner for everything that company created across all industries. We could have chosen any number of companies, but we liked Microsoft's product roadmap. We liked where they were investing in their technologies. And we liked their partner model.

In 2002, we made it official and pivoted the entire organization to focus on Microsoft solutions. Our BHAG—the Big Hairy Audacious Goal I covered in Chapter 3—was to become the most sought-after Microsoft partner in the world. It's no exaggeration to say that decision transformed Catapult's future.

FINDING YOUR ADVANTAGE

As Geoffrey A. Moore describes in his best-selling book *Crossing the Chasm*, most B2B companies stumble when it comes time to make the transition between the early adopters of their product or service and the mainstream market. Mainstream companies want to know that you understand their business needs perfectly and that you have a complete solution to their specific problem. They expect you to have rock-solid references who are of similar size and in the same industry as they are. In other words, they want to know you're the best in the world at helping companies just like theirs. This can only be achieved if you have a laser-sharp focus and know exactly who you are as a company. You have to be known by your clients for doing "one thing" extraordinarily well rather than for doing many things unremarkably.

This is true for every type of business. If I am looking to hire a maid service for my condo, I want to know if they are the best cleaning service in my area. I want references from people who have condos downtown, preferably in my building. I don't care if they clean commercial buildings in Round Rock out in the suburbs. I want to know that homeowners just like me choose their service and feel it's the best. I want to know that their focus is on cleaning condos just like mine and if they excel at it.

That being the case, where should you turn your focus in your own company?

Just like Switzerland built on the natural advantages of its terrain to create an impenetrable unfair advantage, most businesses already have natural advantages they can build upon. It's all a matter of discovering what that advantage is—or could be.

When Juan Rodriguez approached me about investing in his company FlashParking, he was as unclear on this point as anyone. When I asked him what his company was best in the world at, I heard all kinds of answers at first. I asked who his customers were, and like my early experience at Catapult, they were all over the map. So we refocused. I asked which customers were the most natural fit for FlashParking. Which were the most profitable? Which were the easiest to close? Which ones could use his product right out of the box? Which customers called the support lines the least?

As we dug in, a clear pattern emerged. And that's where we turned our focus. We developed an ideal target customer profile that could benefit the most from our products out of the box. This profile included industry, company type, facility size and complexity, number of locations, equipment purchase life cycle, and geographic location. The more we differentiated ourselves from the competition, the more we narrowed in on our target clients, the faster we grew.

This process was not so different from the one Jim Collins introduces as the "hedgehog concept" in his book *Good to Great*. A hedgehog concept is a simple idea that comes from the intersection of three key questions. Slightly rephrased, those are:

- What can you be the best in the world at?
- What drives your economic engine?
- What are you deeply passionate about?

As you move from the shotgun approach of a startup, taking any business that comes your way, answering these questions allows you to grow most effectively. But only if you continue to redirect focus around those answers. Like the core values we covered in Chapter 3, you have to live by it. At Catapult, our focus on becoming the number one Microsoft partner in the world meant I turned down a $3 million contract to implement an IBM solution for an existing client. At FlashParking, we turned down projects at large airports that required time-consuming custom features for our product. The projects were lucrative, but they were ultimately a distraction.

This can feel counterintuitive, but in the end, it works. Catapult grew more than 70 percent per year for the five years after we implemented our unfair advantage. And FlashParking is now valued above $1 billion.

AN ADVANTAGE IS NOT A STRATEGY

Knowing our unfair advantage at Catapult did not give us the roadmap to get there. It just told us where to focus our attention. In other words, an advantage is not a strategy: it's an endpoint. Strategy is how you get there.

To give you a sense of the difference, Catapult's strategy included:

- Exiting all non-Microsoft business within a year
- Only pursuing customers who had already made the decision to use Microsoft tech
- Only hiring Microsoft consultants
- Only training on Microsoft technologies
- Incentivizing our consultants to become Microsoft certified
- Driving toward more Microsoft competencies as a Microsoft partner than anyone else in the world
- Diversifying our services beyond app dev to include software integration and networking
- Launching a series of in-person presentations and webinars to

educate more customers and prospective customers on the latest Microsoft technologies

- Building relationships with the top one hundred influencers at Microsoft (more on this in Chapter 25)

I include this example only to illustrate that finding your unfair advantage is just the beginning of this process. Strategy requires far more attention than I can provide in this book. Once you have your focus, I recommend you read *Blue Ocean Strategy* by Renée Mauborgne and W. Chan Kim and *Good Strategy, Bad Strategy* by Richard Rumelt to start taking those next steps into strategy.

TAKE THE TIME TO UNCOVER YOUR ADVANTAGE

To find your unfair advantage, you have to build time into your personal schedule to think about this challenge. As with your core ideology, you don't just want to write down what sounds good off the top of your head. This should definitely take time. At every quarterly offsite planning meeting, set aside an hour or two to ask all the questions raised in this chapter.

Better yet, create a "Council," as described by Jim Collins in his book *Good to Great*. A Council is a group of employees who meet periodically to discuss important issues facing the company. It usually consists of five to twelve people, including certain members of the executive team, as well as other subject matter experts. This informal, standing body should meet as often as weekly or as infrequently as quarterly. It does not have the authority to mandate changes but rather acts as an advisory board to the CEO.

Whether refining these ideas in your senior leadership team or your Council, until you can clearly articulate your unfair advantage, this has to be an agenda item. At Catapult, it took us more than half a year, and that timeline was accelerated by crisis. We had to have an answer, or we'd go out of business. We were discussing this topic weekly. In calmer times, it usually takes closer to a year.

Once you have your answers, you have to commit to them—at least so long as they are giving you momentum.

But the world does change. Industry needs shift; customer expectations evolve. You have to be ready to do the same. So this isn't a "set and forget" task. It requires dedication upfront and a willingness to return and reexamine those answers when they stop moving your company forward.

KEY TAKEAWAYS

- Every successful company has a unique aspect that sets them apart—what you do better than anyone else. Focusing on this "unfair advantage" is key to growth and market differentiation.
- Companies that attempt to be everything to everyone often stagnate. It is important to narrow your focus and specialize, thereby creating a distinct value that makes your business indispensable.
- To find your unfair advantage, ask yourself three questions:
  - What can you be the best at?
  - What drives your economic engine?
  - What are you passionate about?
- Focusing on the intersection of these three questions will help define your company's unique strength.
- Practice turning down projects that distract from your focus, even if they are lucrative in the short term. It may sound counterintuitive, but your company will grow faster.
- An unfair advantage is not a strategy. A strategy is required to fully achieve that advantage and involves defining specific actions, investments, and focus areas to align your operations accordingly.
- Build in enough time to think through the questions that define your unfair advantage. This is a long process—one you have to be willing to return to if and when the business environment changes.

- Once you understand your unfair advantage, build it into your elevator pitch. Ask yourself: "What is the one thing I want a prospective customer to remember about my company after a short interaction?"
- As I discussed in Chapter 2, make sure everyone in your organization understands your unfair advantage and memorizes your elevator pitch.

FURTHER READING

Blue Ocean Strategy: How to Create Uncontested Market Space and Make Competition Irrelevant by Renée Mauborgne and W. Chan Kim

Crossing the Chasm: Marketing and Selling Disruptive Products to Mainstream Customers by Geoffrey A. Moore

Good Strategy, Bad Strategy: The Difference and Why It Matters by Richard Rumelt

Good to Great: How a Few Companies Make It…and Why the Rest Don't by Jim Collins

CASE STUDY

OrganiCare's Unfair Advantage

Caroline Goodner began her career in marketing at PepsiCo. There, she quickly realized that she needed to work for a more mission-driven company, so she left to pursue an MBA at Rice University. During an entrepreneurship class at Rice, she developed the business plan for her first company, Identigene, which she founded in 1993. Leveraging scientific advancements pioneered by her father, the world-renowned geneticist Dr. Charles Thomas Caskey, Identigene focused on DNA testing for paternity and forensic identification. Caroline successfully ran the company for fourteen years before selling it.

After another successful stint in leadership, this time at UpSpring-Baby—a company focused on health and wellness products for mothers—and some time off with her family, Caroline reentered the entrepreneurial space when she cofounded OrganiCare with David Shockley and Franco Papa in 2016. The company's first product, CUROXEN, was an all-natural, nonantibiotic competitor to Neosporin. Created using a highly oxygenated olive oil from Italy, this all-natural ointment had been successfully used in Italy for chronic wound care, and Caroline and her team saw an opportunity to bring it to the US market.

Despite its many advantages over its name brand competitor, Organi-Care struggled to gain a strong foothold in the market. Neosporin was simply too well established.

Still seeking its competitive niche, OrganiCare expanded into other applications with its core ingredient, particularly in feminine health. In 2019, the company launched FemiClear, a product aimed at treating yeast infections, which offered superior efficacy compared to traditional treatments. Through rigorous third-party testing and clinical trials, FemiClear proved to be a more effective, natural alternative in a highly competitive market. This, combined with OrganiCare's patent for the product and the general lack of innovation in the space, suggested the company had found its unfair advantage.

By 2020, Caroline and her team had realized they'd truly caught a gear in the feminine health market. Therefore, OrganiCare made a strategic decision to focus exclusively on that market. The company introduced additional products under the FemiClear brand, including treatments for genital herpes outbreaks and bacterial vaginosis. Both products had significantly better efficacy than their competitors, including prescription treatments, which helped the company stand out in the market.

FemiClear products quickly gained traction. Today, FemiClear is sold in major retailers such as CVS, Walgreens, and Walmart.

This success has not slowed the company's focus on innovation. Instead, it has led to even greater focus on product quality. A crucial part of OrganiCare's success has always been its ability to listen to customer feedback and continually improve its products. For example, after receiving complaints about a burning sensation from 15 percent of customers, the company reformulated FemiClear from an ointment to a cream, reducing side effects to just 2 percent of users.

This commitment to customer satisfaction, combined with the company's unique and powerful unfair advantage over its competitors, has solidified OrganiCare's position as a leader in the feminine health market.

Chapter 6

The Best Defense Is a Good Defense

DIFFICULTY: 5/5

The motto of the Swiss Army is "Si Vis Pacem, Para Bellum." For those of you who skipped Latin in high school, that means, "If you want peace, prepare for war."

The Swiss take this motto to heart. We live in a constant state of readiness should a foreign aggressor attempt to invade our country. We are determined to defend our borders at any cost, and we anticipate war as a matter not of "if" but "when." We prepare now because we believe we will need to defend our sovereignty again, just like we did in World War I and World War II.

Of course, plenty of people have argued that Switzerland is a little paranoid, that war in modern, prosperous, peaceful Europe is highly unlikely. Frankly, for all my enthusiasm for the Swiss military, I might have at least partially agreed in the past. I certainly never thought that I would see another land war in Europe. But then Russia invaded Ukraine in February 2022, just 750 miles from the Swiss border.

To ensure our readiness in case of conflict, Switzerland has a system of compulsory military service for men. Every male citizen is trained and then called upon to serve periodically throughout their adult life, creating a robust army of militia. Incredibly, Switzerland can mobilize 625,000 men in forty-eight hours or less. Since every Swiss male is an active soldier until the age of thirty (fifty for officers), Switzerland has one of the largest armies in Europe.

The Swiss Army is not just impressive in size; it is also equipped with modern weaponry and technology, including advanced rifles, armored vehicles, and sophisticated air defense systems. Switzerland also invests heavily in cybersecurity measures to protect against digital threats and ensure the integrity of its command-and-control systems during any future conflict.

Along with rigging all infrastructure with explosives and building modern cannons into the mountains, the Swiss have hangars and other installations inside mountains that have enough fuel, ammunition, and food to last up to a year of war without resupply.

The Swiss civil defense is as impressive as the Swiss military. Today, almost every Swiss citizen will find a place in a hardened nuclear shelter in case of war. Each new residential building and even certain nonresidential buildings built in Switzerland must include a civil defense shelter.

In addition, there are medical service facilities, protected operation rooms, and emergency hospitals hidden within the mountains. Every industry in the country, as well as every government office and official, has a predefined reassignment in case of war.

Incredibly, all of these efforts are entirely defensive. We have no ability to conduct warfare fifty miles beyond our borders. We don't have the supply lines, transportation, or weaponry to take offensive measures.

We prepare for the worst, and that means we have the best possible defense if—and when—things go wrong.

DEFEND AGAINST A RECESSION

"Winter is coming." The Stark family motto in *Game of Thrones* has a dramatic if slightly paranoid flair to it at the beginning of the series. By the end, though, we all know that the Starks were proven right.

When I started Catapult, I never expected winter to come. I had gone most of my life without witnessing a recession. The last one had occurred when I was a teenager. Such events felt almost hypothetical in my own industry, where we were riding these technology inflexion waves that created more demand than there was supply. Running a tech services company at the dawn of the internet meant there was always more work than we could respond to. Our focus was solely on attracting and retaining the best talent—noble goals, but ones that left us exposed.

In 2000, we found this out the hard way when the tech bubble burst. Within six months, we'd lost 50 percent of our revenue. One of our crucial mistakes was to over-invest in startup companies. This had made a lot of sense at the time. Startups paid the best because they had a ton of venture capital funding. Why diversify? In an instant, I knew the answer—as all those startups disappeared overnight.

A year later, the terrorist attacks of September 11, 2001 made things even worse. The country slipped further into recession, and our business shrank even further. With no other options, we took emergency measures. We went through two rounds of layoffs. Everyone who remained at the company took a pay cut. We shut down our San Antonio office and moved into a smaller office in Austin. We retracted to our defensive position and survived on rations.

Even with all that sacrifice, we barely survived as a company. Frankly, we just got lucky. Catapult was hemorrhaging money, but Inquisite, our software product company, maintained positive cash-flow. That was a happy accident, not a well-constructed plan. If not for Inquisite proving unexpectedly recession resistant, I'm certain Catapult would have crumbled.

As we came out of the recession in 2003, I was determined to be ready the next time a downturn came along. The sun came out, the wind was once again in our sails. But I now knew the truth: a sunny sky doesn't guarantee easy sailing. Winter would be coming again—and probably sooner than I would have liked.

From 2003 onward, I made sure to always make that preparation a priority at Catapult. In fact, I retooled our entire strategy around this idea. In Chapter 5, I laid out one of those changes: a focus on the unfair advantage we could build into the company that could make us a dominant player in a particular technology niche. This was only the beginning, though. From then on, we would have no single customer who represented more than 5 percent of our revenue. If one account grew too big, we'd stop growing it. We simply stopped taking new business. It was too dangerous.

We also focused on geographic and industry diversification. We wanted to be spread across enough industries—from manufacturing to services, banking, high tech, and low tech—that we could protect ourselves in leaner times. If one industry struggled, another might be thriving. That diversity could save us. The same was true of locations. One state might be in a recession while another wasn't. We needed to be spread across every region.

Luckily, these two initiatives were strategically complementary. The industries prominent in Dallas were different from those in Phoenix or Seattle. Or DC, where we paid extra attention because we wanted 20 to 25 percent of our business to come from state, local, and federal government. Even though the government pays less, it always still has a budget when a recession hits.

Finally, I made sure we always had a three-month financial runway, including cash in the bank and an available line of credit. That way, we'd have far more room to maneuver the next time some of our customers disappeared overnight.

Within five years, we had our first test of these new defensive measures. From 2008 to 2010, the economy went through an even bigger recession. The headlines every day dwelt on the risk of another Great Depression. But it had little to no impact on our business. Catapult experienced no layoffs. We remained profitable throughout. All the recession did was slow our growth.

ACCEPT THE WEATHER

The theologian Reinhold Niebuhr composed the Serenity Prayer in the early 1930s: "God, grant me the serenity to accept the things I cannot change, the courage to change the things I can, and the wisdom to know the difference." In the decades since, it's featured on everything from Hallmark cards to the twelve-step program followed by Alcoholics Anonymous. It has value for executives and entrepreneurs as well.

We can't control the weather. We can barely predict it. The same is true of the economy. You can't control when the next recession occurs—whether across the entire economy or in your specific industry. All you can control is how you prepare for it and how you respond to it. To do that successfully, though, you have to accept this reality.

I remember a twenty-four-hour march I was once on with the Mountain Grenadiers at the beginning of survival week—a whole week spent out in the wilderness. Only a couple hours in, it started pouring down rain. At that moment, my comrades and I had only two choices: either endure it begrudgingly or choose to embrace it.

In an instant, I decided to do my best to love being cold and wet for seven days—because it was better than being miserable. I had no other choice.

The same is true of recessions. They will come. You can choose either to accept this, embrace it, and prepare—or be miserable. The choice is yours.

KEY TAKEAWAYS

- Another recession or downturn in your industry is inevitable, whether you like it or not. It's your job to prepare your company for it.
- Every company's approach to diversification will be different. It may or may not include diversifying your customer base, your product/service offerings, and your geography.
- Develop long-term relationships with clients that are less vulnerable

to economic downturns, such as government sectors. These clients can provide stability when private sectors face budget cuts.

- Maintain a three-month financial runway (including cash and credit) to give your company enough room to manage an unexpected crisis.

PRO TIPS

- Simulate financial stress by imagining different scenarios like losing key clients or facing a recession. Identify weak areas and create plans to shore them up before an actual crisis occurs.
- Once a year, have your executive team come up with a plan to cut 20 percent of their expenses in their respective business units. That plan should include actual names and real budget cuts. Once you're satisfied they have a real plan, have them file it away.

CASE STUDY

Tom Rhodes and the Resilient Growth of Sente Mortgage

After graduating from Duke University, Tom Rhodes started in the movie industry before transitioning to the real estate investment sector, working with a real estate investment trust. In 2006, he moved to Austin and entered the residential mortgage industry, initially as a loan originator. A few years later, Tom cofounded Sente Mortgage with three other partners after the owner of their previous mortgage company decided to shut down. Currently licensed in twenty-two states, the company originates, funds, and services its own residential mortgages.

Despite the challenges of starting in a competitive market, they launched with twenty-six employees and began originating loans from day one, self-funding the company and establishing themselves as an independent mortgage bank. While the looming global financial crisis of 2008 spelled doom for many mortgage banks, it benefited Sente Mortgage. Because they had no legacy loans and could capitalize on the low-interest-rate environment, the company was able to make money during its first few years in operation.

Despite this initial success, Tom soon realized that he had not built a resilient company. His first lesson in how to change that fact came in 2009, when a liquidity crisis caused the warehouse banks funding mortgage loans to freeze their credit lines across the industry. Thanks to relationships they had established with three warehouse banks, rather than the industry standard of just one, Sente avoided going out of business.

This experience taught Tom the importance of diversification and redundancy, particularly when dealing with critical providers, prompting him to ensure the company always had at least three or four options for vital functions.

The company's second crisis struck in 2013 when rising interest rates led to a significant drop in mortgage volume, causing Sente Mortgage to lose money for two consecutive years. Only their strong capital reserves allowed them to weather the storm. Once again, Tom took some valuable lessons from the experience, this time recognizing the cyclical nature of the industry, the importance of cutting expenses early and deeply when necessary, and the need to track key metrics consistently to identify trends and adapt quickly.

Tom also began to recognize another important form of diversification that added resiliency to his business: income streams. He expanded Sente Mortgage's loan servicing business, which involved retaining the servicing rights to their loans instead of selling them, thereby generating a steady stream of income from servicing fees.

While this aspect of the business was initially difficult to grow due to its cash-intensive nature, it proved to be a crucial component of Sente's long-term strategy. During the COVID-19 pandemic in 2020, when interest rates dropped to historical lows and mortgage volumes soared, the value of loan servicing dipped. Yet Tom held onto this part of the business, believing it would be invaluable when interest rates eventually rose again. This decision proved wise, as by 2023, when interest rates hit a thirty-year high, the income generated from their loan servicing operations provided significant cash flow, helping the company navigate the crisis while over a hundred national mortgage companies went out of business.

Several other strategic decisions further strengthened Sente Mortgage's capabilities to weather economic downturns. Tom prioritized building a strong balance sheet and earning interest on their cash, a tactic that became highly profitable when interest rates rose again. Moreover, he consistently reinvested profits back into the company rather than distributing them to partners when times were good, ensuring the business had sufficient capital reserves to endure lean periods. This financial discipline proved vital, allowing Sente Mortgage to use its own money to fund mortgages rather than relying on warehouse banks, which in turn generated higher returns during periods of high interest rates.

Tom's ability to anticipate business cycles, maintain flexibility, and make strategic investments in the company's long-term stability has enabled Sente Mortgage not only to survive but thrive during economic downturns. Thanks to his careful planning, financial discipline, and adaptability, he's built a business that's proven resilient and recession proof.

Chapter 7

Recruit the Best

DIFFICULTY: 3/5

Recruiting for the Swiss military is easy: everyone has to sign up. There's no need to aggressively market to potential candidates; everyone is showing up for basic training. But challenges do exist in the system, particularly around placement for those new recruits—or whether they belong in the military at all.

To determine aptitude, the Swiss military tests their endurance by having each recruit run as far as they can over twelve minutes. They have everyone do push-ups and sit-ups to test strength. There are similar tests for speed, agility, and climbing ability. Recruits are further tested for vision, hearing, and psychology, all to determine whether the individual is capable of living up to the responsibilities of a soldier.

Once the military is satisfied every new recruit has the physical and mental qualities to succeed, the recruiters investigate if they have any preexisting skills that might precondition them for success in a particular area. If you are a truck driver as a civilian, perhaps you should drive trucks for the military. If you're a cook, likewise, and the same if you're trying to become a pilot.

The military is so deliberate in these efforts because they know that first impressions and appearances can be deceiving. On my first day with the Mountain Grenadiers, the instructors lined us up from shortest to tallest. I was the fourth tallest. Three places up from me was a guy who looked like he had come right out of central casting for a big, tough, loud member of the special forces. Every one of us assumed he'd easily get through basic training. He was what we imagined a Mountain Grenadier should look like.

At the opposite end of the line, there was this short, quiet, scrawny guy. If we assumed the first recruit was born to be a Mountain Grenadier, we all assumed this small guy was destined to drop out before the end of the first week.

We were wrong on both counts.

The big guy washed out in three weeks. He may have looked tough, but he cracked quickly and easily under pressure. That little guy, on the other hand, was made of hardened steel. What we didn't know at the time was that he had grown up on his family's vineyard on the side of a mountain. He had been carrying baskets full of dirt, rocks, and grapes that weighed more than him up and down that mountain his entire life. He was one of the toughest characters I have ever met, and he breezed through basic training like it was just another day at the vineyard.

A COSTLY MISTAKE

Peter Drucker, the management consultant, educator, and author, coined the phrase "culture eats strategy for breakfast." In my opinion, neither matters unless you have the right people.

Even though this makes intuitive, even obvious, sense, most employers largely underthink their recruitment process. They hire based on instinct—or hand the task off to someone in HR who then… hires people based on instinct. The problem with this is that most people tend to hire those who look and sound like them, a decision they make based on an unreliable first impression.

There are few courses on hiring. The typical college courses in human resources focus on the organizational or legal aspects of hiring rather than how to make these delicate decisions. Companies throw managers into the process without any formal training.

Yet hiring is where managers often make their costliest mistakes. When the wrong person is introduced into an organization, productivity and quality are impacted, team morale suffers, and client satisfaction drops. For most companies, a hiring mistake can cost anywhere from $20,000 to $60,000 when you take into account recruiting, interviewing, onboarding, and training costs—not to mention client goodwill.

These mistakes can set an entire company back. So if growth is important to your business, you should have a system in place that removes your current haphazard hiring practices, ensuring the best people are the ones who ultimately land the job.

RECRUITING IS ITS OWN FUNCTION

Before diving into the system I built at Catapult, I want to start with another hiring and organization point. If recruitment is a priority for your company, you should have a dedicated internal hiring person or team. Don't just hand this off to HR.

I know this is counterintuitive to many of you, but hiring is not actually a natural function for HR. With its quotas, outbound calls, and candidate follow-ups, it's closer to sales. In reality, though, it shouldn't even reside there. In my opinion, this is a strategic function that should report directly to the CEO or COO. If you're smaller—or filling specialty jobs—an external recruiting firm is a good partner here, but they are expensive. Ultimately, you want to bring this in-house for most positions.

However you set up your recruitment function, your best channel for new talent is always going to be your current employees. Make sure they know you are hiring and reward them for anyone they refer who gets a position and stays for ninety days. At Catapult, we paid $1,500 to $5,000 per referral, depending on the role we needed to fill. In fact, for those truly crucial jobs, we offered a bounty of up to $10,000.

This is almost always money well spent. The truth is, no one knows your company and what your company needs like the people who already work there. If you're building a great culture, the best way for it to grow is for those who are already bought in to bring in more people who believe in those ideas.

This is the engine for your growth, and it should be running at all times. If you're not actively hiring, you should always be recruiting. This is another reason to make hiring a separate function. This isn't something HR should do for a season and then neglect. When positions aren't available, you can still build a pipeline of those who are enthusiastic and qualified to work for you.

A SYSTEM TO SCREEN FOR THE BEST

With your new recruiting function in place, you can build a system that brings the best candidates into your organization. Much of my own approach is adapted from the excellent book *Topgrading* by Brad Smart and Geoff Smart, so go there for more detail. Brad Smart's most recent book (this time with Chris Mursau), *Foolproof Hiring*, is also excellent, as is. *Who* by Geoff Smart and Randy Street is also just as effective and an easy read. Regardless of your own preference, what's most important is that you establish and follow a standardized interview process for your company.

That said, let's start with changing your expectations around this system. We're not looking to do one or two interviews for most positions. At Catapult, most positions required five to eight interviews. These interviews were run by the best A players on our team. A players like to hire other A players because they want everyone to drive the company to the top. B players hire C players because they want to avoid the competition.

Along the way, any one of our interviewers could raise the red flag and say a particular candidate was a poor fit.

The process begins with a job description and a scorecard. The job description is a brief overview of the job that includes primary responsibilities, required qualifications, and skills. The scorecard documents exactly what you want a person to accomplish in the role. It defines the role's mission, measurable outcomes, and required competencies. Your recruiter and interviewers use the scorecard to evaluate each candidate.

All applicants will enter into a series of interviews. These can fall into different categories with different aims attached to each:

- Phone screen interview: a fifteen-minute call by the internal recruiter to review the candidate's interest and fit for the job, verify employment status and willingness to relocate, clarify salary expectations, and evaluate the candidate's communication skills
- Screening interview (optional): an hour-long call by the internal recruiter or hiring manager when you're considering relocating a candidate to understand a candidate's career goals, professional strengths and weaknesses, and professional interests, while also giving the candidate the opportunity to ask questions about the job
- Competency-based interviews (two or three interviews): a series of forty-five minute interviews over the phone or in person performed by one or more subject matter experts to assess a candidate's proficiency in the desired competency
- Open-ended interview (optional): a more casual interview often held over lunch to further assess culture fit, probe any outstanding concerns, or "sell" the candidate on the position
- Group interview (optional): a forty-five minute interview usually conducted by several members of the hiring manager's team to assess the candidate's ability to present in front of a group of people, evaluate their level of preparedness and understanding of the company, and gauge the team's level of comfort with the candidate
- Topgrading interview: a two to three-hour in-depth interview conducted by the hiring manager that covers high/low points from

the candidate's time in high school and college and answers the following questions for each job since college:

- Employer name and location
- Job title
- Start and end date
- Roles and responsibilities
- State of affairs when joining
- Results and accomplishments
- Mistakes and failures
- Most enjoyable and least enjoyable aspects of the job
- Manager's name and phone number
- Manager's strengths and weaknesses
- What the manager would say about the candidate's strengths and weaknesses
- Circumstances that led to the candidate leaving

For all interviews, keep in mind that the best predictor of future performance is past performance. And everyone should screen for a candidate's cultural fit with your company.

SPEED AND TRANSPARENCY

You don't have to implement all of these interviews into your own organization. Your system doesn't have to be this complex to be successful. The key is to create a structure that allows you to identify the best people. With that in mind, be sure that no matter how many interviews you conduct, you cover different things in each one. We call this "divide and conquer." So often, organizations will have a candidate go through three or four interviews only to have each interviewer ask them the same questions over and over again.

Each interview should provide you with new information. Give coders a test or project to demonstrate their skills. Have a sales candidate give a presentation. Ask a potential executive to prepare a high-level ninety-day plan.

At the same time, whatever your eventual process, you have to prioritize speed and transparency. The interview process I laid out above may seem extensive—and it is—but we always aimed to complete it in a single day. After the initial screening interview(s), we would fly a candidate in and complete four to six interviews the same day. We'd then let them know if they got the position the very next day.

We were always transparent about what the process looked like and when they would know our decision. If we were still considering other candidates for the job, we were up-front about that. And if that meant we needed more time, we let them know when they would hear from us.

Speed matters. Candidates are more than likely considering other job opportunities, and you want to move the process along as quickly as possible.

Ultimately, when done right, this process can help secure the top talent and leave others reapplying for another chance. At Catapult, we reached a 90 percent success rate with our hires through this rigorous interview process.

KEY TAKEAWAYS

- Having the right people in your organization is more critical to success than strategy. And a bad hire is one of the most expensive mistakes you can make.
- Recruiting should be a strategic priority. Don't just hand it over to HR. Establish a dedicated hiring function that reports directly to leadership.
- Current employees are your best source for new talent, as they understand your company's culture and values. Establish a referral bonus program to encourage your employees to refer high-quality candidates.
- Keep recruiting even when not actively hiring. Maintain a pipeline of potential candidates even if positions aren't immediately available, so when opportunities arise, you're ready.

- Unless you have a standardized interview process, most managers will hire candidates based on first impressions. A structured interview process will ensure consistency in how candidates are evaluated. Use scorecards for clear, measurable criteria during each interview stage.
- Only have your best employees participate in the interview process. A players hire other A players. B players hire C players.
- Even if you don't have a formal interview process in place, at a minimum make sure that your interviewers are asking different questions and focusing on different competencies.

PRO TIPS

- How a candidate treats your receptionist or a waiter speaks volumes. Leave them in your lobby for fifteen minutes and ask your receptionist how they interacted with them. Take the candidate out to lunch and see how they interact with the waiter.
- The best predictor of future performance is past performance. If you ask a hypothetical question, you will get a hypothetical answer. Ask the candidate to give a real example of how they actually handled a situation, not a hypothetical one.

FURTHER READING

Foolproof Hiring: Powerful, Proven Keys to Hiring HIGH Performers by Brad Smart and Chris Mursau

Topgrading: How to Hire, Coach and Keep A Players by Brad Smart and Geoff Smart

Who: The A Method for Hiring by Geoff Smart and Randy Street

CASE STUDY

The "People First, Process Second" Philosophy at Addison Group

Tom Moran's journey into the human capital industry began unexpectedly. Initially studying accounting at Illinois State University, Tom quickly realized that his passion lay not in numbers but in people. After an internship in auditing, he transitioned into sales within human capital, where his natural talent for building relationships shined through. Tom's career took him through various prominent roles, including a tenure at Robert Half International that proved pivotal in expanding the company's operations across the Midwest. His success and expertise in the industry eventually led him to Monster.com. There, he spun off and turned around the company's global $1.1 billion e-resourcing business. Tom later moved into private equity as an operating partner at Frontenac before becoming CEO of Addison Group in 2011.

Under Tom's leadership, Addison Group became a powerhouse in the human capital industry. The company has established itself as a true leader in talent solutions and consulting services specializing in information technology, accounting and finance, nonclinical healthcare, and digital marketing.

Tom's guiding philosophy, "People First, Process Second," has been instrumental in the company's success. This philosophy emphasizes attracting top talent and providing employees with the training, processes, and tools needed to succeed. Tom developed this philosophy through years of experience, understanding that while processes are crucial, people drive a company's results.

Tom implemented this philosophy by focusing on recruiting and retaining top talent, which he believes is the key to scaling a business. In particular, hiring recent college graduates is a foundational element of Addison Group's hiring strategy. Representing 60 percent of all new hires, recent graduates are crucial for protecting the company culture that emphasizes communication, collaboration, and transparency.

With new employees trained thoroughly on Addison's processes and key performance indicators (KPIs), the company is able to promote from within—a practice Tom calls the "pyramid effect." New hires start as recruiters, where they gain experience within the business from the ground up, often moving into sales roles and, for some, eventually opening new offices. Thanks to this approach, the company maintains a consistent and vibrant company culture and drives growth and continuity across the organization. It has led to an astonishing 98 percent promotion rate from within the company.

To support its people-first approach, Addison Group developed a proprietary interview process designed after analyzing over a thousand past interviews. One fundamental discovery focused on what happens when too many interviewers are involved in the interview process, leading to analysis paralysis without any meaningful improvement in interview accuracy. Additionally, the prolonged process occasionally caused the company to lose strong candidates. Addison Group found that a shorter interview process involving just two interviewers—each spending one hour with the candidate—was ideal for their target demographic. If both interviewers reached a candidate rating of 80 percent or above, the interview accuracy rate proved to be 90 percent.

Recognizing the effectiveness of this streamlined approach, Addison Group has since trained all their hiring managers to implement this interview process, ensuring consistency and efficiency in identifying top talent. By focusing on attracting and developing the best people and ensuring they are aligned with the company's goals, Tom Moran has driven Addison Group to unparalleled success in the human capital industry. "People First, Process Second" has been crucial in transforming Addison Group from a company generating $68 million in revenue with seven offices to a billion-dollar enterprise with twenty-eight offices nationwide.

Chapter 8

Organizational Structure

DIFFICULTY: 3/5

Organizational structure is essential to every military, and the Swiss are no different. The Swiss Army has a hierarchical structure that would be familiar to any soldier around the world. It is organized into units, ranging from division, brigade, battalion, company, platoon, squad, down to individual fire teams. Each unit has a single leader at the helm who is ultimately responsible for all the decisions made within that unit.

Each unit is also structured in such a way that there is a clear second-in-command who can make the tough calls if the primary leader is unavailable. Each leader has a rank associated with the scope of their responsibilities, the size of their units, and their years of experience, from generals down to corporals. Every Swiss colonel, for instance, has a similar level of responsibility and a similar level of experience.

The value of such organization is obvious in the military setting. You know where every service member is and how they fit into the overall structure. It's clear who is responsible for what, and if you need something from another unit—say, artillery or air support for a particular mission—you know who to go to for that help.

One final benefit is the ability to systematically train different units and then place them across the military organization where they can do the most good. For instance, each territorial division of the Swiss Army has its own company of Mountain Grenadiers. While Grenadiers train together and to the same standards, a company is assigned to each division. We report directly to our respective divisions, who engage us as they see fit.

With the same training, the same skills, and the same best practices, each Mountain Grenadier company can provide the same capabilities across the entire army. That type of matrix organization can become extremely chaotic at scale—unless you have a high level of organizational structure and clear lines of accountability.

STRUCTURE IS ALWAYS THE RIGHT CALL

On the surface, org structure feels like such a boring topic. For a while, I wrestled with removing this chapter entirely. Doesn't every business already have an org chart?

On a recent trip, though, I discovered how wrong that assumption was. I was speaking to a couple friends—both professors of economics—who brought up how rarely they see companies with clear, well-considered organizational structure these days. Even at their own prestigious university, the org structure was byzantine and opaque. They had no idea who was in charge of various departments and initiatives or what responsibilities each person actually had. Such ambiguity made it impossible to hold anyone accountable or to introduce policy across a department, let alone the whole school.

In other words, this is not an academic problem, in any sense. Many large companies have messy org structures. Others fail to communicate that structure to employees. And this isn't just an issue with established businesses either. Many small companies consciously choose to avoid implementing a concrete structure, feeling it's stodgy and outdated.

Considering all this, I want to be particularly clear here: there are many different ways to structure your company, but there must be a structure. In fact, one of the most important decisions a CEO makes is how the company is organized. CEOs decide who reports to whom and what each person's sphere of responsibility and authority is. The nature of that structure can have an enormous impact on a company's growth and success.

THE MOST IMPORTANT RULE OF ORGANIZATIONAL STRUCTURE

There are many ways to organize your company. I want to focus on the rules you should keep in mind, no matter what structure you choose to implement. Not coincidentally, these are the same rules we already saw in the way the military organizes. In particular, only one person should be in charge of each business unit. You can't have two leaders with the same level of authority and responsibility for the same business unit. I've made this very mistake myself. When we opened our first expansion office in San Antonio, I decided I wanted the sales team in our new San Antonio office to report to my centralized VP of sales. Meanwhile, I asked all of our new consultants to report to our head of delivery in Austin. In other words, there was no single person in charge in that office.

This was an abysmal failure. I had a geographic business unit with each side pointing the finger at the other and no single person with the power to make a call and clear things up. No single person was accountable for success or charged with the responsibility to make decisions.

In the end, I realized my mistake and installed a general manager to run the San Antonio office—a person that both regional sales and regional delivery would report to. I gave that general manager full P&L authority and full accountability for results.

This is the second half of the rule of one leader per unit. Once you've placed someone in charge of a particular business unit, you need to give them the authority necessary to succeed. They need the power to hire and fire. And, if possible, they need full P&L authority for that business unit. That's the only way they can actually succeed.

While some leaders are resistant to tying their hands with any structure, following this rule still allows flexibility. For instance, at the same time I appointed that general manager, I installed the same matrix organization I'd seen in the Swiss Army, leaving training in the hands of the VP of sales and head of delivery without giving them direct authority in the new office. Like the Mountain Grenadiers, salespeople and consultants would receive the best possible training and then work under a local authority who knew how to deploy them best.

SHARE THE ORGANIZATION

Implementing a clear structure isn't enough; you also have to communicate that structure across your entire organization. After all, it wouldn't do much good if the Swiss Army had a clear hierarchy but left that hidden from the average officer. It's important to understand rank and responsibilities—who to call and what they can do for you. In other words, everyone needs to know where they fit in the organization—and where everyone else fits as well.

You don't have to share this structure externally, but everyone inside your organization needs to know it.

Communicating your structure is easier with job titles. I know job titles have fallen out of favor. In this new era, no one wants to put a label on anything. But people need to know who is in charge. They also want to see a clear roadmap for their own professional growth. If they do well in their current position, they want to know what the next step up is. They want to know how many steps remain to climb to the top of their profession.

To create this clarity, titles have to mean something. You should define each position clearly and stick to those definitions. Just as the rank of colonel tells every soldier about how much experience and authority a person has, each title should communicate similar information. Don't just throw titles around. If everyone is a VP, then the role of vice president means nothing. At Catapult, if you were a technical architect, it had a very clear—and very prestigious—meaning. You had to have a certain amount of experience and expertise. To earn the title, you had to have your work and progress reviewed by two other technical architects. Receiving that title meant you were an absolute expert in your field.

Similarly, titles should be clearly tied to compensation. Moving into a new position should come with clear benefits that match the new level of experience and authority.

Combining all these ideas together, then, everyone in your organization should have access to your org chart, which has position titles at every level that are tied to responsibilities, authority, and compensation. Again, these are basic, well-established concepts, but trust me, your company will function far more effectively with them in place.

KEY TAKEAWAYS

- Every company needs a defined org structure, with clearly assigned responsibilities. Determining who reports to whom and what is each person's sphere of responsibility and authority is one of the most important decisions a CEO will make.
- There should be no ambiguity in leadership roles. Each unit must have one leader with full authority to make decisions, avoiding the confusion that arises when different parts of a business unit report to different leaders.
- Implementing a matrix organization for training ensures that employees receive standardized, high-quality training, even if they report locally to different authorities.
- Business unit leaders should have the authority necessary to make impactful decisions, including hiring, firing, and financial oversight.
- It's not enough to establish an organizational structure; it must

be communicated throughout the company. Employees need to understand where they fit in, who they report to, and where to turn for specific issues.

- Job titles are important for clarifying authority, hierarchy, and career progression within a company. Titles should have well-defined meanings, help people understand growth opportunities, and be tied to corresponding compensation.

--- **PRO TIPS** ---

- Have your business unit leaders get together (in person or virtually) once or twice a year to learn from one another and share best practices.
- Most human resource management (HRM) systems have the ability to maintain and produce an org chart. There are also a number of inexpensive software tools dedicated to that task.
- If you're struggling to create the ideal org structure for your company, read the chapter on the Accountability Chart in *Traction* by Gino Wickman.

FURTHER READING

Humanocracy: Creating Organizations as Amazing as the People Inside Them by Gary Hamel and Michele Zanini

Traction: Get a Grip on Your Business by Gino Wickman

CASE STUDY

Organizational Adaptation and Growth with
Holly Turner and Stampede America

During law school, Holly Turner interned at a district attorney's office, where she realized that the legal system was not quite what she had imagined. Young and idealistic, Holly pivoted toward politics, where she immersed herself in political campaigns, providing legal and consulting expertise. It was during these years that she realized the inherent challenge in scaling a political consulting firm: everyone wanted to engage with the consultant directly, making it nearly impossible to leverage other team members effectively.

In 2013, Holly partnered with her cofounder, Chris, to launch a new venture, Stampede America. The idea was simple yet ambitious: to make a difference by providing scalable political campaign staffing on a grassroots level. Stampede America specialized in getting canvassers to knock on doors, educate voters, collect data, and encourage voter turnout. The organization's unique twist was a focus on military veterans and their families, making them the backbone of their workforce for conservative causes and candidates. This approach not only offered disciplined and mission-driven personnel but also gave veterans meaningful work.

Early on, the company experienced some growing pains. The business model had to adjust to the cyclical nature of political campaigns, which saw a significant surge in staffing needs every two years during midterm and presidential elections. To attract high-quality employees for such short stints, Stampede America offered well-above-market pay rates, creating a highly competitive workforce. However, Holly and Chris quickly found that they needed to rethink their organizational structure multiple times to keep up with operational demands and growth.

At the local level, Stampede America initially structured their operations with one field manager overseeing around twelve canvassers per region. This model quickly showed its flaws. Managers were underutilized, and the limited scope of oversight made scaling difficult. Holly and her team pivoted to a new model where one field manager would oversee up to one hundred canvassers, gradually hiring and training new team members as they expanded. This change increased efficiency and allowed Stampede America to scale much more rapidly.

At the national level, Holly organized Stampede America geographically, with one operations director managing an entire state for multiple clients, including elected officials, candidates, political action committees, national committees, and associations. This structure created confusion for larger clients who were running campaigns across multiple states, as they had to work with different operations directors. It was also challenging for operations directors who needed to navigate the varying needs and technologies of multiple clients.

To address these issues, Holly and her team pivoted to a customer-centric model where each operations director focused on one or two key customers across multiple states. This shift allowed for more specialized and tailored support. As a result, Stampede America boosted their effectiveness and client satisfaction.

This customer-centric approach proved incredibly effective during the 2016 presidential election, enabling Stampede America to scale up to over three thousand canvassers. Building on this momentum, the company has continued to grow rapidly and was ranked eighty-eighth on the Inc. 500 list of fastest growing companies in the US in 2021.

Chapter 9

Measurable Objectives

DIFFICULTY: 3/5

We measure absolutely everything in the military, and we track the progress of every soldier over time. Whether it's how fast and far you can run, how many push-ups and pull-ups you can do, how accurately you can throw a grenade and shoot your assault rifle, how fast you can disassemble and reassemble a submachine gun, or how accurately you can distinguish foreign tanks and helicopters: whatever it is, it has defined metrics, and it is measured.

These metrics exist not to create needless paperwork but so we can set targets for each soldier to achieve in every discipline that matters for combat readiness. Speed, accuracy, and adherence to proper protocol can be the difference between life and death, so the military has a vested interest in laying out clear expectations and tracking progress over time.

A Mountain Grenadier may not be expected to be marksmen on day one, but their shooting scores should show clear improvement over time as they move toward that goal.

This applies not just to soldiers but officers as well, who are measured on the organization and effectiveness of their unit. As a lieu-tenant, I was measured on my ability to bring my platoon up to a high level of combat readiness and mission success. I was tested on this in a number of ways, from safety and risk management, communication, leadership development, operational planning, and performance on our training missions. In each category, I had clear measurable objec-tives, I understood what was expected of me, and the military made sure I met those expectations.

OBJECTIVES AND PRIORITIES

In business, using metrics, setting goals, and tracking progress are well-established practices for certain types of jobs. Take sales. Almost every business already sets targets for its sales team. Most salespeople have benchmarks, whether those include cold calls, closed opportuni-ties, revenue, or what have you. They know the number they have to hit, and they can track their progress over time. But too often, businesses fail to expand this process to other parts of the organization.

This is a mistake. Think of the clarity these measurable objectives provide to your sales team as well as the value you gain from the data you track. You not only measure overall sales and efficiency, you compare numbers across your whole team and reward around those metrics. Why not incorporate that into every part of your business?

The value here isn't just theoretical. I've found that setting measur-able objectives is the number one way to improve performance across your company. Not only do measurable objectives allow you to track progress more successfully, they also force conversations that need to happen between managers and their people. While some managers are naturally skilled at setting expectations and holding their team members accountable, others find it more challenging. Implement-ing a framework of setting measurable objectives for all employees across your organization provides managers with the tools they need to actually be managers.

With that framework in place, every manager can discuss with every person on their team what their objectives are, how they are performing, where there is room for improvement, and what to focus on in the next quarter. Everyone can be aligned on objectives and priorities. These are healthy conversations for every department.

Imagine, for instance, you're preparing a big push to sell your main software product to a larger audience. Before this sales push, you need to fix the bugs still lingering in that product. Without setting clear measurable objectives, it's easy for the new directive to get lost across the organization. How do you know if every programmer has pivoted to fixing bugs? Are everyone's individual objectives aligned with this initiative? Is everyone performing in their role? Or are some people still creating new functionality rather than repairing bugs?

The only way to be sure everyone is on the same page and doing their part is to set clear measurable objectives and track their progress over time.

KEEP IT SIMPLE

There are some wonderful advanced frameworks available if you want to really maximize the value of goal setting in your organization. In particular, I recommend OKRs, or "objectives and key results." This is the gold standard in goal setting and accountability. I won't spend time on it here, but if this interests you, go read *Measure What Matters* by John Doerr immediately.

However, you don't have to invest in OKRs to reap many of the same benefits. This process can be far easier to implement than many leaders assume. Setting clear objectives and tracking metrics for each position doesn't have to be a bureaucratic nightmare. You don't have to purchase a performance management system. It can be simple and lean. In fact, you can get started with nothing more than Microsoft Excel or Google Sheets.

To get started, all you really need to do is follow five simple steps:

1. ALIGN OBJECTIVES WITH BUSINESS GOALS

Ensure that employee objectives are directly linked to the overall strategic goals of the company. If your goal is to release a new version of your software product, and to do so you need as few bugs as possible, make sure every programmer involved has objectives tied to fixing bugs.

Importantly, you shouldn't just hand out objectives without explanation. You should communicate the company's mission, vision, and goals to all employees, providing context and alignment. Not only does this provide the background reasoning behind their objectives, it also gives your people something to get behind while they work toward their objectives.

2. INVOLVE EMPLOYEES IN OBJECTIVE SETTING

While individual objectives should be aligned with your company's overall strategic goals, it's important to engage employees in the objective-setting process. This increases buy-in and commitment.

At each objective-setting meeting (which we'll discuss in step 5), discuss and agree upon objectives collaboratively to ensure they are understood and accepted. Everyone is more willing to be held accountable if they have been part of the conversation around their own targets.

3. KEEP THE LIST SHORT

It can often be tempting to set objectives for every aspect of a team member's job. But it's far more productive to keep the list short. I recommend setting no more than three to five objectives for each employee. This makes it easier to keep track of performance and focus on those areas that really matter.

4. SET SMART OBJECTIVES

I don't want to spend too much time on this, since it's already very well-understood across most industries, but each goal you set should be SMART. That means they should be:

- Specific: Clearly defining what is to be achieved
- Measurable: Offering clear criteria to measure progress and success
- Achievable: Setting realistic objectives that are attainable with available resources
- Relevant: Aligning with the employee's role and the company's objectives
- Time-bound: Establishing a clear time frame for achieving the objectives

5. PROVIDE REGULAR FEEDBACK AND REVIEWS

To influence the positive returns on these objectives, managers have to spend time individually with their people. That's why it's so crucial to schedule regular check-ins and performance reviews to discuss progress and provide feedback.

These meetings are opportunities to troubleshoot, adjust goals when necessary, and recognize achievements. When possible, these meetings should be held in person unless the team member works remotely.

Meetings should take place across several timescales and with different purposes.

Weekly or Bi-Weekly Meetings

Meet with each person once a week or at least once every two weeks. These can be five- to ten-minute chats.

Purpose: For more informal updates, day-to-day progress discussions, and quick feedback.

Monthly Check-Ins

Slightly longer and more engaged, these meetings are a chance to catch developing issues.

Purpose: To discuss short-term objectives, address any immediate challenges, and provide ongoing support

Quarterly Reviews

A quarterly review is the perfect time for more engaged discussions around objectives and potentially to pivot into the next quarter. They are usually thirty-minute discussions with each team member.

Purpose: To assess progress toward objectives, provide constructive feedback, make any necessary adjustments, and set the objectives for the next quarter

This process is straightforward enough that any company can implement it. Eventually, we implemented a performance management system to help manage this process at Catapult. However, that's not a prerequisite for success with objective setting. You can just as easily follow this process and adjust it manually. The important thing is that every employee has a set of objectives to work toward that match company priorities, and that each manager has regular meetings with each member of their team to review their progress toward these goals.

As a quick side note, the terms "goal" and "objective" are often used interchangeably. I know I often do. But they have distinct meanings worth pointing out. A goal is a broad, long-term aim that an individual seeks to achieve. Goals are typically qualitative and focus on the big picture, setting the overall direction. They are more abstract and are often inspirational in nature. An objective, on the other hand, is a specific, measurable step that you take to achieve a goal. Objectives are more concrete and detailed than goals, outlining what needs to be done, and within what time frame.

- Setting clear and measurable objectives for employees is one of the best ways to improve performance across the company. It provides clarity on expectations, enables progress tracking, and encourages accountability.
- Implementing a performance management process doesn't need to be complex. Start by using simple tools like Excel or Google Sheets to track goals and progress. You can later upgrade to a more sophisticated system if needed.
- Employee objectives should be directly aligned with the company's strategic goals. Providing context on how their objectives tie into broader company goals helps employees stay motivated and committed.
- Engage employees in setting their own objectives. This collaboration increases their buy-in and commitment to achieving those objectives, making them more likely to succeed.
- Objectives should follow the SMART framework—Specific, Measurable, Achievable, Relevant, and Time-bound. Limit the number of objectives to three to five per employee.
- Regular check-ins, whether weekly, monthly, or quarterly, allow managers to monitor progress, troubleshoot challenges, and adjust objectives as necessary.
- Implementing a framework of setting measurable objectives forces essential conversations between manager and employee about what each person is focusing on and how that aligns with company strategy.

PRO TIPS

- Implementing measurable objectives won't work unless everyone across your entire organization participates in the program, including you and your executive team. Unless you join in, no one will take it seriously.
- Some objective setting methodologies recommend that you make

everyone's objectives visible to the whole company, including the CEO's objectives and the objectives of the entire executive team. I don't think that's necessary. So long as objectives are known by the manager and employee and carefully tracked, further visibility offers limited benefit.

FURTHER READING

Measure What Matters: How Google, Bono, and the Gates Foundation Rock the World with OKRs by John Doerr

CASE STUDY

Company-Wide Measurable Objectives at Oliva Gibbs LLP

Rob Lynch, a former member of the US national rowing team, transitioned into the business world after working as a schoolteacher in New York. His second career led to remarkable success, as Rob became the CEO of three Austin startups: ClearCommerce, Between Markets, and Innography. Each company achieved a successful exit under his leadership. For the past twelve years, Rob has applied his experience as a Scaling Up coach, helping CEOs and the executive teams of various companies scale their businesses effectively.

One of Rob's clients is Zack Oliva, the cofounder and managing partner of Oliva Gibbs LLP, a law firm specializing in transactional, litigation, and regulatory work for oil and gas companies across the United States. After reading the book *Scaling Up* and realizing he needed help implementing the recommended structured framework at his firm, Zack sought Rob's expertise. Together, they embarked on a journey to embed company-wide measurable objectives—referred to as "rocks" in the Scaling Up framework—into the firm's operations. This strategic partnership was pivotal in transforming Oliva Gibbs LLP from a small practice into a rapidly growing national firm with fifty attorneys and offices in multiple states.

Rob's first act as coach was to help Zack establish a business impact statement for each rock. The written statement would define the impact of successfully completing a rock for the company. He also emphasized the importance of identifying two numbers: a *critical number*—the one key performance indicator (KPI) most essential to the rock's success—and a *counterbalance number*—another KPI ensuring no unintended negative consequences arise from focusing too heavily on the critical number.

For example, while establishing a rock to start a new litigation practice at Oliva Gibbs LLP in 2023, the critical number was hiring six litigation lawyers, and the counterbalance number was the revenue generated from the new practice, ensuring that the new hires actually contributed to the firm's financial goals.

Under Rob's guidance, Oliva Gibbs LLP adopted these practices rigorously. Each rock was assigned a single owner and supporting team. Progress was monitored through weekly executive meetings, where milestones were color-coded (green, yellow, red) to track progress and take corrective action if necessary.

This structured approach allowed the firm to focus on its goals methodically, leading to significant growth. Since implementing measurable objectives with Rob, Oliva Gibbs LLP has grown fivefold, underscoring the effectiveness of using an outside coach and following a proven framework in driving sustainable business success.

Chapter 10

Real-Time Intelligence

DIFFICULTY: 3/5

In the military, getting real-time intelligence is a matter of life and death. Imagine the risk of approaching a target without knowing the approximate size of the enemy forces. Or imagine the difficulty of removing a threat when you can't trace its location. Even an elite military unit can set itself up for disaster without good intel.

For this reason, the military employs a variety of methods to gather real-time intelligence. It uses surveillance, such as aerial drones, reconnaissance aircraft, and satellite imagery, to monitor enemy positions and gain detailed views of the battlefield. It employs human intelligence, such as spies and informants, as well as techniques like interrogation, to gather firsthand, critical information about the enemy.

Signal intelligence, another resource, involves electronic eavesdropping and radar to intercept communications and monitor the movement of enemy vehicles. Meanwhile, cyber intelligence allows the military to monitor networks and hack enemy computer systems, tracking and disrupting their operations. As Mountain Grenadiers, we were trained to conduct deep reconnaissance and direct action missions to obtain critical intelligence behind enemy lines and report back to headquarters.

Our troops rely on geospatial intelligence that provides mapping and analysis, as well as 3D terrain models that provide crucial information about the terrain when planning an assault. When electronic mapping isn't available, we're trained to build 3D models in the dirt. A little rock can stand for a particular hill. A line in the dirt can stand for a river. We use pebbles and sticks to detail enemy positions. Primitive but effective.

These methods, often used in combination, provide a comprehensive picture of the battlefield, enabling military commanders to make informed decisions rapidly.

BUSINESS INTELLIGENCE AT ANY SIZE

Most business leaders are aware of the value of business intelligence (BI), they just assume it only exists at enterprise scale. BI, according to this thinking, is too complicated, too expensive, and generally reserved exclusively for large companies that can afford it. This misconstrues what business intelligence is at its root, how we obtain it, and when we use it.

In essence, they assume business intelligence as defined by the world of information technology—generally referring to a set of technologies and practices to help companies better understand the vast amount of business data they generate every day—is the only form of BI available. This can, as many assume, be costly and complex. However, on a basic level, business intelligence is much simpler than that. It's really any process that allows you to get the **right information** to the **right person** at the **right time** so they can make the best possible decision.

In the same way the military gathers intelligence in incredibly sophisticated ways alongside very simple methods, business intelligence is available at a much smaller scale than you might believe.

And you almost certainly already have the means to begin using it today.

A BUSINESS INTELLIGENCE STRATEGY FOR EVERY COMPANY

Introducing business intelligence to your company doesn't have to be complicated or cost a lot of money. With five simple steps, you can begin using it across your organization.

1. LESS IS MORE

Your car dashboard has a number of gauges. There are perhaps a dozen lights that can pop on from time to time. However, most of the time, when glancing down at the dashboard while driving, you only really need to look at the speedometer. Occasionally, you might also take a quick peek at the fuel level. Every other gauge is rarely checked.

I'm a private pilot, and I can tell you, the same is true of flying. Even though there are dozens of complex instruments on an airplane dashboard, a pilot only focuses on a select few at any one time—usually the altimeter, artificial horizon, and oil pressure. How high am I? Am I flying straight? What is my oil pressure? Those are the key questions they usually need to answer.

There's value in having access to those other gauges, but most of the value you gain comes from the gauges you check most often. The same is true of business intelligence. There is a ton of data out there, and there's value in having access to dozens of metrics, but for the most part, you only need a few data points to inform your decisions.

Additionally, there's real risk in overwhelming yourself with too much data. Most executives and managers are swimming in data. They struggle to make sense of it all or to integrate it into their thinking. What they really need are the few metrics that influence most of their decisions.

This is the first essential component of a successful BI strategy: figure out what *critical numbers matter* to your organization or department. Those numbers should total between one and three. They will be different for every business and every business unit, but the amount is almost always the same.

To unearth those metrics, ask yourself:

- What critical numbers drive your organization?
- Which ones are most effective at measuring the current and future health of your department?

If I'm running the regional office of a professional services organization, then I probably want to know what my utilization number is. I also want to look at my backlog of signed work because I need to know how far I'm scheduled out. Finally, I need to know my weighted sales pipeline.

That doesn't mean there aren't other numbers I could track. But I'm not looking at those other numbers every day. Particularly at a smaller scale, I don't need a fancy system that updates those other numbers for me all the time.

2. SETTLE ON A SINGLE TRUTH

It is common for business data to come from multiple systems or sources. It's also fairly common for different people to have different definitions of the same metric or to pull from different sources for the same critical number. This can prove disastrous. It can make a big difference how you calculate your average deal size or where you pull your revenue projections from. If different people in sales have a different sense of what that number looks like, they might as well be living in different realities.

It is essential, therefore, that everyone in an organization or department agree on a single definition of the truth and the sources used to derive that truth. Then, you have to stick with it.

Define the meaning of the term you are tracking and the sources you'll use to calculate it. If I say "utilization," what do I mean? Where do I draw from to determine that number?

From then on, everyone has to follow the same definition and use the same sources.

3. TREND IT

Once you've identified your one to three critical numbers and the data sources for those numbers, you have to define what success looks like for each one. Occasionally, you can define an absolute range as a health indicator for your business. For example, there is an optimal range for utilization and gross margin.

Most of the time, however, a number by itself is not that meaningful. Is one thousand units shipped good or bad? That really depends on whether it's up from 950 or down from 1,050. In other words, most critical numbers need to be trended over time to give them context and meaning.

Is your sales pipeline growing or shrinking over the last two quarters? Has your backlog crept up this quarter or is it running flat? To make any sense of the numbers you're tracking, you have to trend them over several quarters.

With a trend set, all updates should simply add the next datapoint onto your graph or chart, giving everyone an easy way to eyeball the current state of business. Much like glancing at the speedometer, it will only take an instant to know exactly how fast the company is moving.

4. PUT IT ON DISPLAY

That final point about eyeballing the trendline is important. Critical numbers are useless unless they can be seen by those people who can impact them. Don't make this information hard to find. Display your critical numbers front and center. Post them on the wall, write them on a whiteboard, or highlight them on your intranet.

At FlashParking, we targeted our support call process. To keep our customer support levels at an elite level, we maniacally tracked how long it took to resolve each support call. But that information was only valuable because we made sure the numbers were extremely conspicuous. They were kept in front of everyone's face. If the goal was to resolve an issue within two hours, we wanted everyone to see when we fell short. If it took us two days to address the problem, that needed to be painfully on display for all to see—from leadership down to the front lines of that department.

Once again, this is easier to do than you might assume. It doesn't require an expensive system. You can just write the number on a whiteboard. You can send a quick email every day to the whole team with the updated graph.

And make sure the updates are simple and straightforward. Like your speedometer, keep the visual language easy to interpret at a glance. By far, the most effective way to grab people's attention and make these numbers easy to understand is to display them graphically. Use charts, graphs, gauges, meters, icons: anything to help your audience visualize your critical numbers. Line up, good. Line down, bad. Red number, bad; black number, good. With cues that simple, everyone can track how the company or department is doing.

5. AUTOMATE

Nothing I've discussed so far requires the purchase of expensive software to be implemented successfully. You can take this system pretty far by simply appointing one person to be in charge of updating and sharing your critical numbers for the company or the department.

At some point in a company's evolution, however, it makes sense to automate this process through technology. It doesn't have to be complicated or expensive, and not every critical number needs to be automated at once. But the more this can be automated over time, the better. Just know, you don't have to start there.

HUMAN INTELLIGENCE

In the previous sections, I have focused on quantitative intelligence—the critical numbers that drive an organization or department. Qualitative data, while not as straightforward to collect, is equally important. This type of intelligence comes from engaging with people and conducting targeted research. I typically focus on five areas of human intelligence:

- Employees
- Customers
- Competitors
- Suppliers/Vendors
- Projects

EMPLOYEES

This should be your first stop when gathering human intelligence. After all, your employees know your company—its greatest assets, its limitations, and its potential—better than anyone. For this reason, I have dedicated Chapter 18 to discussing how to assess employee morale and engagement. Therefore, I will skip this topic here.

CUSTOMERS

Customers have the best outside view of your company. They know when your company is living up to its promises and providing the highest-quality service. To gather customer intelligence, the gold standard is the Net Promoter Score (NPS) as described in *The Ultimate Question 2.0* by Fred Reichheld. There is really no substitute. This method centers on a single pivotal question: "On a scale from zero to ten, how likely are you to recommend us to a friend?", where zero is not likely at all, and ten is extremely likely. Respondents fall into three categories:

- Promoters (9–10): Happy, loyal customers who will buy from you time and time again.
- Passives (7–8): Customers who got what they paid for from your company and nothing more. They are indifferent and not likely to be long-term loyal customers.

- Detractors (0–6): Dissatisfied customers who are likely to disparage your company with friends and colleagues.

Your company's NPS score is calculated as: *% of promoters – % distractors*. Passives are ignored in this formula. For example, in 2013, Catapult had an NPS score of seventy-three. That same year, Apple's NPS score was seventy-eight, and Amazon's was seventy-one.

Many companies will use an online survey tool to gather this information. That might work for high-transaction industries, but many customers experience survey fatigue and are increasingly less likely to respond to an online survey or email.

At Catapult, we found that calling our active customers once a quarter was a better approach. One afternoon a week, our receptionist called a list of customers that were due for a check-in. She followed a very simple script: "Hi, this Leslie with Catapult's customer experience team. Do you have thirty seconds to provide us some quick feedback?" She asked the NPS question, listened attentively, recorded their NPS scores and comments, and avoided attempting to resolve issues on the spot. Customers always elaborated, especially if things weren't going perfectly. These insights were consolidated into a dashboard and reviewed weekly, providing actionable intelligence.

COMPETITORS

While I never agonize over what the competition is doing, and I don't benchmark our company against them, it's still important to keep tabs on them. You don't want to be blindsided if your competition enters a new market, changes their prices drastically, introduces a game-changing feature, raises a big round of funding, or acquires another company. To avoid that, you need real-time intelligence on their activities.

There are many ways of collecting this intelligence, including talking to your competitors' customers and vendors, meeting directly with them at trade shows, spending time on their website, and setting up Google Alerts to find out when they are mentioned online. You can also have someone on your marketing team comb through your competitors' websites once a quarter. If one of their employees interviews with you, that can also be a treasure trove of information.

Your salespeople are great at collecting this kind of intelligence, but so are your other frontline employees. Make sure that everyone in your organization knows who your top competitors are and are trained to inquire about them if given the opportunity. To gather all this information in one place, you can create a Wiki page on your intranet where your employees can write down anything they hear about a competitor. At Catapult, we reviewed competitor intel once a quarter during our executive offsite meetings.

SUPPLIERS/VENDORS

It's not usually as important to monitor your vendors or suppliers, unless they are integral to your operations. If you do need this information, you are usually looking for big changes that could massively affect your business.

At FlashParking, for example, we used a ruggedized tablet PC in our parking kiosks. When COVID-19 first broke out in 2020, we assumed that global supply chains would be disrupted, and since our tablet PC vendor relied on parts from China, we knew we were potentially at risk. If we ran out of components to manufacture our kiosks, we would have nothing to sell. So we preemptively purchased their entire remaining inventory to give us as much runway as possible. This decision proved vital, and we were able to continue running our business uninterrupted during the pandemic.

PROJECTS

Most companies don't systematically gather qualitative intelligence from their frontline employees, relying instead solely on quantitative metrics. The problem with this is that managers have deadlines and quotas and are often tempted to report only good news. If a project falls behind or experiences quality issues, a manager might hesitate to sound the alarm because they believe they can resolve the issue on their own. This can have catastrophic consequences, as you might not find out about an issue until it's too late—when you receive a low NPS score, have to recall a product, or worse.

The irony is that someone on the front lines likely knew about the issues all along. They were simply never asked.

We experienced this firsthand at Catapult. When we were small and only running a few projects at a time, it was easy to keep tabs on everything. If something wasn't going well, we knew about it immediately. However, as we grew geographically and started delivering over a hundred projects simultaneously, we had to rely on our project managers to keep us informed. On several occasions, a project manager was overly optimistic, thought they could fix the problem on their own, and failed to raise the red flag. By the time the problem was finally escalated to the executive team, the customer was furious, and it cost us a fortune to get the project back on track.

To address this issue, we implemented a system requiring every Catapult consultant to provide us weekly feedback on every client engagement they were working on. We asked them how they *felt* about each project using a zero to ten rating scale—like the NPS survey—with an opportunity to leave a short comment. This was one of the most impactful processes we ever implemented at Catapult. When a project occasionally experienced challenges, we always found out about it immediately, allowing us to rapidly address the issue long before it escalated into a bigger problem.

KEY TAKEAWAYS

- At its core, business intelligence is any process that allows you to get the right information to the right person at the right time so they can make better decisions.

- Identify one to three critical metrics that drive your business or department and focus on monitoring these regularly.
- Agree on a single definition of each critical number and the sources used to derive that critical number.
- Track your critical metrics over time to understand whether the trend is positive or negative, giving insight into how the business is performing.
- Ensure that the key metrics are prominently displayed and easy to understand. By keeping them front and center, everyone in the organization knows where they stand.
- Represent critical metrics graphically—charts, gauges, and colors (e.g., red for negative, green for positive). This allows everyone to easily understand the current performance at a glance.
- Appoint someone responsible for regularly updating and sharing the metrics. As your company evolves, automate the tracking and sharing of your key metrics.
- Engage with people and conduct targeted research to gather intelligence on your employees, customers, competitors, vendors, and projects.

PRO TIPS

- You can track critical numbers down to each individual, not just at the department or company level, especially once you automate. For example, what is the personal utilization and average bill rate of an IT consultant?
- When identifying your critical numbers, it's helpful to have some focused on your past state (like your financials), present state (like number of cars parked or shipping volume), and others focused on your future state (like reservations or sales pipeline).
- Gathering intelligence about your competitors and strategic vendors can now increasingly be automated through the use of AI.

CASE STUDY

Aquasana: Leveraging Real-Time Data to Drive Growth

Todd Bartee's journey into data-driven decision-making began at Dell Computer Corporation, where he initially worked as a quality manager for their consumer product line. In this role, Todd was responsible for analyzing field failure data to identify trends and proactively address product issues. Later, as a member of Dell's consumer forecasting team, Todd gained deeper expertise in leveraging data to inform strategic decisions, particularly around optimizing marketing expenditures.

When Todd was promoted to run Dell's consumer sales division—overseeing three thousand agents across seven locations—he had to identify the right key performance indicator (KPI) to drive sales without sacrificing customer experience. Todd settled on "margin per call" as the crucial KPI. He not only surfaced the KPI in real time to every sales agent, he also linked it directly to their compensation. This strategic alignment of metrics and incentives helped drive performance and accountability across the division.

In 2010, Todd was recruited by a private equity firm to serve as CEO of Aquasana, a direct-to-consumer residential water filtration business. The company operated with a recurring revenue model by selling replacement water filters. As a result, Todd was able to estimate the lifetime value of each customer.

Todd recognized that, in a direct-to-consumer environment, marketing expenditure was the most significant lever for growth. He applied his expertise from Dell to track contribution margins across customer segments and to identify the most effective metrics to drive the business forward. Aquasana's primary KPI became "return on ad spend," which measured the revenue generated for every dollar invested in marketing.

This KPI was more accurate than the traditional customer acquisition cost metric because Aquasana sold a range of products—from a $69 shower filter to a $1,500 whole house filtration system—and they were willing to spend more to acquire a higher lifetime value customer. A return on ad spend metric would allow Aquasana to evaluate the marginal return for each marketing dollar spent, helping the team determine where to best allocate resources for maximum impact. For instance, the business adjusted its marketing channels—moving dollars from paid search to direct mail, or vice versa—based on where the highest return was at any given time. This data-driven approach would allow Aquasana to strategically balance growth and profitability, adjusting investments based on the diminishing returns of each marketing channel.

Aquasana's disciplined marketing strategy also emphasized incremental improvements. Todd implemented a practice where 10 percent of the marketing budget was dedicated to testing and experimentation, assuming no return on these dollars to avoid risk-averse budgeting. This creative resource allocation allowed Aquasana to find new scalable marketing channels, such as expanding into Amazon and refining their direct mail campaigns. By continually measuring, learning, and optimizing, Todd's team created a systematic way to unlock new growth opportunities. Through this data-driven strategy, Aquasana's revenue surged from $10 million to over $100 million in just eight years.

Chapter 11

Checklists

DIFFICULTY: 2/5

After graduating from Texas A&M, I received my orders from the Swiss defense department to return to Switzerland for officer candidate school. Along with my marching orders, the Swiss Army provided a checklist for everything I needed to do before showing up on base. Whether it was completing my medical evaluation, filling out my paperwork, or retrieving my assault rifle from the local arsenal in Fribourg, it was all on the list. The checklist also reminded me to gather my military-issued combat boots, dress uniform, backpack, all the way down to my belt buckles. There was even a list of personal effects I would need to bring with me, such as socks, underwear, and toiletries.

The military loves checklists. Whether a situation is stressful and chaotic, or repetitive and boring, a checklist always helps reduce mistakes. In the Swiss military, we had checklists for mission planning, combat patrol, vehicle maintenance, camp setup, live fire exercises, supply delivery, inventory management, radio communication, and medical evacuation. If it was something we had to do and it involved a process, there was a checklist for it.

Some of these lists were in writing, such as the one I followed when preparing for officer candidate school. Others, though, were memorized. When you learn to load an anti-tank rocket launcher, for example, each step is repeated verbally over and over until it's ingrained in your mind. One, safety on. Two, load the rocket. Three, check your rear. Four, safety off. And so on. This way, whenever you're loading and firing a weapon in dangerous, high-stress situations, you intuitively follow the checklist that's running in your head. That leads to fewer mistakes, and no one gets blown up accidentally.

A BORING, USEFUL TOOL

Starting out in business, checklists often feel unnecessary because the founder and their core team is doing everything. They have to learn on the fly, and once they do, they feel they know the process. Why waste time drafting a list or checking items off when they figured out the process themselves?

But even when you're the only one following the process, there's still value in codifying it in a list. I learned this lesson in 1997, the year Catapult launched our flagship software product, Inquisite. Eager to reach a large audience of potential customers, I realized the best way to get the word out about Inquisite was to attend some trade shows. One of the natural target customers for our online survey platform was HR departments that conducted employee surveys. And they all attended the Society for Human Resource Management trade shows. So I signed up as a vendor at the national trade show, as well as several of the society's regional events.

Without a sales team in place, it was left to me to work the booth, and I noticed pretty quickly that there was a fair amount of complexity to attending a trade show as a vendor. I had to keep track of registration deadlines, shipping deadlines, what needed to be shipped, and making sure we had enough marketing collateral printed in time for shipping. I also had to figure out what equipment I needed to bring, all of the booth components, and basic logistical concerns like hotel reservations, flights, and transportation—all while holding down the CEO role for Catapult.

For the first couple of trade shows, I consistently found myself forgetting *something*, often a deadline or a piece of equipment. I'm sure, in time, I would have mastered all this and reduced the number of errors I made simply through repetition. But I already knew the value of a checklist from my days in the Swiss Army, so after those mistakes, I created a comprehensive trade show checklist. It included all the tasks I had to complete and all the items I had to bring with me.

The mistakes disappeared overnight. And that wasn't the only benefit. When we eventually did build up a software products sales and marketing team, I was able to delegate trade shows to them. Instead of that team starting from scratch, they attended their first trade show using my checklist. Over time, they added their own items to the list to match changes in process and personal preference. In other words, it became a living document, evolving with the team.

IF IT'S COMPLEX, IT NEEDS A CHECKLIST

Any process that is sufficiently complex and important in your business should have a checklist. Even if it seems like everyone knows the process, I'd still recommend creating one. They allow you to reduce errors, ensure consistency, and enhance efficiency and accountability. I'm such a believer in checklists, in fact, I use them in my personal life. I own a lake house on Lake LBJ about forty-five miles outside Austin. I often let friends and family use it. When someone asks to spend a weekend there, though, the first thing I send them is my lake house checklist. It includes everything they need to do from arrival to locking the door on the way out. It has instructions of where everything is and how to use the boat and jet skis. The final step on the departure checklist is to text me a picture of the master water shutoff valve in the closed position. This checklist allows me to hold my guests accountable while also keeping them safe and ensuring they know how everything works.

Even if you aren't sold on checklists in your personal life, they are an immense help in business—and not just in tech either. Checklists are the easiest way to document your process, no matter the department. At Catapult, for instance, once we started on checklists, we added them everywhere, including:

- Project Management, for project initiation and close
- Human Resources, for employee onboarding, performance reviews, and employee offboarding
- Finance and Accounting, for monthly closing procedures and audit preparation
- Marketing, for campaign launches, as well as the previously mentioned event and tradeshow planning
- Sales, detailing the sales call process and customer follow-up
- Customer Service, for ticket resolution and collecting and analyzing customer feedback
- IT and Security, for system maintenance, backup procedures, and incident response

And that isn't even a complete list. Like I said, anywhere the process was complex and important enough, we added a checklist.

CHECKLISTS ARE WORTH THE TIME

Not everything in business requires a checklist, of course. For actions that are simple and relatively unimportant, there's no reason to waste time on filling out a form. However, if you're concerned about bureaucratic time wasting, let me assure you, a checklist is often worth the minor inconvenience that comes with the paperwork.

For instance, like all manufacturers, FlashParking has a checklist to ensure quality control at each stage of the assembly process. This is standard procedure in manufacturing, but it's often the only checklist those companies employ. We changed that and added a checklist for our third-party installers. FlashParking installs equipment in garages across the country, which means we have to rely on construction workers and certified electricians to get our installations right. In our business, even a relatively small mistake can be very costly.

In order to ensure that our installers perform the work correctly and test everything thoroughly, we require that they fill out a thorough project completion checklist. They have to check off each item on Google Sheets and upload about thirty different photos to prove they've done everything correctly.

From the outside, this may seem like overkill. It may feel like bureaucratic inefficiency. But before we added that checklist, the most expensive issue we faced with our product was returning to a job site because we missed something during installation. Sure, our installation checklist slows down our contractors a little bit, but the money we save avoiding errors—and our ability to hold partners accountable—is worth it.

For any process sufficiently important to your business—any process you can't afford to get wrong—you need a checklist.

KEY TAKEAWAYS

- Checklists help eliminate errors in complex processes, ensuring consistency and quality.
- Documented processes and checklists make it easier to delegate tasks to others.
- Checklists are not static—they should evolve over time to reflect changes in processes, incorporating new learnings and preferences from different team members.
- Checklists are also a tool to hold people accountable, whether inside your organization or with third parties.

- Begin with a checklist for one important process in your business, then expand to other areas. This helps establish a culture of process improvement without overwhelming your team.
- When creating checklists, involve team members who execute those processes. They can provide insights into key steps and help ensure the checklist is practical and effective.
- Consider using digital tools like Google Sheets or specialized apps to manage checklists. This enables easy tracking, updates, and sharing with relevant stakeholders.

FURTHER READING

The Checklist Manifesto: How to Get Things Right by Atul Gawande

CASE STUDY

Julio Torres and the Importance of Checklists

Julio Torres's love for both construction and aviation began at a young age. By the time he turned seventeen, he had earned his private pilot's license. One pivotal moment during his early flying days—when he discovered a loose belt on his plane's alternator during a preflight inspection—instilled in him an appreciation for safety measures, particularly checklists. This could have led to a catastrophic failure midflight had he not caught it, but a checklist saved him.

Later in life, while earning his MBA at Kellogg, Julio encountered another example of the power of checklists through a case study on reducing mortality rates in hospitals. The healthcare industry had drawn lessons from aviation, implementing checklists to reduce errors and saw substantial improvements in patient safety.

In 2005, Julio founded Tordec, an engineering, procurement, and construction company in Monterrey, Mexico. In the early days, Julio was a one-man operation, handling everything from sales to supervising construction sites. As the business grew, Julio began to hire more staff, but he soon noticed that the results from his team weren't as consistent as when he managed tasks himself. Recalling his aviation training and his MBA case study, Julio decided to implement checklists throughout his growing organization to create clear expectations, reduce the chances of errors, and improve communication across departments.

Julio's first step was to develop detailed checklists for core business processes, including hiring, estimating large projects, invoicing for partial payments, and closing out projects. By standardizing these processes, Tordec began to build a reputation for quality and reliability, delivering consistent results across every project.

The use of checklists became a cornerstone of Tordec's success, allowing it to manage complex projects efficiently. Tordec continued to grow, expanding into large infrastructure projects for both private and public sector clients, including roads, bridges, waterworks, and industrial developments. Tordec now employs over five hundred people and operates throughout Mexico, with a reputation for delivering turnkey solutions that consistently meet high standards.

Julio continues to evolve his checklists and his company. Still an active private pilot, he just got certified on his new TBM 850 aircraft. During his recent training at a simulator in Scottsdale, Arizona, Julio was introduced to the concept of "flow" in aviation. "Flow" refers to a systematic, intuitive sequence of actions that pilots follow during preflight, in-flight, and postflight procedures. These actions are often done without referring to a physical checklist, following the layout of the aircraft's controls, switches, and instruments in a logical and smooth pattern, designed to ensure that nothing is overlooked. Inspired by this new approach, Julio is now planning to implement a similar flow-based system at Tordec, streamlining operations even further. This evolution will allow his team to execute complex tasks efficiently while maintaining the same high standards of consistency and safety that have driven Tordec's success.

Chapter 12

Decentralized Decision-Making

DIFFICULTY: 2/5

In any special forces unit, the ability of individual team members and small groups to respond rapidly to dynamic and unpredictable situations without waiting for approval from some higher command is crucial for operational effectiveness and mission success. This "decentralized decision-making" allows for adaptability and flexibility at the speed of battle, enabling units to exploit fleeting opportunities and counter threats with great responsiveness and agility, essential traits for the high-stakes, time-sensitive nature of special operations.

I experienced the value of this concept myself as a lieutenant. Our Mountain Grenadier company was on maneuvers at the time in the Gotthard Pass region, a rugged patch of mountain in southern Switzerland. My platoon was given specific orders to engage and capture a mock command post near the summit of the pass at exactly midnight in two days' time. We were not told how to accomplish the mission; that was up to us. A different platoon was tasked with repelling any assault over the next few days without instruction on how to do so. They also didn't know the exact date and time of our attack.

With significant freedom, we had some important calls to make. We could definitely approach this task "by the book." Reviewing the terrain map, the obvious choice was a two-sided attack, one coming up from the valley and the other descending from the top of the pass. We knew this was the approach our instructor likely assumed we would take—and the approach the other platoon was likely to prepare for. It was also a fatal plan. With both sides of the pass guarded, following that plan would turn this operation into a suicide mission.

During our reconnaissance of the area the day before the scheduled attack, though, we hit a lucky break. Two of my corporals and I noticed a flaw in the other platoon's defenses: they were not guarding the rear of the command post. This was not due to any particular oversight on their part. The command post was built into a two-hundred-foot vertical cliff. There was no obvious way to attack from the rear. But we noticed a hiking path on the map that led right to the top of the peak overlooking the post. This was the unexpected advantage we needed to change the odds on this mission.

I split up my platoon into three fire teams. The first two were instructed to approach from the valley and mountain pass as expected, mainly as a diversion. The third fire team, meanwhile, would hike up the back of the cliff and quietly rappel down in the dead of night, ending up on the roof of the concrete command post. I personally led that team.

I'm not going to lie, rappelling down a two-hundred-foot cliff in pitch darkness when you're not completely sure that your climbing rope is long enough was pretty scary. It took us about an hour, but we managed to lower nine men onto the top of the bunker without being detected. The whole team was in place by 23:00, an hour before we had to take the post.

Most of that hour was spent in concentrated silence, putting all our effort into avoiding making any telltale sound that would alert the platoon below us. At 23:45, the instructor arrived, and the other platoon knew something was coming. They increased their readiness. From our vantage point, I could see the instructor glance down at his watch. He looked a little frustrated, perhaps because he saw no sign of our platoon yet. He must have assumed we had failed the mission.

At exactly midnight, we lowered two of my men head-first by their harnesses. They threw practice grenades into the command post through the open windows while the rest of us shot the opposing platoon recruits (with blanks, obviously) who were facing away from the roof, watching the path. At that exact same moment, my two other fire teams advanced rapidly from the valley and the pass.

The whole thing was all over in a couple of minutes. The other platoon was decimated, the command post was captured, and we didn't suffer a single casualty.

TEAMS DON'T NEED A MICROMANAGER

If we'd been told exactly how to do that mission, we would have failed. My commanding officer would have asked us to follow the "by the book" plan, attacking from both sides of the road. With the terrain advantages the other platoon had, they almost certainly would have mowed us down. It was only because our commanding officers trusted us to make the call ourselves that we were able to come up with a strategy that Mountain Grenadier instructors still talk about to this day.

In any organization, part of the reason you hire people is so they can take on the responsibility of making important calls without involving you. But this is a tough lesson for entrepreneurs to absorb. When a founder starts a new company, they have their hand in every aspect of the business—because they have to. They perform every job across the organization and develop every process, procedure, and department over time. If they don't do it all, it won't get done. There's simply no one else to do it. As a result, the founder is intimately familiar with every role and function in the organization, from accounting and human resources to sales and marketing.

This is an asset in the beginning. But as a company grows, becomes more complex, and starts hiring others to run those functions, this intimate understanding of every nook and cranny of the business can actually limit potential growth and success if the founder doesn't step back.

I fell into this trap myself. I was twenty-six years old when I started Catapult Systems, and I had to learn every aspect of running a business. As the company grew, I struggled to let go of true control. It's not that I felt my people would fail without me, I just felt compelled to be a part of every single meaningful decision we made as a company. Honestly, I even held on to a number of responsibilities that weren't meaningful at all. For instance, I insisted on personally hanging the whiteboards in every new office conference room because I felt I was the only one who could get them "just right."

None of this was intentional. I felt confident that I was being a good leader. I led by example, working tirelessly ninety hours a week and displaying great resilience and emotional fortitude for all to see. I was certain I was making good decisions that were leading the company in the right direction. Unfortunately, what I couldn't see at the time was that my command-and-control management style was actually holding our company back. My micromanagement was unintentionally stifling the capabilities of my team.

Then fate intervened. In 2000, my father was diagnosed with cancer and was told he had six months to live. He resided in Munich, Germany, at the time. I did what any loving son would: I packed my bags and prepared to leave immediately. Out of necessity, I told my management team that I would be unreachable for a month. They were in charge now.

Until that moment, I had never taken more than a few days off from work and had never been out of reach for more than a day or two. My team was stunned and didn't know how to react at first.

"How will we make decisions?" one of them asked me.

"You'll figure it out," I told them. "I trust you."

And it's true. I did trust them. I knew I had good, experienced people working for me. I knew they could do it. I had just never thought to give them the chance before. Now, I had no choice. This was in the era before Zoom—a time when an international call was eye-wateringly expensive. I did have email, but I barely checked it. During my time away, I only read through and approved one document. I made no changes.

That month with my father was great. Though his cancer would eventually take his life, it was not as aggressive as the doctors thought at first, and we had another eight years together. That wonderful surprise was still ahead, but another one met me when I returned to Austin after my time away. Much to my amazement, my company was not just running as well as it had when I left, it was running better—and not by a little. Without me in the way, my leadership team discovered talents they never knew they had. Because I wasn't there to review every decision, they had stepped up and taken full accountability for their actions. Over the course of those weeks, they grew more confident, took more initiative, and started trying new approaches. Everyone around them felt more empowered as well.

I have to admit that, at first, my ego didn't quite know how to grapple with feeling somewhat marginalized. But I quickly got over it. After all, I'd put that team together. I knew I had people I could trust to own their positions. Like my own commanding officer, I'd taken a chance giving them decentralized decision-making authority—and it had really paid off.

CREATING A TEAM YOU CAN TRUST

As we discussed in Chapter 7, hiring is an incredibly important function within your organization. You have to have the right people in place to succeed. But if you have the right people, you should be able to hand them the authority to make decisions in their department. The results will often quickly speak for themselves. In fact, despite struggling to let go of decision-making control across the rest of my company, I actually learned this lesson pretty early at Catapult.

When we started out, I had my next-door neighbor, Alice Werchan, help me with the books. I handled day-to-day accounting back then, but once a quarter, I'd sit down with her, and she helped me file the company's taxes. I always joked with her, "Someday, we'll be big enough to hire you full-time." And she'd always laugh it off. Eighteen months later, though, I got the last laugh and brought her into the company full- time.

One of the best days of my life was handing accounting over to Alice. At that point, it'd been a year since I had reconciled our bank statements with our transaction records. You can imagine how eager I was to get this task permanently off my desk. While I was at it, I also gave her HR. We were so small at the time, both functions could be handled by one person.

But we kept growing. Eventually, Alice was working eighty hours a week, and she was as far behind on accounts as I had been when she came on board. The situation was untenable. I told her she'd have to choose one function, and I'd hire someone else for the other. Much to my surprise, and I think hers, she chose HR.

That's when we brought in Mike Albe. Mike loves accounting. I'm almost allergic to going over the books, but he genuinely enjoys it. He was better than I could ever be at that job from day one. While I made sure to regularly check in and review things like expenses (an annual inspection that I'll explain in detail in Chapter 15), I mostly left him to handle the accounting as he saw fit.

At its core, handing over decision-making authority is as simple as trusting the people you've hired to know their role and what that role requires. That doesn't mean you refuse to support them; you just don't get in their way. Set the overall strategy, then give them the freedom to do what they do best. Accept that they'll make mistakes and sometimes get things wrong. With a little trial and error, most will rise to the occasion.

A FRAMEWORK FOR EMPOWERING YOUR PEOPLE

When handing over increased authority, it can be useful to create a structure around decision-making. For me, the best and simplest structure is the "Rules of Empowerment." Jack Daly lays these rules out in his book *Hyper Sales Growth*. These rules are really questions. If a person on your team is unsure whether they have the authority to take an action in a particular situation, all they have to do is answer these five questions:

- Is it right for the client?
- Is it right for our company?
- Is it ethical?
- Is it in line with our core company values?
- Are you willing to be held accountable for it?

If the answer to all five is yes, just do it. There's no need to ask your manager. We made it clear that no one would ever be punished for getting something wrong if they'd run the scenario through the Rules of Empowerment.

To further entrench our people's decision-making authority, we also gave everyone a budget. This included, at the lower end, a $100 "make it right" allowance. Every customer-facing employee could spend up to $100 on anything that would correct or improve a client situation. No questions asked. If they were working late with a client and wanted to order everyone pizza, no need to call a manager for permission—just order. If a client's mother passed away, don't ask, just send flowers.

This "no questions asked" budget scaled up so that managers had thousands of dollars set aside, and VPs had even more.

Decentralized decision-making ended up becoming so important to Catapult that we placed these ideas front and center, adding them to our boot camp under the title of "Freedom & Responsibility." From day one, everyone knew we expected initiative and accountability, and we'd give them the space to make their own calls. Overwhelmingly, our people proved they deserved that trust.

WHAT YOU CAN'T DELEGATE

Once you start successfully delegating key aspects of your company, you might be tempted to hand over everything to your executive team. After all, why not? If it's worked so well so far, perhaps you could hand over most of the rest of your responsibilities and enjoy an early retirement.

Unfortunately, there is one thing you can't delegate. As my business mentor Verne Harnish cautioned me, "A founder can delegate (or outsource) everything except the soul of the business." For example, Steve Jobs famously never delegated or outsourced product design and user experience at Apple. He was deeply involved in ensuring that every product reflected his vision of simplicity, elegance, and functionality. Jobs believed that the design and overall experience of Apple's products were the "soul" of the company, and he maniacally maintained a hands-on approach in this area.

At Catapult, I was focused on building an efficient, well-run company. You might even say I wanted to run my business with Swiss Army precision. Process automation was a key component of doing this at scale. Therefore, I delegated every aspect of the business over time except for our internal app dev team. That continued to report directly to me.

That's how I continued to drive efficiency and productivity across the entire organization, even as we scaled to hundreds of employees. That was the soul of our business.

KEY TAKEAWAYS

- Businesses run more successfully when authority is handed down to the people who need to make the call in each situation.
- Founders often struggle to let go of control, which can limit growth. Trusting the right people to make decisions without oversight helps unlock their potential, enabling them to grow more confident and take greater ownership.

- A framework, such as the "Rules of Empowerment," can help employees determine when they have the authority to act.
- Create an environment where mistakes are accepted as a part of learning. Empowering employees means accepting some degree of risk.
- To further entrench decision-making authority at your company, give everyone a budget. That budget is different at every level of your organization, but will empower your employees to make decisions that benefit customers without seeking approval.
- Embedding decentralized decision-making into company culture, from onboarding onward, sets clear expectations that initiative and accountability are valued and rewarded.
- A founder can delegate or outsource everything except the soul of the business.

PRO TIPS

- Recognize and celebrate instances where team members successfully make independent decisions that benefit the company. This positive reinforcement encourages others to take initiative as well.

FURTHER READING

Hyper Sales Growth: Street-Proven Systems & Processes. How to Grow Quickly & Profitably by Jack Daly.

Outrageous Empowerment: The Incredible Story of Giving Employees Their Brains Back by Ron Lovett

CASE STUDY

Implementing Decentralized Decision-Making at Trident Proposal Management

Jeff Everage, a former Navy SEAL with a background in systems engineering at the US Naval Academy, founded Trident Proposal Management in 2009 after a diverse career that included stints at Booz Allen Hamilton and PricewaterhouseCoopers. Trident Proposal Management specializes in providing business development services for large and medium-sized government contractors, including proposal management and writing, training and advisory services, and capture management. Jeff's company quickly gained a reputation for handling high-stakes proposals, often valued at billions of dollars.

Despite its early success, Trident eventually hit a plateau, which prompted Jeff to seek the help of a business coach. During a session with his business coach, Jeff realized that he was the primary decision-maker for nearly every aspect of the company, significantly slowing down operations and hindering growth. The coach introduced Jeff to the Entrepreneurial Operating System (EOS), which provided the framework for evaluating and evolving his organization. Jeff worked with his coach to develop a comprehensive org chart that included roles beyond just operations, such as business development, marketing, sales, HR, and finance. This exercise highlighted that Jeff was overly involved in almost every area of his business, prompting the need for a more distributed approach to decision-making. To address his over-involvement, Jeff created a leadership team who took over significant portions of the organizational responsibilities. He then introduced a decision matrix to clearly define who was responsible for making specific decisions, ensuring that authority was appropriately distributed. This matrix was regularly updated to reflect the evolving roles within the company.

After these structures were in place, Jeff had the opportunity to take a three-month sabbatical to get reenergized and rethink his role at Trident. During his absence, the leadership team successfully managed the company, proving that the decentralized decision-making system worked. Upon his return, Jeff found that he no longer needed to be involved in most daily decisions, allowing him to focus on higher-level strategic planning. The company has thrived ever since, quadrupling its annual revenue and increasing its profit margins.

Chapter 13

Always Be Training

DIFFICULTY: 3/5

In Switzerland, it sometimes seems that all we do is train. Because our active duty soldiers are functionally similar to most countries' reserves, ongoing training in the Swiss Army is paramount for maintaining a high level of readiness and operational effectiveness. Our continuous training sessions, known as repetition courses, ensure that we stay proficient in crucial skills and up-to-date with the latest tactics, equipment, and procedures long after basic training.

Repetition courses last three weeks each year and are required until the age of thirty for soldiers and fifty for officers. They encompass a variety of activities, including advanced marksmanship, tactical maneuvers, survival skills, and leadership training. Over those three weeks, we also engage in simulated combat scenarios with other divisions—which hone our ability to respond to real-world threats with agility and precision—participate in physical fitness programs to maintain peak condition, and run teamwork exercises to reinforce unit cohesion and communication.

By regularly revisiting and refining our skills, Swiss militia soldiers remain a formidable force, capable of rapidly mobilizing and effectively protecting the country—even as we spend the other forty-nine weeks of the year living otherwise normal lives.

EDUCATION SHOULD NEVER END

There are some careers where we expect professionals to engage in lifelong continuing education. Doctors, lawyers, CPAs, pilots, therapists—essentially everyone with a professional license—also have to engage in regular courses that update and reinforce their knowledge. Yet in a business setting, most professions require no further education once a diploma is handed out. And because it isn't required, many assume once that final course is completed, they never have to learn anything again.

When I was CEO of Catapult, it always surprised me how few business professionals engaged in continuing education. During the interview process for new hires, I always asked each candidate about the most recent nonfiction book they'd read in their field. Management, leadership, sales, marketing, human resources, whatever they did—whatever they wanted to do at Catapult—I wanted to know what they were studying now. If they could name a book, I'd ask what they had learned from it. Far more often than I would have ever expected when I came up with this question, though, the candidate couldn't name a single book. So I'd broaden it out. I'd ask about the most recent article or blog post they'd read. Again, most would stumble. They couldn't come up with a decent response. While failure to answer this question was not immediately disqualifying for a candidate, I considered it a pretty big red flag.

There was one exception. One class of candidate never had any difficulty answering this question: software developers. In fact, they would often pull a book out of their backpack, one so technical I had to take their word for it when they explained what they were learning. That field, of course, is the great exception to the general licensed/unlicensed divide on continuing education. The culture of software development not only encourages ongoing professional training, it essentially requires it.

That's because it's very clear to people in IT how quickly skills degrade and people fall behind. Most people in business, though, feel this doesn't apply to their field. They mistakenly believe that they already know everything there is to know about their profession—and what they don't know, they can learn on the job. This misconception gets exacerbated by early professional success and further ingrained with each year of hands-on experience that goes by. Because no one requires them to learn more and their peers and employers don't expect them to learn more, they never check to see if there's more they could know about what they do. If they can keep being successful without reading another book, they will.

This is unfortunate because every profession benefits from outside ideas. Every industry and occupation has thought leaders, emerging trends, innovative methods, and new best practices. The most successful people I know, in any field, have an insatiable appetite to keep learning.

Deep down, I think everyone realizes this is true. I've never really received pushback on the value of training and education. Most agree with the well-known sentiment of Verne Harnish: "Those who can read but don't barely have an advantage over those who can't." Instead of arguing a counterposition, I hear excuses. I hear that people already have plenty on their plates. They're too busy, they tell me; they can't find the time; they're always putting out a client emergency; the dog ate that white paper they were going to read.

Everyone has an excuse because the culture of their workplace tolerates those excuses. So the only way out of this is for leaders to lead the way, creating an environment where education isn't just an option, it's expected.

TRAINING ON A BUDGET

One of the reasons candidates struggle when asked to name a book they've read recently is that many people aren't really readers. If they don't think they have to read, they won't. They need a structure that makes learning easy, useful, and essential. For any leader who wants to up the level of their team, this is where you have to start.

Luckily, getting started doesn't have to be expensive. Undeniably, there are expensive educational options out there. You could send everyone on your team to a conference or two every year. But many strategies are much more affordable and easier to get off the ground. At Catapult, for instance, we ran a book of the month club where every manager read the latest best-selling business book. I set a deadline, and then we'd all get together for a couple of hours to discuss what we had learned and whether we could apply any of those ideas to our company.

To make sure everyone participated, I often asked attendees at random to present a chapter to the rest of the group. For those eager to read more, I installed a bookshelf as an office library. Anytime someone finished a good business or technical book, they could add it to the shelf. Before long, we had quite a selection. This made it easy for people to recommend books or read a chapter over lunch to see if a certain author interested them. Simply being around books can encourage people to pick one up and give it a try.

Education isn't just about books, of course. We also brought in local speakers, business leaders, and even vendors to share their insights on various topics. For those employees lucky enough to go to a conference, we created a "lunch and learn" program where those employees would create courses around what they had learned. We'd record all those lessons and put them online. Eventually, we were able to create an archive of all these educational events that we called Catapult University.

We supplemented these homegrown courses with a subscription to the "all you eat buffet" of professional education offered by Verne Harnish's Growth Institute. The program has a huge catalog of online executive education classes, and we'd regularly meet for a pizza lunch to watch and discuss videos together.

Finally, once a year, we invested in taking the entire executive team to one of Harnish's Scaling Up conferences so that we could hear in person from the authors and thought leaders we'd been learning from.

This approach to education was invaluable in helping us "think outside the box" and further differentiating Catapult Systems from our competitors. And most of the resources we funded were low cost or free. Ongoing professional learning is a muscle that will atrophy unless it is used regularly. All of these programs helped us flex it, and for less than a gym membership.

EXTRA VALUE

The obvious value of encouraging or even requiring further education is that everyone in your company remains at the top of their profession. They know all the latest ideas, and they think about those ideas regularly. But this is not the only value these ideas can offer your company. For instance, having educational resources available can improve employee retention. One of the reasons people choose to stay with their current employer is they feel they're growing in their career compared to peers at other companies. Education provides a clear path toward improvement for those most eager to reach the top.

It can also give new purpose to work. At FlashParking, we found ourselves in a surprisingly strong position when COVID-19 hit. While the rest of the parking industry was laying off 90 percent of its employees, we had just finished a big round of fundraising. Coffers freshly filled, we didn't need to let anyone go, but that didn't mean everyone could remain busy in the way they usually were. In particular, our salespeople suddenly had a lot of downtime. Without the ability to do in-person sales meetings, they had far more hours to sit around twiddling their thumbs.

That was a recipe for lower morale, so our CEO, Dan Sharplin, came up with an idea. We called it "Squats in January," based on a quote from quarterback Vince Young. After his team, the University of Texas, narrowly defeated the University of Michigan in the 2005 Rose Bowl, a reporter asked Young how he was able to pull off his miraculous touchdown run at the end of the fourth quarter. With less than a minute left and on fourth down and five, Young shook off three defensive players and ran the ball into the end zone. How did he do it?

Young answered with a single word: "squats." Dan interpreted that to mean that Vince had put in the reps. He'd trained as hard as possible. When the time came to outmaneuver and outsprint the defense, he was ready.

Our "Squats in January" program had a similar ethos. If someone didn't have anything else to do, they should be training. They could read, go practice their cold calling, or tweak their skills overcoming objections. Instead of sitting around with nothing to do, they could fine tune their sales pitch. We set up mock customer calls to train the whole team.

We kept everyone busy, increasing comradery while giving them something to do instead of sitting around worrying. And when the economy recovered from COVID-19, we had a fully staffed, fully trained sales team ready to get back to work and sprint into the end zone.

KEY TAKEAWAYS

- Many professionals become complacent once they finish their formal education. Training and continuing education should be encouraged or even mandated for every position to help individuals stay at the forefront of their fields.
- Effective education doesn't need to be costly. Book clubs, "lunch and learns," and recorded presentations are affordable options that make training available to all employees without significant expense.

- Use your own team's knowledge as a training resource. People generally love to share their knowledge if given the opportunity.
- Training and ongoing professional development is one of the main reasons employees stay at companies.
- If your team has any downtime, train.

PRO TIPS

- Recognize employees who actively engage in continuing education and certifications. Offering incentives, such as a small bonus or public acknowledgment, can motivate others to follow suit.
- Allow employees to learn about areas outside their direct responsibilities. This cross-functional education can create more well-rounded employees and foster better collaboration across teams.
- Training is more fun and engaging when done in groups. Whether you're taking a class, discussing a book, or watching a video together, always finish with a conversation about how this new knowledge can be applied at your company.
- Incorporate personal development topics into your training programs like financial planning, stress management, health and wellness, public speaking, personal time management, parenting workshops, emotional intelligence, first aid and CPR, and personal branding and social media management.

FURTHER READING

Scaling Up: How a Few Companies Make It…and Why the Rest Don't by Verne Harnish

CASE STUDY

Cyrill Eltschinger and the Power of Continuous Employee Training

I have known Cyrill Eltschinger since I was four years old. He was my next-door neighbor when my parents moved us to Fribourg. Born on the same day two years apart, he was the older brother I never had. And like brothers, we got into our share of trouble growing up together. Cyrill went to the same high school and enlisted with the Mountain Grenadiers a year before I did. With a little help and encouragement from my father, Cyrill also went to college at Texas A&M University. I joined him there a year later. Sadly, as brothers sometimes do, we had a falling out halfway through college, and we didn't speak for a couple of years. The next time I saw him was when I showed up for officer candidate school at Chamblon. I didn't even know he would be there, but it made for a great reunion.

Cyrill's professional journey began unexpectedly on a delayed flight from London to Zurich on his way home from Texas A&M, where he was fortuitously upgraded to business class. Seated next to him was the Strategic Business Unit president of Electronic Data Systems (EDS) Europe. This encounter landed Cyrill his first job at EDS, working directly for the president.

Cyrill's career at EDS took him around the world, including Zurich, Antwerp, Munich, London, Singapore, and finally Beijing, where he worked directly for EDS' parent company, General Motors (GM). While at GM, he identified a significant gap in the communication and teamwork skills of Chinese employees working with Western companies. To bridge this cultural gap, Cyrill developed the Footsteps training program, which focused on equipping Chinese employees with the technical and soft skills required to thrive in a Western corporate environment.

In 1998, Cyrill founded his own IT consulting company in Beijing, I.T. UNITED, alongside six of his colleagues from GM. The firm specialized in software development, systems engineering, and network computing, eventually growing to over three hundred employees with offices in Beijing, Shanghai, Xi'an, and several international locations, including San Francisco, Tokyo, and Toronto.

At I.T. UNITED, he introduced the concept of "training for life" to counter the pressure Chinese employees often felt to change jobs after their first year, leading to high turnover rates. Cyrill's training program went beyond technical education to include marketing, communication, and business development skills. This holistic approach not only produced highly skilled consultants, it also significantly improved employee retention.

By positioning ongoing training as a core value of the company, I.T. UNITED became an industry leader in employee development. Competitors soon began targeting Cyrill's employees, recognizing the exceptional training they had received. Despite these challenges, I.T. UNITED retained most of its talent and grew to become a benchmark in IT outsourcing and employee development.

Chapter 14

Show Your Colors

DIFFICULTY: 1/5

Like all other military institutions around the world, insignia are an important component of the Swiss Army uniform. Insignia are symbols that denote an individual's rank, role, achievements, and affiliations within the military. They can come in the form of patches, badges, stripes, or pins, each with a specific design and set of colors that signify different aspects of a military career.

All branches of the Swiss Army wear their respective unit insignia with pride. It provides them with a physical representation of the community and camaraderie they feel for that unit. It's something they earned. The insignia I wore was, of course, for the Mountain Grenadiers. The image is of a yellow stylized grenade with a spherical base and a flame-like top on a bed of green, and it usually appears on the collar of a dress uniform. This iconic symbol dates back to the French grenadiers who served under Napoleon. I still have a framed picture of this insignia near the desk I'm sitting at right now.

This sort of lingering affiliation is not uncommon for service members. Many veterans wear T-shirts and caps with their unit's military insignia long after returning to civilian life. Drive down any street in America, and you'll probably see a retired Marine's Semper Fi bumper sticker on the back of a car. The use of insignia in this case is meant to display lasting pride, but it also acts as a means of introduction. When you encounter a fellow soldier from your military unit out in the "real world," it provides an opportunity to connect, share experiences, and maybe even forge a new relationship.

DEVELOP YOUR OWN INSIGNIA

Insignia is not just for the military. Though we don't use that specific term, we have a version of it in civilian life. If you've never been a soldier, you might have a sense of how insignia works if you've ever traveled while wearing clothing or jewelry with the name of your university on it. As a graduate from Texas A&M University, the Aggie ring is the most visible symbol of my school affiliation. Awarding the ring to students who have completed ninety credit hours or more is a time-honored tradition with roots dating back to 1889.

Worn proudly on the right hand, the ring serves as a powerful symbol of connection, instantly recognizable and respected among Aggies across the globe. When you see someone wearing an Aggie ring, it's customary to walk up, shake their hand, and introduce yourself with your name and the year you graduated. I have run into Aggies across the globe. Whether it's Chicago or Singapore, if there's an Aggie nearby wearing that ring, we've shaken hands and exchanged stories. Frankly, I've lost count of how many connections I've made that way.

These connections through insignia are possible because people have so much pride in the institutions they have been a part of. Like the military, people feel a large part of who they are is wrapped up in the school they attended. And there's no reason that pride—and the power of those insignia—shouldn't transfer to where they work as well.

Before digging into how you can utilize this principle in your business, I want to briefly state that though this chapter is about corporate branding, I'll be sticking to the visual component of that brand here. Developing and maintaining a strong corporate brand involves a multifaceted approach that combines strategic planning, consistent execution, and continuous adaptation. This isn't a marketing book, so I will leave all of that to one side.

Instead, I want to focus on the power of developing a strong visual identity that offers the same potential value as insignia. This visual identity should include a company name, logo, color scheme, and messaging that ensures that your brand is easily recognizable, resonates with your target audience, and gives people associated with your business the opportunity to wear your "swag" with pride.

For those of you who lack these elements at the moment, I have good news. It's never been easier to develop them quickly and cheaply. Thanks to AI, you can design a logo or choose colors for your company in an instant and for free. If you'd rather have a more personal touch, ask the most artistic member of your family to design these elements. That's what I did at Catapult. I had my mother, Marci—an accomplished artist in her own right—design our logo in 1993.

I want to stress here that it's better to have *a* logo than to delay this process so you get the perfect one. It's great if your logo is really cool, but even if it's mediocre, most people will still wear it, and as we'll see, many of your employees will wear it with pride.

Once you have a unique visual identity, you need to represent these brand elements uniformly across all touchpoints, from your marketing materials, website, and social media to customer interactions and employee communications. In short, when people see your brand, they should know it belongs to your company. You don't want any inconsistency to muddy the visual message.

Once you have consistent branding across all aspects of your company, you can begin to leverage that image in creative ways—in particular, by giving that image away on lots of *stuff*.

THE POWER OF SWAG

While spreading the visual elements of your brand far and wide is important, one of the easiest and most cost-effective ways of promoting your company is by giving away clothing and swag with your logo on it. In most industries, company uniforms have been out of style for some time—thank goodness. At this point, even the "professional uniform" is disappearing. When we started Catapult Systems in 1993, the standard "uniform" for an information technology consultant was still a suit and tie. Thanks to the tech boom of the '90s and influence from Silicon Valley, the dress code for technology workers, even IT consultants, has rapidly become more casual. Many other industries have followed suit.

This change has made workwear more comfortable, while also providing an opportunity to introduce your company through the clothes on your employees' backs. These days, workers at tech companies wear the company's swag all the time. Providing employees with company-branded clothing and swag is more than just a gesture of goodwill. It's a strategic investment, one with numerous potential advantages.

In the first place, swag can play a crucial role in building a cohesive and motivated workforce. Employees want to feel that they are part of something. When they don apparel adorned with your company's logo, it fosters a sense of belonging. This tangible connection to your brand enhances their identification with your company's mission and core values, reinforcing their role as integral members of the team. Giving away branded clothing helps nurture a strong internal culture where employees feel valued, important, and united.

Beyond these internal benefits, branded clothing acts as a powerful marketing tool when worn outside the workplace. Employees sporting the company logo in public become walking advertisements, increasing your business's brand visibility and recognition within the community. In the same way a pizza delivery car detailed out in Domino's branding acts as a moving billboard, your own staff can spread the word about your company just by wearing your logo on their shirt.

This organic form of marketing can pique the interest of potential customers who may inquire about your company, leading to new business opportunities. We've won an unbelievable amount of business over the years simply through introductions that started when someone noticed the Catapult name and logo on an employee's shirt and asked what we did as a company.

As I mentioned in Chapter 2, we trained everyone during boot camp to do an effective elevator pitch for the company precisely for this reason. If someone asked about the logo, they knew what to say.

You can also create some viral online marketing through this swag. At Catapult, we had a traveling branded hat. It was just a normal baseball cap with a Catapult logo, but the team began to take pictures of it everywhere they visited on vacation. Before social media, the hat became a meme, as employees positioned it next to the Great Wall of China, on one of the Galapagos Islands, at the top of the Eiffel Tower, and so on. This same potential is available today—with the benefit of social media and email newsletters to share the results with the world.

Finally, having company-branded clothing out in your community can attract potential recruits. When your people are proud to wear your swag, potential applicants will assume your company is a desirable place to work. This makes it easier to attract top talent.

That's a lot of benefit just for giving away a few caps and T-shirts.

HOW TO SHARE SWAG WITH YOUR TEAM

Let me start out by repeating that your logo doesn't need to be part of a uniform. You don't have to require anyone to wear it. Some of your people won't want to wear anything with your company name on it, and that's fine. You don't want those people answering questions about your company with potential clients or applicants anyway.

However, that group is almost always the minority. If you're generous in giving away swag, most people will take it and use it. Sometimes, that generosity can be as simple and straightforward as handing out free hoodies. Other times, you might offer a gift certificate. At Catapult, every new employee received a $150 clothing allowance at Lands'

End to purchase anything they wanted, as long as it had the Catapult logo on it. We gave them another $150 allowance after three years with the company. Whether they were looking for T-shirts, polos, jackets, hats, beanies, or anything else, they could pick it up for free.

We also gave away swag for special events. We handed out Catapult T-shirts at every family event. Whenever someone in the office had a baby, Catapult sent a gift basket that included a onesie with a Catapult logo—pink for a girl, blue for a boy. Each month, we printed up "100% Pure Catapult" swag that we gave to our consultants who made the "100 Percent Club" (a reward I explain in detail in Chapter 16).

Once a year, we also printed unique, one-off T-shirts with our annual theme. You could only get one if you were part of the company the year it came out. We put a lot of effort into the design for these. One time, we designed a shirt that resembled the Harley Davidson logo. It looked very cool. Years later, I still wear that shirt. And I'm not the only one. These unique designs turned the shirts into collector's items. After a few years, they were essentially vintage.

These efforts were not expensive. It was relatively cheap to design and print each of these items. But people loved them, and they generated real, measurable benefits for the business.

SWAG AMBASSADORS

The power of swag extends beyond the boost to company culture and free advertising you get with your employees. There's a whole secondary market for swag: your clients. Giving away branded items to clients is a strategic move that can enhance loyalty and brand recognition. Clients often appreciate these thoughtful gestures, viewing them as tokens of recognition for their support. And they'll often leave these items out in the open, or even display them. Nothing used to make me happier than walking into a client's office and seeing a Catapult logo on a mouse pad, desk clock, pen, or phone charger.

When a client uses or wears branded items, it subconsciously reinforces their connection to your company, creating a sense of allegiance.

These objects serve as a subtle yet powerful reminder of the positive experiences they associate with your company. Additionally, when clients proudly display your branded merchandise, it acts as a visible indicator to competitors of the strong relationship you have cultivated with them.

Depending on who your clients are, these swag items may need to be more expensive and nicer than what you give to your team. If you work with elite law firms, for instance, a branded T-shirt may not end up in their regular wardrobe rotation. But a nice clock, a fancy desk calculator, a leather-bound notebook—those are the sort of items that end up sitting on a desk for months or even years.

At FlashParking, we gave away branded Yeti mugs right when that company was really taking off. As a bonus, Yeti is an Austin-based company, so we were boosting local business while also strengthening relationships with clients. It was a win for every company involved— and definitely worth the cost.

KEY TAKEAWAYS

- Creating a unique and recognizable brand identity—including a logo, color scheme, and messaging—ensures that your brand is easily recognizable. This visual identity forms the foundation for creating company "insignia" that employees can wear with pride.
- Providing employees with branded clothing and company swag fosters a sense of belonging and strengthens their connection to the company. Employees wearing the company logo feel like part of something bigger, reinforcing internal culture.
- Employees wearing branded clothing and swag act as walking advertisements, increasing brand visibility and attracting attention. This can lead to new business opportunities, as people inquire about the company when they see the logo in public.
- Encourage employees to share photos of themselves with company swag on social media. This can help boost online engagement and broaden the reach of your brand in a fun and authentic way.

- Provide employees with the ability to choose their own swag. Offering a branded clothing allowance allows them to pick items they're excited about wearing, ensuring greater usage.
- Creating unique, event-specific, or limited-edition swag can make these items more desirable. People are more likely to use or wear "collector's items," which further promotes the brand and builds a sense of exclusivity.
- Providing swag to clients not only strengthens relationships but also subtly promotes your brand within their office environment.

PRO TIPS

- Unless your company name is short enough to stand alone with a stylized font (like DELL or Ford), design a logo along with your company name. That way, on some swag, you can use your logo on its own. For example, the iconic Apple logo stands on its own without the word "Apple."
- Designing a logo is inexpensive. If you want a more personal touch than AI can provide, crowdsource it with a company like Crowdspring (https://www.crowdspring.com/).
- Once you have a logo-company name combination you like, trademark it.

CASE STUDY

Visual Branding Strategy at Mama Fu's

Randy Murphy's exposure to the food and beverage industry began during his time at the University of Texas, where he worked at various restaurants and bars to put himself through college. After graduating, Randy spent fourteen years in the tech industry, including stints at Price Waterhouse and several startups. However, he always harbored a desire to start his own business and return to the restaurant industry.

In 2004, he purchased the Austin Mama Fu's franchise. The fast-casual pan-Asian restaurant served a blend of Chinese, Japanese, Thai, Vietnamese, and Korean dishes, all prepared from scratch. Dissatisfied with the lack of support he was receiving from the franchisor, Randy raised capital and acquired the entire Mama Fu's brand in 2008. His vision was to transform the brand and expand its reach throughout the Southwest.

In 2014, well on his way to growing the franchise to thirty locations, Randy commissioned a brand awareness study that revealed 70 percent of customers discovered Mama Fu's by seeing its signage on a restaurant. Randy immediately realized the potential to grow delivery sales, which accounted for only 20 percent of their business at the time. He drew inspiration from NASCAR's branding strategy and decided to create a visual identity for Mama Fu's delivery vehicles. Back then, delivery drivers used their personal cars with only small plastic toppers bearing the Mama Fu's logo. To enhance brand visibility, Randy piloted a program that deployed ten company-owned Nissan Versa Notes branded with the Mama Fu's logo, along with logos from some of their vendors like Kikkoman and Sriracha. Some of these brands even helped cosponsor the cost of the vehicles.

The results were immediate and impressive. Delivery sales at the test locations increased from 20 to 35 percent, with delivery orders yielding higher ticket averages than dine-in orders. The visually branded cars also generated significant buzz on social media, with customers posting pictures of the cars online, further increasing brand visibility. Satisfied with the initial results, Randy expanded the program to all of Mama Fu's locations, deploying a total of eighty branded delivery vehicles. This initiative led to a sustained period of growth, with Mama Fu's achieving double-digit year-over-year growth for thirty consecutive months.

Chapter 15

Inspections

DIFFICULTY: 3/5

Inspections are a routine part of military life, especially when you're on base. Every morning, our instructors closely inspected our barracks before we were permitted to head to breakfast. The floor had to be spotless, and all of our gear had to be stored correctly. There were twenty-four beds per room—in two rows of twelve—and each one had to be perfectly made. Not only that, they had to be so perfectly aligned that the inspecting officer could stare down each row without spotting a single irregularity. If a blanket showed a wrinkle or a single sheet was out of alignment, the instructors would flip over several beds at once, and we would have to start all over again. None of us could go to breakfast until the entire room passed inspection. Sometimes, this process took so long we missed breakfast entirely.

A similar inspection took place at the end of each day. In the evening, after many hours of hiking up and down mountains, crawling through the dirt or snow, and performing endless weapons' drills, we would have to meticulously clean all of our equipment before we could go to sleep. When we were ready, our instructors would scrutinize every combat boot, canteen, helmet, and assault rifle. If they found even a speck of dust or rust, we all had to remain in the cleaning area for another thirty minutes. As with our beds, the process would repeat endlessly until everything was spotless. There were some nights my head didn't hit the pillow until 3:00 a.m.

Those were our daily inspections. Once a month, we had yet another one. This time, our instructors would conduct a complete and thorough inspection of all of our military gear. This didn't just include the gear we used over the past day. It was everything the Swiss Army had ever issued to us. We carried every item over to a parking lot and laid it out on a small tarp. Rifle, helmet, gas mask, uniforms, boots, rucksack—everything down to our belt buckles had to be perfectly arranged and symmetrically aligned with every other soldier's gear in our platoon. This exercise took several hours to complete at the best of times. Inspections could only begin when everything was perfectly organized and displayed. If a soldier lost something, they either had to find it or pay for it.

While every soldier in those barracks dreaded inspections, they played an integral role in our training. These weren't arbitrary tasks designed to punish us. They helped reinforce our training in maintaining discipline, efficiency, and readiness. In war, details matter; precision matters. And inspections drove that point home as much as anything. To this day, I still make my bed every single day, clean my boots after every hike, and wash the dishes before going to bed. I never misplace anything. That's all a result of those seemingly unending inspections.

TRUST BUT VERIFY

Inspections often have a slightly negative connotation in business, particularly with young entrepreneurs who worry they suggest leadership doesn't trust its people. This is unfortunate because inspections should play a crucial role in maintaining operational efficiency, ensuring compliance, improving quality, and fostering a culture of continuous improvement. And once employees get used to them, they can even come to appreciate them.

We can see this in many companies today—because some aspects of business already live with regular inspections. They are common and even welcome in occupations like software developer. Architecture and code reviews are an integral part of the software development process and serve to assess the quality of a new system, ensuring it meets predefined standards and development guidelines. Catapult's process was no different in this regard. As with everyone else in the tech industry, code reviews were required for all our consulting projects, as well as for our Inquisite research and development (R&D) team.

Inspections are also common in manufacturing. Because FlashParking manufactures its own equipment, for instance, we regularly inspect our assembly facility. Using detailed checklists (an important tool with any complex process, as we learned in Chapter 11), auditors or managers run inventory audits, safety inspections, and quality control checks.

Finally, internal and external audits are a common and necessary practice for finance and accounting to ensure compliance with standard accounting practices and regulations. But this isn't just about compliance. When, once a year, I would sit down with Catapult's CFO and go over every company expense, we would always find savings. Simply by reviewing the books, we'd discover subscriptions we'd meant to cancel still on the books or expenses we'd intended to rein in but failed to implement.

For all those professions, inspections are an important part of business life. We may not always call them inspections, but inspections they are nonetheless. And all of those professions understand that those inspections are a useful tool to reduce mistakes and improve quality. So why don't we inspect every aspect of business?

Regular inspections and peer reviews can have a similarly positive impact on every department. They reinforce a commitment to quality and standards, boosting employee engagement and fostering trust across all stakeholders. They're an opportunity to get everything in tip-top shape. They drive home that quality control matters and that you don't cut corners. Knowing that you have to show your work to someone else is an amazing way to up your standards and hold yourself accountable.

And for these reasons, given a little time to adjust, I've found that most employees come to welcome the opportunity to showcase what they are working on to their managers and peers, whether it's a new marketing campaign, sales proposal, product roadmap, or business initiative. While inspections can be initially uncomfortable, most people want to rise to the occasion.

We saw this in our annual employee performance review process at Catapult. Each manager had to present their reviews for their whole team to a review committee to ensure consistency across the organization. Every manager had a slightly different style, but this gave them a chance to present their vision for the team as well as their opinion on the quality of each team member's work. As they presented their assessments, they were able to justify and nuance why they gave a particular rating and why they made certain comments. They detailed what each employee did well and where they needed to improve in order to be a bigger asset to the company.

In this way, managers shared their perspective, while we were able to create consistency across all our managers. We could see who was too lenient and who was too tough. The process was time-consuming, but it made our entire organization better.

SETTING STANDARDS

While you want to introduce inspections across your entire organization, that doesn't mean you have to run them yourself. Having senior leadership set standards and spot-check progress across an entire company can lead to a poorly considered inspection process and needless distraction. While you should be involved in helping establish some of the higher-level points of any review process, every department should nuance their own process and inspect their teams themselves.

This is so important because inspections must find the balance of being regular but not burdensome for workers, managers, and leaders. You don't need to review every line of code. You may not need to check every proposal. Instead, inspections should be common enough and cover tasks important enough that you are sure good work is always being done without constantly looking over everyone's shoulder.

In some departments, this may look like a graded process. Perhaps at your company, proposals below $100,00 require no review. Those above $100,000 might be reviewed by a manager. Those above $500,000 might have to be checked by a small committee. And proposals above $1 million might require a VP to put eyes on it.

This way, inspections aren't happening every day or even every week. They aren't a taxing bottleneck, but quality is insured when it really matters.

This is going to look different in every department in every company. To make sure it runs efficiently, you have to work in partnership with management in those departments, and then let them run the process themselves.

KEY TAKEAWAYS

- Regular inspections, whether of facilities, products, or processes, help maintain high standards of quality, discipline, and efficiency.
- Inspections are often viewed negatively, but they should be seen as an opportunity to reduce errors, improve quality, and foster accountability. When properly implemented, they can help employees showcase their best work and build a culture of pride and responsibility.
- Senior leadership should help establish high-level standards for inspections but allow departments to implement and nuance their own processes. This ensures that inspections are effective without becoming onerous.
- Inspections should be frequent enough to uphold standards but not so frequent that they become burdensome. A graded process based on importance or value can ensure quality while maintaining efficiency.

- The word "inspection" can have a negative connotation. Call it a "review" instead.
- The best kind of review is a peer review.
- Frame inspections as a chance for feedback and learning rather than punitive measures. This approach helps employees grow and see inspections as beneficial for their professional development.
- When teams pass an inspection with flying colors, celebrate that achievement.

FURTHER READING

Flawless Execution: Use the Techniques and Systems of America's Fighter Pilots to Perform at Your Peak and Win the Battles of the Business World by James D. Murphy

CASE STUDY

Inspecting Expenses at Double Line Partners

Zeynep Young grew up in Turkey before moving to Houston with her family. She completed her undergraduate studies at Rice University and later earned her MBA from the Kellogg School of Management. Zeynep then spent eight years as an analyst at McKinsey, where she developed a deep appreciation for data analysis and the importance of going beyond surface-level insights to uncover hidden trends. This analytical mindset shaped her approach to leadership, particularly during her time at the Dell Foundation, where she focused on K–12 educational data.

Her passion for using data to drive meaningful change in education led her to found Double Line Partners in 2008, a company dedicated to providing data analytics solutions for K–12 education agencies and school districts. Double Line developed dashboards for teachers to track student performance metrics, helping schools make data-driven decisions.

Given that Zeynep bootstrapped Double Line, she was acutely focused on managing expenses. To ensure financial efficiency, she developed an inspection process. Twice a year, she sat down with her CFO to review every single payment the company had made. This review involved going through thousands of payments and flagging any that seemed unclear. Typically, thirty to a hundred expenses would be identified for further scrutiny. Zeynep would then meet with her CFO and department heads to examine each expense, identifying inefficiencies or unnecessary costs. This detailed inspection process consistently uncovered avoidable expenses, ranging from unused software subscriptions to redundant service retainers. By systematically questioning the necessity of each cost, Zeynep ensured that Double Line operated as leanly as possible without sacrificing effectiveness.

Importantly, Zeynep's inspection method wasn't just a cost-reduction tool—it provided her with an intimate understanding of how the business operated from the ground up. By reviewing the data at a granular level and having value-driven conversations with each department head, she was able to align the company's spending with its strategic priorities. Zeynep's strategy also combined this aggressive cost-cutting with reallocating funds to more productive areas, resulting in significant financial improvements.

This inspection process became a hallmark of Zeynep's leadership style. After selling Double Line, Zeynep took on CEO roles at three other companies and implemented the same approach. At one organization, the expense review process led to doubling the company's EBITDA within nine months.

Zeynep's approach is a powerful example of the principle "trust but verify." While leaders may trust their teams to manage budgets responsibly, conducting regular, detailed inspections can uncover inefficiencies that are easily overlooked. Zeynep's process was not about micromanaging but about ensuring that every expense added value. It also fostered collaboration, as department heads were invited to provide input on which expenses were necessary and which could be eliminated.

Chapter 16

Awards and Recognition

DIFFICULTY: 2/5

Every military has awards designed to recognize the work and sacrifice of service members for acts during war and in peacetime. Wartime recognition places a significant emphasis on acts of valor, bravery, and heroism under fire. Medals for gallantry, citations for combat excellence, and honors for leadership in battle reflect the extraordinary circumstances and high stakes of wartime operations.

Technically, Switzerland has awards for these situations on the books like every other country, but since we have been at peace for several hundred years, recognition in the Swiss Army tends to focus on training accomplishments, professional development, and contributions to unit readiness and efficiency. We have awards for exceptional physical fitness, exemplary leadership, outstanding marksmanship, superior performance during combat training exercises, and excellent conduct in day-to-day duties.

Whether awarded for actions in peace or war, these honors serve the same purpose: they are powerful tools to motivate soldiers and reinforce desired behaviors. All the awards usually come in a physical form, such as commendation medals or special badges. These are worn with pride, just like the insignia we covered in Chapter 14. However, though these objects mean a great deal, nothing is more impactful than the moment you receive one of these awards. Receiving a commendation or verbal praise in front of your peers is something you never forget.

This was certainly my own experience. In addition to the many individual aptitude tests during officer candidate school, we had three team challenges, called "patrol races," designed to test our physical and mental endurance, map reading skills, and team cohesion. All three races started at night and were held in the mountains, with increasing levels of difficulty, from thirty kilometers to sixty kilometers and, finally, one hundred kilometers. This last race took place at the end of survival week and marked the effective end of officer candidate school—for those who managed to finish it. Those who didn't finish failed to graduate and would not become officers.

So the stakes were high, and that made the first step in the patrol races all the more important. As part of the exercise, we had the opportunity to select our own teammates before the first race. There were only three Mountain Grenadiers in that year's officer candidate program, so we naturally gravitated toward one another. We then carefully recruited three other officer candidates who had displayed strong endurance and mental toughness. Without bragging too much, I think it is fair to say we put together the Dream Team for that year. And like the Dream Team, our team won everything. We swept all three patrol races, which had never been done before, and at sixteen hours twenty-four minutes, we set a new record for the one-hundred-kilometer race.

As a result, our team was recognized for our achievement in front of the entire officer graduating class a few weeks later. We received a simple challenge coin bearing the school's insignia. That was definitely one of the proudest moments of my life. And every time I pick up that coin—which is still in my desk drawer—I am reminded of it.

EVERYONE LOVES AN AWARD

Rewards are an effective tool in management for a very simple reason: everyone likes getting an award and some public praise. Even those who are shy and introverted want their colleagues, family, and friends to see that they are excelling in their work. They may not want to go up on stage or give a speech, but like everyone else, they enjoy having their name read out for their achievements. Nothing is as powerful as the hit of dopamine that comes from being recognized in front of your peers.

It's hardly surprising, then, that awards play the same role in business that they do in the military: they reinforce desired behaviors, values, and outcomes, encouraging employees to maintain high levels of performance and align their efforts with the company's goals. They also serve to validate employees' hard work, dedication, and achievements, fostering a positive and motivating work environment.

Ultimately, a business that recognizes your efforts is just a nicer place to work. When employees feel appreciated and acknowledged for their contributions, it enhances their job satisfaction and boosts morale, leading to increased engagement. This culture of appreciation can also foster loyalty and reduce turnover. Employees are simply more likely to work harder and stay longer with an organization where their efforts are visibly valued, even if they have other options available.

TYPES OF AWARDS

There's no limit on what acts you can reward or how you reward them in your own company. Recognizing your people doesn't have to involve a huge win or a huge prize. Awards don't have to include an eighteen-carat gold medal or two tickets on a Caribbean cruise. That challenge coin I earned in the military is probably worth less than a dollar. It's what it symbolizes that matters.

At Catapult and FlashParking, we tried to recognize and celebrate our employees as often and as publicly as possible. We found that awards didn't lose value because we gave them out often. Nor did appreciation for the little achievements reduce the significance of bigger accomplishments. Everyone enjoyed small wins and looked forward to the major ones.

In the end, we landed on a variety of forms of recognition for everything from simply staying with the company to outselling an entire office. We broke these awards down into four different categories.

REAL-TIME RECOGNITION AWARDS

Not every award or moment of recognition has to be a huge deal for it to be effective. Sometimes, it's nice to just get a shout-out from a fellow employee for a job well done. At both Catapult and Flash-Parking, we gave our employees the tools to recognize or thank one another anytime they wanted on a company social media feed.

Whatever platform you use, whether Slack, MS Teams, or some alternative, you can create a channel that exists solely to recognize people. This real-time feed allows anyone in the company to post a quick comment praising a colleague.

There are definitely some more advanced tools on the market you can play with to get even more value here. WorkTango, for instance, has a whole system for employee recognition where you give and receive points throughout the month. But you don't have to invest anything to set this kind of system up. A free channel on Slack is more than good enough for most companies.

PROGRAMMATIC AWARDS

At Catapult, we made a point of acknowledging every employee's birthday and the tenure of their time with the company during our monthly company meetings. We also posted them on our intranet. These are not necessarily awards. They're more about basic recognition, letting everyone know that you see them and you appreciate them just for being with you.

You don't have to do anything special for these moments of recognition, other than publicize your appreciation, but we took it a step or two further and mailed birthday cards to every employee's home on their birthday. Each card was signed by the entire executive team. They even sent me one each year, getting it signed in private when I wasn't looking.

We also showed appreciation for joining and sticking with the company. Recognition for working for the company began in boot camp, where we gave every new employee their own dog tags with their name, the name of the company, and the date they started. These were dollar-store trinkets, but they were a fun reminder we cared that they were joining us.

Work anniversaries were also celebrated in a fun, public fashion. As I will detail more in Chapter 18, our one-year "Bronze Club" members were invited to a private meeting, where between five and ten of them would sit down with me to talk about their experience at Catapult. We'd also commemorate people at three-year (Silver Club), five-year (Gold Club), seven-year (Platinum Club), ten-year (Diamond Club), and amazingly, twenty-year (Double Black Diamond Club) anniversaries.

Most of these anniversary "clubs" were just fun names to make the employees feel special, but that ten-year Diamond Club anniversary actually came with a secret perk. This perk was kept hidden from employees until they hit that anniversary. As that date approached, though, they and their significant other would get an envelope in the mail with an invitation to a private dinner.

This dinner was hosted at an expensive restaurant and attended by the company founders and every other Diamond Club member (along with their significant others) who was still with the company. We hosted these dinners in a city where we had at least one Diamond Club employee.

Everyone invited made a big deal out of this meal. It was strictly suit-and-tie and strictly secret—something just for those who had been truly loyal to the company.

If that wasn't enough, our Diamond Club members also received a $500 allowance to buy something at the Swiss company Victorinox.

These, admittedly, were more expensive rewards than we gave out for most other achievements, but I've always felt that kind of long-term loyalty deserves significant recognition.

REINFORCEMENT AWARDS

These awards are designed to bolster the type of behaviors you hope to see in your workers. They usually include small perks that show how much you appreciate that little bit of extra effort someone has been putting in.

For our consultants at Catapult, we created the 100 Percent Club. All it took to win this award was to bill 100 percent of their billable hours for a month. That may not seem like much, but consultancy is not a forty-hour-a-week job. It involves a number of nonbillable responsibilities. In a given week, I might ask someone to step in and help out with an interview. There might be several meetings to attend. And they might need to engage in some training. In other words, to reach the average 160 billable hours each month, a consultant had to stay a little longer, finish a little late, and put more time and effort in.

This award simply showed our appreciation for that. Our system calculated the hours automatically each month, and when someone hit 100 percent, we gave them some 100 Percent Club swag and an extra $100 in their paycheck.

For sales, we had a policy of publicly celebrating every time a deal was closed, no matter the size. It was a nice shot of peer recognition to go with the commission. But FlashParking took this appreciation even further. Our VP of Sales founded a sales award banquet. It was a multihour affair with recognition for many accomplishments in the department. He gave awards for most improved, best performing region, biggest deal… There were dozens of these awards, and some salespeople would collect multiple trophies.

There was no additional financial compensation, just glass statues and a round of applause from colleagues. But as with celebrating wins and the 100 Percent Club, the public recognition is what meant the most to people.

It's hard to overestimate the value of that recognition. Once, when congratulating a young salesperson who had just won four awards, he said to me, "You know, Sam, I was in the audience last year. I had just started, and as I watched people go on stage one after another, I became determined to win one of these next time. And now I've got four!"

Imagine that level of motivation, all stoked by a buffet dinner and an evening receiving appreciation from colleagues.

EMPLOYEE-NOMINATED AWARDS

Personally, these are my favorite awards because they allow peers to recognize one another. These awards aren't earned by staying in one job, and they aren't awarded by leadership. It's people celebrating people they admire—in a way that goes far beyond just praising someone on Slack.

At Catapult, we had core value awards that we announced during our monthly company meetings. It was only possible to earn one when nominated by a colleague or manager. We took this further at FlashParking, where we made core value poker chips that were not so dissimilar from my challenge coin. You could only get one if you were recognized for that particular value by a peer.

Employees coveted these. Technically, they also received a $25 Starbucks gift card, but that was never the focus. It was those little pieces of plastic. They meant the world to people.

We also had an annual employee of the year award that was voted on anonymously by the whole company. Everyone got one vote. We had a single trophy—a one of a kind item, like the Stanley Cup. Each year, the previous year's winner came up on stage to present the trophy to the new winner, who got to keep it for the whole year until it was their turn to pass it on.

Once again, this wasn't about money. There were no huge perks. But people treated this award like it was an Oscar. It meant that much to them.

No matter how you go about this process, whether with dozens of awards or a few elite ones with big prizes, the key is to make these moments as public and visible as possible. That's where the real value is for your people.

This recognition can be done in person or over Zoom. You can even do it over email. We always tried to acknowledge people at the end of our meetings and in our emails recapping those meetings. When it comes to praise, you can never be too public or do it too much. Because after the paycheck, that's really what the work is all about.

KEY TAKEAWAYS

- Public awards and recognition help boost employee morale and motivation. Whether it's a small token or a formal award, the act of recognition—especially in front of peers—helps reinforce positive behaviors and values.
- Not all awards need to be large or costly. Recognition can range from real-time shout-outs to formalized programs, celebrating achievements big and small. This variety ensures that employees feel acknowledged frequently and consistently.
- Peer-nominated awards can be particularly meaningful since they reflect recognition from colleagues.
- Celebrating milestones like work anniversaries helps foster long-term loyalty.
- Simple items like custom coins or poker chips can carry significant emotional weight when tied to specific achievements or company values. Employees will collect and display these items.
- Ensure recognition is visible throughout the organization. Announce achievements in company meetings, over emails, or on a dedicated social media channel. The more public the acknowledgment, the more valued employees will feel.

- Come up with fun names for your awards. For example, in addition to our monthly core value awards at Catapult, we gave out a "Badass" award.
- When giving out a peer recognition award (like a core value award), always have the nominating employee publicly share the reason why they nominated the recipient.

FURTHER READING

Bringing Out the Best in People: How to Apply the Astonishing Power of Positive Reinforcement by Aubrey C. Daniels

CASE STUDY

The Power of Employee Recognition— Insights from Willo Crenshaw

Willo Crenshaw has always felt at home in a blue-collar work environment. His father, Will Crenshaw, founded The Modern Group in 1963, an industrial equipment and services company serving various industries including oil and gas, agriculture, and power generation. Willo and his two brothers, Casey and Colby, grew up immersed in the business, learning firsthand the values of hard work and perseverance. At the age of twenty, Willo joined one of his father's manufacturing plants as a quality control employee. When the plant director unexpectedly resigned, Willo was asked to step into the leadership role. One of the veteran welders didn't hesitate to let him know that he was too young and inexperienced for the job. Determined to prove himself, Willo worked hard to build rapport with the team, especially by acknowledging individual contributions, a lesson he learned from his father, who often said, "catch them doing something good and promote that."

Willo quickly learned that recognition meant more when done publicly in front of the employee's coworkers. It offered a significant positive impact, not just for the individual but for the entire team. While Willo initially found such group appreciation challenging, he soon improved in those efforts.

However, he also learned a hard lesson when he praised one out-standing employee too often. This left the employee feeling alienated from his peers, and he eventually resigned. This taught Willo the delicate balance of acknowledgment in a team setting—understanding that praise must be equitable and inclusive. To spread recognition around, Willo began celebrating not just exceptional work but basic behaviors he wanted to reinforce, like consistent attendance. In that blue collar environment, he found that public approbation for these small successes could make a difference. By recognizing and rewarding these behaviors, he helped model the desired work ethic for others in the plant.

In 2005, Willo left the family business to start his own company, Austin Outhouse. With a used truck and some portable toilets, he entered the porta-potty business, a venture that many saw as unglamorous. Nevertheless, Willo applied the same principles of employee recog-nition, acknowledging and rewarding his team for their efforts. This approach helped him grow the company to over fifty employees. In 2010, he successfully sold the business. Shortly after, he rejoined the family business, where he was tasked with repurposing and growing one of the business units within their Dragon Products vertical.

The environment at Dragon Products was extremely safety-focused. The oil fields and offshore rigs they served were dangerous and required strict adherence to safety protocols. As a result, employee recognition programs were centered around safety accomplishments. Monthly and quarterly awards were given during all-hands meetings, and remote recipients were called to ensure they felt acknowledged. One of the most prized awards was a preferred parking spot near the plant entrance—particularly valuable at large facilities spanning dozens of acres. Willo also instituted group awards for project milestones and maintaining good safety records. These group recognitions often involved small gatherings at the plant, where employees could take a break, enjoy food and drinks, and bond as a team.

Perhaps the most unique and sought-after recognition came in the form of gold lapel pins—an award that was created by accident. One of the employees showed Willo's brother, Casey, a custom-made gold pin engraved with the company logo. Casey loved it and had the employee order twenty-five more, only to find out later that they cost over $300 each. To justify the expense, they decided that these pins would be reserved exclusively for their most influential employees across the organization, symbolizing induction into the company's "inner circle." Once a year, The Modern Group invited between seventy-five and a hundred team members—out of their four thousand employees—to the industry's largest trade show. During the first morning, they held a company meeting where Casey would deliver a state-of-the-company address, followed by the awarding of gold pins to the new inner-circle inductees. This ceremony was always highly emotional, as the recipients felt a profound sense of achievement—like they had truly "made it."

Chapter 17

Get the Families Involved

DIFFICULTY: 1/5

Switzerland doesn't really do much for its military families—for the simple reason that almost every man in the country is a part of the military, making every family a military family. At the same time, our armed forces are almost entirely made up of reservists. We don't shift soldiers from base to base around the country, let alone around the world. After each year's three-week repetition course, we all just go home. We aren't separated from our families for months, nor are we engaged in any wars that would put our lives at risk.

For this chapter about institutional responsibility to the families of soldiers and employees, therefore, I'd like to make an exception and talk not about my own experience in the Swiss Army but about a different military experience: that of my good friend Amy Gerrie.

Amy met John in March 1999 on a dance floor in San Antonio. John was training to become a navigator in the US Air Force at the time, a nonstarter for Amy, whose father had been in the military. She'd vowed never to marry into a military family herself, but John somehow changed her mind. She gave him a chance, and their relationship flourished. They got married and eventually had three beautiful children: Emily, Jack, and Katie.

Like most military families in America, Amy's family moved frequently, transferring from base to base as John's career progressed, from KC-135 navigator to electronics warfare officer on the C-130 for special operations. These moves, although still challenging, were made smoother by the robust support system provided by the military. This support began well before the family relocated each time, with detailed information packets about the new location, including insights into local schools, traffic patterns, and amenities. The military also offered the services of movers who came in, helped to pack and box everything up, and shipped it to the family's new home. Upon arrival, Amy's family was assigned a sponsor—another military family who helped them acclimate, often lending a hand with the move-in process and providing essential guidance. Additionally, military housing offices assisted by providing temporary housing and finding suitable long-term accommodations. Temporary furniture was also made available if needed.

And that wasn't the end of the Air Force's support either. They also organized numerous activities and events for Amy and other military families. Monthly happy hours, spouse clubs, family days, and seasonal celebrations fostered a strong sense of belonging and mutual support. These events were not just social gatherings but essential components that helped build a resilient and cohesive community that Amy came to rely on.

Military spouses often take on significant responsibilities. The day they arrive, their husband or wife in the military is busy. They're on base, working long, tough hours. And that's when they're home. There's always the chance they'll be deployed for months on end. That means a military spouse like Amy has to do all the unpacking, get the kids settled, cook that first family dinner, and prepare everyone for their new lives. The military's culture of support ensured that Amy never felt isolated, creating an environment where she and her family could thrive despite the challenges of that lifestyle.

That commitment to helping families thrive extended to access to comprehensive training, good medical coverage, counseling, financial planning, and flight benefits. These all made a huge difference to Amy, John, and their kids.

There's hard data behind this approach. Families improve the overall readiness and morale of service members. Equally importantly, they also play a key role in the decision to reenlist. Every four years, each service member chooses whether to sign up for another four years or walk away. The military knows all too well that service members with families are far more likely to re-up than those who are single.

This fact might seem surprising at first, but it makes a lot of sense. The military requires significant sacrifice—even in the best of times—for what is, in the end, mediocre pay. The work is dangerous, the demands high, and there are innumerable career paths out there for a young man or woman that can offer more upside. It's families that often make the difference. They come to appreciate the community, camaraderie, and support of military life. They can't get that anywhere else. By supporting families, then, the military can turn what was initially a four-year stint into a lifelong career.

In the end, I believe military support is heartfelt as well as mutually beneficial. This was certainly Amy's sense as well. In 2016, she received the worst news imaginable. John was deployed overseas at the time, and she found out that he was never coming home. But the military's robust support system throughout her family's journey—from their first years together through the loss of John—left Amy looking back fondly on those years she and John shared as a US Air Force family. The military had been there for her and her family, and she was glad she had been and would remain a part of that community.

DON'T IGNORE FAMILIES

The military sees the value in focusing on family, yet so many companies feel they can completely ignore this side of their employees' lives. The thing we have to remember is that if there's a choice between work and family, most people will choose the latter. In other words, if the family is unhappy, the employee isn't going to stick around. So if you want to retain your talent, you have to make sure their families are as excited to be part of your company as the people who actually work for you.

Every time I mention to someone the programs I'll lay out in a moment, they comment on how wonderful it all sounds, but they assume the costs must be astronomical. How could we justify the expense? The truth is it was easy. In the early years of Catapult, our company's strategy was centered around finding, attracting, and retaining the best people in the industry. And just like the military, we found that supporting families really helped retain our best people.

We did the math, and each time we had to replace an employee, it cost us about $50,000 in recruiting fees, interview costs, lost time, and lost revenue. And those were '90s dollars. The way we saw it, if we could convince just one employee to stay with us a year longer, that paid for the entire program. In reality, we did much better than that. With an average annual employee turnover rate of less than 15 percent, we had half the average rate for the IT services industry at the time.

Improved retention rates isn't the only benefit to a family-focused company policy either. Families play a crucial role in the overall happiness and productivity of employees. When companies support families, it fosters a sense of belonging that can significantly boost morale and loyalty. Involving families can help build stronger connections between colleagues, as they get to know each other on a more personal level, which in turn enhances teamwork and collaboration. It can also create a more inclusive and compassionate culture across the organization, as it shows that the company values not just the employee but their loved ones.

At Catapult, we always wanted to create a fun work environment not just for our employees but for what we called our "extended Catapult family." Having worked in corporate positions where we felt anonymous, this just seemed like a natural consideration. It was so important to us that one of our core values was focused on being a fun place to work.

That's not to say we had a complete family-oriented system ready on day one. It developed naturally over many years. At first, we really just focused on employees and their significant others. After all, the other founders and I were all in our twenties and still single when we started Catapult. We didn't have kids yet—and neither did most of our employees. So instead, we set up regular get-togethers like happy hours for employees and their significant others. We had picnics at different parks where we would bring coolers of beer and sandwiches and throw a football around all afternoon. We'd rent out the Alamo Drafthouse movie theater and watch movies together. We'd go bowling. We had a company softball and basketball team—the Catapult Slingers (although we probably should have been the Catapult Bricklayers based on how we played).

Our most ambitious decision was to buy a lake house for the entire team: a place on Lake LBJ that could sleep fifteen people and came fully equipped with a ski boat and two jet skis. We called it the Launch Pad. Employees could reserve it for free for up to one week per year. Reservations were available based on how long each person had been with the company. The person with the most seniority got first dibs on choosing their week, followed by the next longest serving employee, and so on until every week was claimed. Once a year, the whole team went out on the lake for a big Fourth of July party.

As the years passed and leadership and our employees started having kids, we expanded these programs to focus more on families. We began sending out care packages to families when they had a baby—including some newborn Catapult swag, as I mentioned in Chapter 14. And once a year, we loaded up all of our employees and their families onto a bus and drove down to San Antonio for a day at Six Flags Over Texas. We continued this annual tradition even as we opened more offices across Texas—with each new office heading to the amusement park closest to their city.

By far the best family tradition we had at Catapult, though, was Catapult Kids Day. We actually inherited this program when we acquired another company, BSI Consulting, in Houston. They held an annual event where all the kids came into the office to see where their mom or dad worked and to participate in some fun activities.

The idea resonated so much with us, we decided to implement it across our whole company. Each year, our amazing HR team and several volunteers planned the day. They ordered T-shirts for the kids and came up with a set of activities around a new theme. One year it was Military/Veterans Day, another it was Build a Lego Catapult. We had a Welcome to the Jungle Day, Space Camp Day, and more.

The very first Catapult Kids Day was one of my favorites: Entrepreneur Day. We ordered pizzas and taught the kids how to sell slices to employees in the office at a small markup. The kids got to keep all the profits. We split the kids into different groups by age. The older kids learned about basic accounting and placing an order for pizza, while the youngsters drew marketing flyers. It was a huge success. The kids absolutely loved it—and so did our employees.

MORE THAN FUN

I also loved our annual Halloween costume tradition. It was never mandatory, but every October 31, almost every employee dressed up. We took everyone who was in costume out to lunch that day. If their spouse also got into the spooky spirit, all the better. They could come too. And if an employee wasn't in the office, they could share a picture in their costume on our intranet. We turned this into a competition, of course. The best outfit got a Starbucks gift certificate and some of that public recognition that we already discussed is so valuable in Chapter 16.

At some point, some Catapult departments started coordinating their Halloween outfits. My best friend and cofounder, David

Jacobson, and I always dressed up as a pair. We were everything from Men in Black to sumo wrestlers, superheroes, NASCAR drivers, and M&Ms.

It was always a good time, but these programs weren't just about having fun together with our extended Catapult family. We also wanted to make sure that our employees' families felt that they were a part of the company—and that we were there to take care of them.

We began with small courtesies. We collected the email addresses of our employees' significant others so that we could send them our internal company newsletter. We also gave them direct access to our HR team should they have any benefits questions. This was especially useful during the annual health benefits renewal process. So often, spouses are the ones who make the benefits decisions. Having direct access to the necessary information made it so much easier to make the right choice.

We further kept them in the loop at our annual holiday party when I would give a "State of the Corporation Address" that I directed mostly at our employees' significant others. The employees themselves already knew this information, but I felt it was important that the families knew how we were doing and where we were going. For this reason, I was always completely transparent, sharing our high-level financials, as well as our wins and our losses. While these speeches were usually fairly celebratory in nature, they were more solemn when the road ahead was difficult. In 2000, 2001, and 2002, I laid out how hard things were for the company. December 2001, in particular, was a dark time for Catapult, the economy, and America in general after 9/11. But I considered that speech a chance to reassure everyone, employees and families alike, that everything was going to be okay eventually. I think our Catapult extended family appreciated my honesty in those moments.

Finally, I took inspiration from the US military and created the Catapult ambassador program. Just as the military connects new families with those who are already settled in the area, each new Catapult employee was paired with an existing employee for their first three months. This wasn't a training program—and they were never paired with their manager. Instead, it was a way to make our new employees feel welcomed. From day one, they had someone they could go to when they had questions, whether about work or life outside Catapult.

If a new employee had a family and was moving to one of our offices from out of town, we would try to pair them up with another Catapult employee who also had a family, preferably with kids of a similar age. That way, if they had questions about the best neighborhoods or school districts, they would have someone to talk to.

FAMILY FOR LIFE

When your kids are regularly asking when the next Kids Day is or when they are going to Six Flags next, it becomes much harder to leave your job. When your spouse asks if your next employer will be as transparent as your current one, it's difficult to justify moving on. This was a major reason we kept up these programs, but it wasn't the only reason.

To be honest, they weren't just fun for our employees; they made work more fun for all of us. And it made work feel more meaningful and purposeful. To this day, nothing makes me happier when I run into former Catapult employees than hearing how they're still close with the friends they made through the company. That is something I'll take with me for the rest of my life.

And it's something I experienced myself. I made some of my own best friends through Catapult. I don't even know how many hospital visits I made to meet the newborn of one of our employees. I looked forward to those trips to Six Flags as much as anyone because I felt I was going with my friends.

I may not have designed those programs with my own experience and my own family in mind, but in the end, I benefited as much as anyone.

KEY TAKEAWAYS

- By involving families in company activities, you create a sense of belonging for both employees and their families, significantly improving employee retention and loyalty.
- Create activities with the whole family in mind, including the employee, their spouse, and their kids. There should be something for everyone to look forward to on the calendar.
- Providing family members with access to company information—through newsletters, direct communication with HR, and family events—helps build trust and loyalty.
- An "ambassador" program helps new employees and their families integrate into both the company and the community. Pairing new hires with experienced employees ensures a welcoming environment, especially for those relocating.

PRO TIPS

- Provide perks like family day events, financial planning classes, access to company amenities, and tickets to entertainment venues.
- It makes a big difference if you can remember the names of your employees' significant others, but that's hard to do once you get over fifty employees. I had a "cheat sheet" with the names of my employees and their significant others for each office that I memorized before every family fun event and holiday party.
- One of the most cost-effective family events you can plan is a company picnic. Simply meet at a local park and bring some BBQ and beverages. It's remarkably simple, but everyone will have a great time, including the kids.

CASE STUDY

How Rebecca Wayland Transformed Trident's
Support for Its Employees' Families

After serving as a surface warfare officer in the US Navy, Rebecca Wayland joined Trident Proposal Management, a company that specializes in helping organizations craft winning proposals for government contracts. She was seeking a portable career that could adapt to her family's frequent relocations due to her husband's ongoing active duty, and Trident offered her a position with that flexibility. Initially, she worked on proposals as a freelance résumé writer. Over time, her role evolved, and she became a full-time employee, leveraging her skills in writing and project management. As she navigated moves to locations as distant as Sasebo, Japan, she continued to balance work with the arrival of her first child. She also began to recruit others like herself—spouses of active duty military members.

Once she became Trident's chief of staff, Rebecca led the effort to turn this into a company-wide program. To further attract military families, the company's commitment to flexibility expanded to incorporate the need for time off during relocations and accommodate varying work schedules. It also became a completely virtual workforce, allowing remote work from different geographical locations. This approach not only tapped into a talented and resilient workforce but also supported the broader military community by offering stable employment opportunities.

Rebecca also extended Trident's culture of support beyond the flexible work arrangements by acknowledging the contributions and challenges of military families through various initiatives. For example, they sent care packages to deployed spouses, celebrated significant family milestones on social media, and provided practical support like meals and sponsored outings during extended deployments. When the company held their first in-person event in more than five years, Trident invited employees' families to attend and held an awards ceremony celebrating the unique contributions of each employee.

This holistic approach has ensured that employees felt valued not only as workers but also as individuals with families who mattered to the organization. By fostering a supportive environment that accommodates the unique needs of military families, Rebecca has built a resilient and dedicated workforce at Trident. This commitment to employee well-being has translated into higher retention rates, increased job satisfaction, and a strong sense of community.

Chapter 18

Talk to Your Front Line

DIFFICULTY: 2/5

Toward the end of my basic training, my commanding officer, Lieutenant Alexandre Schwab, sat down with me one-on-one, as he had done several times during the previous four months. Normally, these meetings took place out in the field and consisted of reviewing my performance metrics (a powerful tool I discussed in Chapter 9) and giving me feedback on my progress. He also made a point of just getting to know me, while also inquiring about troop morale directly from someone on the front lines, bypassing his corporals. This was his chance to hear what was happening straight from the soldier's mouth.

This particular meeting, though, was different. To begin with, it took place in his personal quarters on base. The purpose was also different. Lieutenant Schwab wasn't trying to get information from me. He wasn't helping me improve my performance. This time, he wanted to present me with an opportunity. He wanted me to enlist in the under-officer training program and become a corporal.

In the Swiss military, everyone starts off at the same level. Unlike the US military system, you can't just go to college and then jump straight into officer candidate school. Everyone starts as a soldier. The military then selects the most qualified individuals to move up in rank. This means every officer has walked in the shoes of their soldiers.

From the pool of recruits in basic training, about 15 percent are selected for under-officer training to become corporals. From that group, 20 percent are selected to become lieutenants. A similar process occurs when selecting captains, majors, and so on, all the way up to general.

Now, Lieutenant Schwab was telling me I was one of the selected. I wasn't exactly surprised by the offer—I knew I was one of the better recruits—but I didn't know how to respond to it. This was a big life decision for a nineteen-year-old. I had never planned to continue on as a soldier beyond basic training. For me, my time in the Mountain Grenadiers had been about proving to myself that I had truly overcome the autoimmune disease that had nearly left me disabled for life. I had never had any aspirations to move up in rank. Changing my mind at that point would entail another six months of intense training—more if I wanted to become an officer—and would mean delaying college.

In the end, it was Lieutenant Schwab's belief in me that convinced me I could "go all the way" and become an officer. His faith in my abilities reassured me it was the right choice. I signed up, and I have never regretted that decision.

In fact, I made a point of becoming the same kind of leader for the soldiers under my command that Lieutenant Schwab had been for me. Several years later, as I commanded my own platoon through Mountain Grenadier basic training, I regularly sat down one-on-one with each recruit, just like Lieutenant Schwab. And just like Lieutenant Schwab, toward the end of boot camp, I selected two of my men for advancement. I met with them to discuss the same opportunity that had been offered to me. Both said yes and reenlisted.

DON'T LET THE GAP GROW

If you've ever cracked open a single book on management, you know the value of regular one-on-one meetings between managers and employees. These meetings allow managers to build strong relationships and trust with their team members. They provide a dedicated time for managers to offer personalized feedback, recognize achievements, and discuss areas for improvement. By maintaining open lines of communication, managers can address concerns and challenges promptly, preventing small issues from escalating into larger problems. Regular interaction also helps managers stay informed about their employees' workload, progress on projects, and overall job satisfaction, enabling them to provide the necessary resources and support to ensure success.

Again, none of this is likely new information for you. But this one-on-one interaction shouldn't be limited to your management team. While most of your meetings will be with your direct reports, part of your job should be keeping a pulse on people at every level of your organization.

Leadership is far less effective when it only exists behind closed doors. If you isolate yourself from the rest of the organization, you remove a key connection your employees have to the culture and vision of the company. So many of the recommendations in this book require that personal touch from the CEO and the executive team. Employees want to feel heard. They want to see that leadership really cares.

Staying in your own office limits your understanding of the company—and your access to new ideas. Some of the best suggestions I have ever received came from employees working on the front lines. By focusing on one or two new ideas a year, I was able to make a huge difference in the company's trajectory. The same can be true of your organization.

MEET YOUR PEOPLE

Creating a personal connection with your frontline workers can begin with the simplest of steps. Open your door and walk around your office. Walk up to different employees and ask questions. If you visit another office, don't just stay in the conference room, go meet your people. In general, you should aim to spend as much time as you can face-to-face with your people, showing real curiosity and interest when you interact with them.

Beyond this basic point, though, I have developed three different initiatives to codify how I learn from and engage with people across my organization.

EMPLOYEE SURVEYS

Every company should run an annual employee survey across the entire organization. My preference has always been for the twelve employee engagement questions developed by Gallup called the Q12® Survey, available at https://www.gallup.com/q12/.

This isn't the only survey out there, but it has the benefit of being short, anonymous, affordable, and repeatable, with good questions that get to the heart of the data leaders are looking for. At Catapult, we compared survey results by office, department, and year over year to find the areas of our business that most needed attention. Like any good business analysis, we trended this data over time to see if we were doing better or worse in our various objectives.

We also shared the results with the entire company for full transparency and so everyone would feel engaged in the process.

BRONZE CLUB MEETINGS

Surveys are great for data, but they lack that crucial personal touch. After all, they are anonymous and by their nature involve a limited number of answers to a limited set of questions. The second method I used to get feedback directly from the front lines allowed for more individual interaction and nuance. Here, I used the club system we developed as a reward (see Chapter 16) as a means of initiating the conversation. Employees joined our Bronze Club after their first anniversary with the company. Being a Bronze Club member included a few gifts—a glass trophy with their name on it, a small bottle of cognac, and a cigar—and lunch with me. But it also involved a discussion about their impression of the company.

We would wait until we had a critical mass of new Bronze Club members—usually five to ten employees in an office—and then my executive assistant, Shelley Roberts, would reach out to the new members to set up an hour-long meeting in a conference room before lunch. During that meeting, I started by thanking them for everything they had done for the company over the past year. They were the best in the business, they had lots of options, and I appreciated they'd decided to stay with Catapult.

Once that moment of recognition was over, I told everyone at the table that they were in a unique position. They'd been with the company long enough to know all the skeletons in the closet. They knew everyone's little ticks and faults, the weaknesses in every process. But they were new enough that they remembered what it was like working somewhere else. That gave them a unique perspective I was eager to hear. So I asked them to share "the good, the bad, and the ugly" about working for Catapult:

- The good: Why are you still here? What do you like about working at Catapult?
- The bad: What can we do better?
- The ugly: Is there anything you think I don't know about but should?

With the questions set, we'd go around the table with each person giving feedback. Inevitably, the first person to answer was always timid. They'd give safe answers about how great Catapult was and how maybe we could improve the snacks we offered in the breakroom.

The next person was usually a little bolder. And by the time we got to the third or fourth Bronze Club recipient, they were comfortable enough to really give me the good stuff. They'd tell me that the 401(k) plan sucked or the laptops were outdated. By the end of the meeting, everyone was speaking up about their deepest thoughts about the company.

I would take all the notes, anonymize them, and put them with all the Bronze Club answers for the quarter. I would then take those notes, look for trends, and review it with the rest of the executive team during one of our monthly strategic meetings (which we'll cover in Chapter 21).

MEETING EVERY EMPLOYEE

This final program was the most difficult to implement and maintain, but it was immensely valuable. I set out to personally meet with every single employee in the company for fifteen minutes every two to three years.

As you can imagine, this was a huge time investment, especially once we grew past a couple hundred employees, but it was completely worth it.

To make time for these meetings, I spread them across six months. I asked each employee to come prepared with answers to the following three questions:

- **What are three things you are working on right now?** These could be projects. They could be areas of self-improvement. Whatever it was, what were they currently doing for Catapult?
- **What do you want to be doing in five years?** This was purposely very open-ended, and I encouraged honesty. It was okay if they wanted to open their own business in that time period. I'd be happy to help them do that. If they wanted to open the new Denver office, I was ready to see if they'd be a good fit.
- **What is the one thing you would do differently if you had my job**

for six months? This was a chance for each person to dream big and offer me their biggest initiative.

I asked each person to email me their responses five minutes before sitting down with me so that I could carefully listen to them rather than take notes. This also ensured they thought through the questions ahead of time. The first two questions were designed to show sincere interest in the employee and get to know them better. The third question opened the door to pretty much anything. I am still amazed by the quality of the feedback I received during these meetings.

My favorite example came from one of our senior consultants, Eric Russell. His answer to question three included a six-page proposal and cost-benefit analysis for the creation of a new role at our company: sales engineer. He had noticed how much billable time was being lost because consultants had to work with salespeople to create proposals and close deals. Not only was this process losing everybody money, many of our excellent consultants weren't particularly good in this area, potentially costing us clients. It would be far better to create a position responsible for this specific need.

Once he made his case, Eric volunteered to be our first sales engineer. Two weeks later, he had the job. The impact over the following years was enormous. We won more proposals, signed more clients, and freed up more consultant time for billable work. The position paid for itself almost overnight.

It was so successful, in fact, we eventually added sales engineers across every market.

- The best ideas to improve your company will come from the front lines.
- Regular one-on-one meetings with employees at all levels are crucial for maintaining open communication and staying informed. Direct contact with frontline workers provides valuable insights and helps prevent potential issues from escalating.
- Put concrete initiatives in place to gather feedback from your employees, including annual surveys, in-person group meetings, and one-on-one meetings with every employee.

PRO TIPS

- Make it a habit for leaders to regularly visit different departments or offices. Visibility is important for establishing rapport with employees and keeping communication channels open.
- I have never seen an anonymous suggestion box (either a physical lockbox in the breakroom or an online form) yield anything useful.
- Instead, we created an online system called "IdeaInbox," where any employee could submit an idea or suggestion—about anything. Everyone else in the company could vote it up or down, as well as submit comments. This yielded some amazing ideas over the years.

FURTHER READING

The One Minute Manager by Ken Blanchard and Spencer Johnson

First, Break All the Rules: What the World's Greatest Managers Do Differently by Marcus Buckingham and Curt Coffman

CASE STUDY

How David Kirchhoff Engaged the Front Lines at WeightWatchers

After working with Boston Consulting Group and PepsiCo, David Kirchhoff was recruited in 2000 as "employee #6" and the head of product and strategy by WeightWatchers.com Inc., a startup funded by the private equity group that owned WeightWatchers International. At that time, WeightWatchers operated mostly as an in-person support group system, where members attended meetings to learn about healthy lifestyles and how to track their food intake. WeightWatchers.com sought to expand that model by offering a digital version of the program through an online subscription service. Back then, David himself was forty-five pounds overweight and joined WeightWatchers meetings to better understand the program. He eventually reached his weight goal, becoming a WeightWatchers Lifetime Member.

In 2004, David was appointed CEO of WeightWatchers.com, and just a year later, after WeightWatchers acquired the two-hundred-person software company, he was made CEO of the parent company, WeightWatchers International. From 2007 to 2013, David led the organization. He understood that his group meeting leaders were mostly women, 90 percent of whom were former WeightWatchers members who had successfully reached their own weight goals. As a result, they had a strong emotional connection to the mission of the company and were highly passionate about helping others achieve the same results.

Understanding the importance of connecting with these employees, David made it a point to regularly visit regional markets around the world, usually twelve to sixteen times per year. During these visits, he would attend group meetings and also hold all-hands town hall meetings with employees. These sessions typically involved a two-hour discussion where David would first talk about the company's vision and strategy, while the second half was always reserved for an open Q&A session. It was during these Q&A sessions that David got his most valuable insights from the front lines of the business. His employees did not shy away from asking tough questions or bringing up challenging topics.

These meetings served as the ultimate skip-level interactions, allowing David to hear directly from those who were most closely connected to the customers. He found that the closer he got to the front lines, the more willing employees were to share what was truly on their minds. The frontline employees felt heard and respected, and David proved not to be some distant CEO, but someone they could relate to and trust. This direct line of communication simultaneously helped shape strategic decisions for the company and reinforced the sense of purpose that WeightWatchers had built through its dedicated staff.

Chapter 19

Gut Instinct

DIFFICULTY: 2/5

During officer candidate school, we learned how gut instinct, often referred to as intuition or instinctive decision-making, can play a crucial role in military operations. Gut instinct, we were told, could make all the difference in the rapidly changing dynamics of a battlefield that demands quick and decisive action. When there is insufficient time to analyze all available data or when the information is incomplete, our gut can be our most powerful ally.

Our instructors, though, were quick to caution the limitations of this ability. One's instincts in the battlefield need to be honed through rigorous training and developed over time through repeated exposure to complex scenarios. If you're new to something, you don't have gut instinct yet. You're just making rash, random decisions. In that case, it's better to slow down and get more information before making a call.

The value of gut instinct was driven home for me most vividly during "advanced mountaineering" week. This was the week all the recruits looked forward to the most. For one week only, we could leave our combat gear behind and spend all of our time in the high mountains learning skills like rock climbing, ice climbing, belaying techniques, and glacier traversing. For those who love the mountains—basically, everyone in the Mountain Grenadiers—this was heaven.

The military brought in outside expert instructors to teach us these advanced skills. They were chosen not for their military experience—some didn't even have a rank—but solely for their experience on the mountain. They were all old, weather-worn mountain men. My group's instructor was Sergeant Major Meier, an alpine guide in his late sixties. On the fifth day of instruction, Sergeant Major Meier marched our unit to the side of a cliff thirteen thousand feet above sea level where we were meant to practice rock climbing techniques. We left at 4:00 a.m. The weather was beautiful—clear sky, light breeze, sun peaking over the eastern horizon. As we made our way up the rock face in the early morning hours, we were all having a blast.

Later that afternoon, something suddenly spooked our instructor. His face turned pale, and a look of deep concern ran across his features. To this day, I don't know what it was—a shift in wind direction, a drop in barometric pressure. I'm not even sure he consciously knew. But he knew enough to trust his instincts. Without a moment's delay, he told us we had to get off the mountain as quickly as possible.

We rappelled down one length of rope at a time. It took us over an hour to get down to the base of the cliff—just as a cold, thick fog swept in and blotted out the previously blue sky. Even as we were still catching our breath, the visibility went to zero. It took us several more hours to fumble our way back to the cabin we had stayed in the night before. By the time we got back, it was dark, and the temperature was dropping rapidly—but at least we could all look forward to a warm bunk that night. If Sergeant Major Meier hadn't trusted his gut and told us to get off the mountain when he did, we would have been stuck on the side of the mountain all night.

TRUST YOUR GUT

Have you ever wondered why some people excel at making business decisions quickly and decisively with limited information, while others get bogged down in "analysis paralysis"? Some people just seem to have a "sixth sense" that tells them when to make a deal and when to walk away or when to push for a sale and when to back off. They seem to be able to predict the outcome of a complex situation without knowing enough to justify their certainty.

We have a lot of words to describe this phenomenon. It's intuition, instinct, a hunch, an inkling, a sneaking suspicion, our Spidey sense tingling. All of these terms refer to the same ability, and effective leaders know how to recognize it and leverage it.

To do so in your own business, you have to acknowledge that gut instinct is a real phenomenon. Malcolm Gladwell details numerous examples of gut instinct in his book *Blink*. There, for instance, he references poker players who know to change their strategy before they can explain why they're doing it. This is the key to gut instinct: it's our brains working faster than our conscious mind can keep up.

In a *Business 2.0* article on gut instinct by Thomas A. Stewart, Harvard professor and psychologist Howard Gardner explains, "Gut instinct is basically a form of pattern recognition." Our brains process more information on a more sophisticated level than most of us realize. And the more experience you have in a specific field, the more patterns you intuitively recognize.

Have you ever started to head down an alley only to stop and feel something isn't right? That wasn't a random guess; it was your subconscious mind picking up on information you didn't consciously notice. It was a sound, a shadow, a smell that told you to choose a different path home. We all have this instinct to some extent, but with training and experience, you can hone it in particular areas.

One of the areas I've learned to trust my own gut instinct is when I'm evaluating a company's potential. After I sold Catapult and returned from a year traveling around the world with my family, I decided to get back into business by investing in and scaling a promising young startup. Over the course of a year, I evaluated over a hundred deals. I rejected them all. Sometimes, there were clear, logical reasons for this, but sometimes it was just a feeling. Then, I sat down with Juan Rodriguez to talk about his company FlashParking.

I met him for what was supposed to be a thirty-minute chat at Starbucks on Guadalupe Street. Three hours later, I made two phone calls on my way home: one to my wife to tell her I'd found the right company, and one to my friend Dan Sharplin to ask him to consider investing with me and joining the board.

Somehow, I knew that this was the right fit for me and that Dan had the right experience to help me guide FlashParking to its full potential. It was one of the best decisions of my life, and I made it with my gut.

WHO HAS GUT INSTINCT IN YOUR ORGANIZATION?

Few people have good intuition about everything, and a great leader knows whose instincts are strongest in each situation. It's your job to see who truly excels at instinctive decision-making and where they employ it best.

I've witnessed this superpower in several members of my team. Sue Darrow was our VP of HR at Catapult. She conducted thousands of interviews over the course of her career, and she always knew within five minutes if someone was a good fit for our company or not. She wouldn't always have a clear reason for it, but anytime I heard her say, "I have a funny feeling about this one; I just can't put my finger on it," I knew to take her word for it. She was right 100 percent of the time. Every time we overruled her, we came to regret it. Without fail, three months later, we had to fire that person.

Another individual with superpowered instinct was Eliseo Diaz, the cofounder and VP of Sales of FlashParking. He also required no more than a few minutes to determine whether a potential client was going to buy from us. If we were in a room with representatives of a potential client, he'd know just by asking a few questions and observing body language if we'd won or lost the deal.

And then there was Catapult's CFO, Mike Albe, who knew instinctively when a customer was in financial difficulty and wasn't going to pay. This wasn't about the numbers. You could have two clients with similar amounts owed and telling us similar stories, and he could tell you which one would pay and which one to stop servicing. Like Sue and Eliseo, he was right every time.

REVERSE GUT INSTINCT

Not everyone has the ability to make those perfect calls on instinct. In fact, some people have what I call "reverse gut instinct." My son, for instance, was born with an inverted sense of direction like his mother. The more confident he is about where he's going, the more likely we should be heading in the opposite direction. Needless to say, he's gotten lost a few times!

For this reason, it's as important to know whose gut *not* to trust when making a decision as who you can rely on. I would ignore anyone but Sue who told me they had a funny feeling about a candidate. If they continued to push, I'd make them justify that claim in a way I didn't with Sue because she'd earned the right to rely on her gut. This approach proved very effective. Usually, this other person's "gut instinct" came down to a negative first impression of the candidate. If I'd relied on that, I would have turned away a number of great employees.

At the same time, I should probably state what may seem obvious: intuition is not always the best tool for the job. If you're reviewing a legal document, architecting a software application, or engineering a new car, decision-making should lie squarely in the realm of reason and rationality.

Gut instinct is there for situations that are complex, fluid, and fast-changing—when you have imperfect information and limited time to find solutions. Whether it's a battlefield, investing in financial markets, or implementing company culture, you often have to rely at least partly on your gut. In these situations, you will never collect enough data or be able to weigh every alternative. That's when you need to know whose gut you can trust. Because their instincts can make all the difference.

KEY TAKEAWAYS

- Gut instinct can be a powerful decision-making tool, especially in dynamic situations with incomplete information. However, this instinct must be honed through experience and training.
- Effective leaders should identify individuals within their organization who have strong intuitive abilities in specific areas, such as hiring, sales, or finance, and trust those instincts when critical decisions are needed.
- They should also be on the lookout for individuals who have poor intuition, or "reverse gut instinct." Preventing poor decisions based on misguided feelings is as important as utilizing gut instinct.
- Gut instinct is useful in rapidly changing, complex situations, but it is not suitable for decisions that require detailed analysis, such as legal reviews or engineering tasks.

PRO TIPS

- Keep a journal of your own gut instinct decisions—in both professional and personal situations—and track your success rate over time. This is the only way to know whether or not you should trust your gut for future decisions in those areas.
- If you're about to make a decision at work and you have a funny feeling in your stomach, that's your gut instinct (or moral compass) telling you to reconsider. Call a mentor or trusted advisor to get a second opinion.
- Just because you've been successful and are great at recognizing trends and patterns in one field doesn't mean you should listen to your gut in others. Tread carefully and gather more data when navigating a new field or industry.

FURTHER READING

Blink: The Power of Thinking without Thinking by Malcolm Gladwell

"How to Think with Your Gut," *Business 2.0*, November 2002 by
    Thomas A. Stewart

CASE STUDY

Gut Instinct in Action: The Entrepreneurial Journey of Kenny Tomlin

A high school debate champion, Kenny Tomlin initially envisioned a future in law. However, after getting married and welcoming his first child while still in college, Kenny needed to work immediately after graduation to support his young family. He found himself in Dallas, working two manual labor jobs as he tried to get his footing in the business world. Then came a pivotal moment: Kenny received two job offers. One was a well-paying position as a call center manager for a paging company. The other was a much lower-paying role as an executive assistant to the director of marketing at a home healthcare company. Kenny's gut instinct told him to choose the lower-paying role because he saw its potential to learn and grow—a decision that ended up shaping his entire professional life.

At the healthcare company, Kenny taught himself to use tools like Macromedia and Photoshop. He built computers, worked with GIS software, managed direct marketing campaigns, and ventured into multimedia marketing. His growing reputation led him into freelance work, and in 1997, he founded ISOFT, where he offered custom development services. While at ISOFT, Kenny incubated his first commercial software application—an e-commerce platform for the golf industry. Though the dot-com bust led to a less stellar outcome than

Kenny had hoped, it caught the attention of Walmart. The retail giant recruited Kenny to build out and run their e-commerce platform.

In 2005, Kenny's intuition pointed him toward another opportunity: cloud computing. He founded Rockfish in Bentonville, Arkansas: a company dedicated to developing enterprise cloud-based software. Over time, Kenny evolved Rockfish into a successful digital agency, developing enterprise software applications, mobile apps, and content management solutions. Continuing to rely on his tech industry intuition, Kenny self-funded and incubated several software products, including YouEarnedIt, Coupon Factory, and Tidy Tweet. By 2011, Rockfish had grown significantly and was acquired by WPP.

Kenny's gut instinct wasn't always perfect. After leaving WPP, he cofounded Elevate Growth Partners in Austin, a venture focused on commercial real estate. This time, Kenny quickly realized that expertise matters more than pure intuition when stepping into an unfamiliar industry. Feeling like a fish out of water, he decided to return to his roots in 2020 when he cofounded CourtAvenue, a digital transformation agency focused on delivering innovative marketing and technology solutions.

Back in a field he understood well, Kenny was once again able to rely on his intuition. As a result, CourtAvenue has been able to secure high-profile contracts, attract top talent, and grow twice as fast as Rockfish. CourtAvenue has been awarded *Advertising Week*'s #1 fastest-growing technology company in the world and was ranked as *Inc.*'s fifty-eighth fastest-growing company in the US.

Kenny believes that successful entrepreneurship relies heavily on gut instinct. He emphasizes that building a game-changing business requires more than just following the obvious path and doing what everyone else is doing. Real innovation, he argues, occurs when multiple trends converge, creating unique opportunities for those who can recognize and act on emerging patterns. For Kenny, "good intuition comes from hard work." It's cultivated by reading diverse materials, listening to a variety of podcasts, and networking both within and beyond one's industry. His approach underscores that intuition isn't a shortcut; it's a skill developed through continuous learning and a willingness to engage with new perspectives, ultimately enabling entrepreneurs to make bold, unconventional decisions that drive success.

Chapter 20

Clear Communication

DIFFICULTY: 3/5

Communication in the military is a highly structured and disciplined process designed to ensure clarity, efficiency, and prompt execution of commands. The reason for this is obvious: communication has to be clear and well understood, or people might die. If troops are stationed in the wrong location or attack at the wrong time, the consequences can be tragic. A single misunderstood detail can change the course of an entire battle.

To prevent misunderstandings, the military has devised numerous forms of communication with processes that ensure full comprehension at every stage. For instance, as recruits, we learned to repeat verbal orders back and get confirmation that we understood them correctly. This is especially important in high-stress, high-stakes situations like calling for artillery fire, but we practice it in everyday military life as well. At first, this repetitive communication process seemed almost silly to me—when you're told to go clean your equipment, it does feel a little ridiculous to repeat those instructions before getting on with it—but experience taught me the necessity of the process.

During a combat exercise involving live ammunition, our Mountain Grenadier company was tasked with overtaking simulated enemy positions on the side of a mountain. We had placed targets at various distances the day before to represent opposing troops. My platoon was ordered to move forward and capture each enemy position while another platoon provided cover fire from an elevated position on the mountain.

As we progressed through the exercise, our fire teams would gradually reach an area that had previously been shot at by the covering team. Right before we reached that position, the covering team was meant to redirect its fire to the next target location farther down range. Unfortunately, on that day, one of the recruits got caught up in the action and didn't accurately repeat his new firing orders. Instead of firing on the next enemy position, he fired on our position—with live rounds. Bullets landed just a few feet away from my men and me.

We immediately waved a red flag, which stopped the entire exercise. Luckily, no one was hurt, but it could have been catastrophic—all because someone failed to correctly repeat an order. A slight miscommunication, a minor misunderstanding, and we'd nearly been caught in a fatal mistake.

MAKING YOURSELF UNDERSTOOD

Entire books have been written about the importance of effective communication in the workplace and the various means of achieving this communication. Instead of being exhaustive here, I will instead focus on three forms of communication that I feel have made the biggest difference in the companies I've run.

In this chapter, I'll cover two of them: company-wide communication (specifically, the all-hands, company-wide meeting) and written follow-ups to conversations. I'll cover a third important communication topic, the executive team's communication rhythm, in the next chapter.

COMPANY-WIDE COMMUNICATION

Frequent and clear communication from the CEO and senior management to the rest of the organization is vital for fostering a cohesive and motivated workforce. Clear communication from the top ensures that all employees understand the strategic direction of the company and how their individual roles contribute to the broader mission. This alignment not only enhances productivity, it also fosters a culture of inclusion and shared purpose, where employees feel valued. When leadership communicates directly with their people, it also creates a sense of transparency and trust, which are crucial for employee engagement and morale.

Communication of this sort can be achieved in many ways. The most common methods include emails, internal newsletters, short videos, intranet portals, and internal social channels like Slack or Microsoft Teams. All of these are valuable and serve their purpose, but none are as effective as the town-hall-style, all-hands meeting.

When I ran Catapult and FlashParking, we used our *monthly* all-hands company meetings to share important updates and engage in Q&A sessions that allowed employees across the organization to voice their ideas and concerns. At FlashParking, these meetings were virtual, but at Catapult, I personally traveled to every office each month for all-hands company meetings. Being physically present for such meetings has become less necessary, obviously, thanks to modern technology like Zoom, but I'd still recommend it—at least from time to time. Visiting our other offices gave me an excuse to walk the halls, meet a few clients, and speak personally to employees I'd otherwise rarely interact with (an important part of leadership, which I outlined in Chapter 18).

Whether your all-hands meetings are in person, virtual, or hybrid, you want to keep them relatively short and follow a clear, regular agenda. Our monthly company meetings lasted sixty minutes and always covered topics in the following order:

- Introduce new employees
- Review of key company metrics and high-level financials

- Review of quarterly objectives
- Provide company-wide updates, including key wins and losses
- Provide department by department updates, led by the head of each department
- Announce Employee Core Value Awards
- Q&A

At Catapult, once we outgrew our training center at our Austin headquarters, we moved our monthly all-hands to the Alamo Drafthouse, the famous local cinema that serves food and drinks with movies. The energy was great. It was friendly, vibrant, and jovial. We even received some good-natured heckling.

We skipped the monthly meeting entirely in December (because we were all getting together for the end-of-year holiday party anyway) and January (because we already had our annual kickoff meeting to attend).

That annual kickoff meeting had a similar but slightly different format. The meeting lasted ninety minutes instead of sixty and looked like this:

- Introduce new employees
- Review the previous fiscal year, covering:
  - Key company metrics and high-level financials
  - Key sales and operations metrics
  - Key customer wins
  - Key milestones achieved
  - List all employee hires
- Preview of upcoming fiscal year, covering:
  - Annual theme
  - Strengths, weaknesses, opportunities, and threats (SWOT) analysis
  - Key initiatives
  - Quarterly objectives for Q1
  - Department by department plans for the year

- High-level financial forecast
    - Key metrics
- Announce Employee Core Value Awards
- Q&A

This structure allowed us to get to everything we had to cover in a relatively short amount of time, while leaving room at the end for participation from everyone in the company. It was quick, clear, direct communication that kept everyone on the same page, moving the company in the right direction.

GET IT IN WRITING

As an IT consultant, you learn very early in your career the importance of documenting everything in writing when working with a client. A written record ensures clarity, accountability, and legal protection for both parties. A project's success requires that everyone is on the same page in terms of scope, timelines, responsibilities, and compensation.

This is all the more important when verbally agreeing to a change after the project has begun. We are trained to immediately update the proposal, requirements document, and/or project plan to reflect that change—and to get the client to approve it *in writing*.

Written documents make all the difference because even if everyone is acting in good faith—which is usually, if not always, the case—people forget details. Was that app meant to be up and running in September or October? Who, exactly, was responsible for that deliverable? Consultants and their clients are very busy, and it's easy for the finer points of an agreement to get fuzzy after a few months. Having everything in writing safeguards both parties' interests by providing a basis for resolving any conflicts that may arise.

An email takes you two minutes, but it ensures that there is a clear, documented record of what was discussed. This document then serves as a reference point that all parties can revisit to confirm details, responsibilities, and deadlines. We believed in this practice so deeply at Catapult we had a saying we introduced in boot camp: "If it's not in writing, it never happened." I have no doubt it vastly reduced the number of misunderstandings with our clients and partners.

This same level of discipline is important for internal communications as well. You should always follow up a verbal conversation (in person, on the phone, or over Zoom) with an email laying out all points of discussion and confirming that both parties agreed to these points. In the same way we repeated each command in the military to make sure we understood it correctly, this is an easy way to make certain everyone is on the same page.

You can also implement a similar process for your all-hands meetings. After each meeting, we always sent an email reviewing the highlights of what was covered. We also published our meeting recordings internally. This provided a level of accountability and demonstrated professionalism and thoroughness, reinforcing our culture of transparency and effective communication.

KEY TAKEAWAYS

- Regular company-wide meetings are crucial for keeping employees informed, building trust, and ensuring alignment. Each all-hands meeting should include new employee introductions, company and department updates, key metrics, and Q&A.
- Using a standardized agenda for all-hands meetings helps ensure consistency and efficiency. A predictable structure allows employees to know what to expect and stay engaged.
- While town-hall-style meetings are most effective for sharing key updates, additional communication methods like emails, newsletters, social channels, and short videos are also valuable for ensuring information reaches everyone in the organization.
- Written follow-ups to verbal discussions with clients and coworkers help prevent misunderstandings and maintain clarity on agreed tasks, responsibilities, and deadlines.

- Be transparent in your all-hands meetings. Share high-level company financials. And don't just focus on good news; share the bad news as well. This will build trust.
- Have everyone on your leadership team present a portion of the meeting.
- Share a recent customer/project case study at every company meeting—and have someone on the project present it.
- Make your all-hands meetings fun and entertaining. We served snacks and drinks, including alcohol. Welcome interruptions, even a little heckling.
- Town hall meetings are the best place to give out employee awards.
- Company meetings are best held in person. Even if you have multiple offices and are broadcasting the town hall meeting virtually, have people get together at those offices to watch the meeting together.

CASE STUDY

Quarterly Business Reviews at AIM Consulting

Mike Mallahan's journey into IT consulting began while studying Management Information Systems at Washington State University. His early exposure to emerging technologies sparked a deep interest in how these systems worked and were integrated. After graduation, he was drawn to the dynamic nature of IT consulting, where he could constantly engage with new projects and technologies.

Over time, Mike transitioned into managing projects and people, eventually leading him to roles at various consulting firms. In 2017, he combined both areas of expertise when he joined AIM Consulting, part of the Addison Group, which focuses on data, digital, and cloud solutions for large and medium-sized enterprises. He initially managed their delivery leadership practice before becoming president. Under his leadership, AIM Consulting has grown to serve over eighty active clients across five regional offices, employing nearly four hundred consultants.

As president, Mike has placed a strong emphasis on company communication, particularly through AIM Consulting's Quarterly Business Reviews (QBRs). These QBRs are more than just routine meetings; they are meticulously designed to engage employees across the company's multiple offices. Mike structures these meetings to avoid the pitfalls of traditional corporate presentations, which are often boring and lead to disengagement. Instead, AIM's QBRs are interactive and inclusive, featuring contributions from employees at all levels, not just executives. By involving team members in presenting new hires, training initiatives, and project case studies, the meetings become a platform for employees to connect with one another and stay informed about the company's progress.

Mike's approach to QBRs also includes limiting the use of charts, graphs, and data-heavy slides, focusing instead on concise communication that highlights key business goals and achievements. Each QBR has a theme that ties the meeting together, making it more engaging for attendees. Themes such as the Olympics and The Great Race have been used to create a cohesive and enjoyable experience. Additionally, AIM Consulting incorporates technology into these meetings, using interactive tools like surveys, quizzes, and live competitions to keep employees engaged. This interactive element not only makes the meetings more enjoyable but also ensures that employees are actively participating rather than passively absorbing information.

To help foster a sense of community, the QBRs feature special segments that further enhance employee engagement and recognition. One such segment is a fifteen-minute spotlight on employees, where team members from different offices are introduced, sharing their hobbies and roles within the company. This feeling of connection is further reinforced through AIM Accolades, where one employee is selected at random from all those nominated for a core value award by their peers that quarter. The Accolades highlight what core value the employee was nominated for and why they were selected.

Finally, the Project Spotlight showcases a recently completed project, detailing the customer's problem, the solution delivered by AIM, and the technology stack used. This not only celebrates the team's success but also educates the rest of the company on AIM's capabilities. The meetings close with a reiteration of AIM's core values, grounding the entire organization in its shared mission and culture. This structured, yet dynamic approach to company-wide communication at AIM Consulting exemplifies how thoughtful, engaging meetings can reinforce company culture, align teams, and drive business success.

Chapter 21

Schedule Everything

DIFFICULTY: 1/5

It's hard to overestimate the complexity and efficiency of Swiss military scheduling. When I was still a senior in high school, I knew exactly when military recruitment day was and when basic training would start the following year. Once I arrived in Isone as a new recruit, I was given a complete calendar including when I could return home on military leave, when my family could visit for Parents' Day, and when I'd graduate. Everything we would do from the first day to the last was already on the calendar.

This experience was not an outlier. In an organization as large and multifaceted as the Swiss Army, the synchronization of various activities is vital to maintaining a state of readiness and operational capability. In order to coordinate its many moving parts, it maintains a master calendar to schedule activities months and years in advance. By planning ahead, the Swiss Army ensures that all boot camps, repetition courses, training exercises, recruiting cycles, maintenance schedules, strategic meetings, international joint exercises, military ceremonies, and disaster response drills are coordinated seamlessly, avoiding conflicts and maximizing the use of available resources.

The Swiss Army takes its scheduling so seriously, that as a Mountain Grenadier officer, one of the artifacts we were tasked with producing during our pre-boot camp planning meetings (see Chapter 22) was a detailed schedule for the next five months including all daily activities, training grounds, troop movements, and joint exercises.

From the moment we had any leadership responsibilities, we were trained to organize and schedule time, men, and equipment. That's how crucial scheduling was taken in the army.

GETTING INTO RHYTHM

Scheduling isn't just a military concern; the efficiency of your scheduling can determine how well run your entire operation is. Even small businesses have so many moving parts that the lack of a well-organized master calendar can lead to missed appointments, scheduling conflicts, and wasted opportunities.

To see how true this statement is, just think about all the scheduling that goes into running even a small, rural high school. If you're the principal at such a school, you have to keep every class in every grade progressing at the same rate. You have to schedule gym time so each class goes once or twice a week but never more or less than every other class. The same is true of the library and the art class and the music room. You have football teams that need to practice— sometimes on the same field as the soccer team. Then you need to coordinate a whole season's worth of games with the other schools in the area. Then you have to do the same for your basketball team and your tennis team. You have school plays to put on and jazz band performances, often requiring the same space for concerts. You have standardized tests, PTA meetings, parent-teacher conferences, and more. You have to fit it all in, and you can't afford any conflicts or too many activities scheduled in one part of the year.

Once you start breaking it down, the logistics are intimidating.

And the same is true for your business. Even if it feels like your company is small enough to run without a master calendar—and even if everything is running smoothly—you're creating more friction and risk than you probably realize.

Employees, like everyone else, function better with a clear schedule and set routines. We all already organize our lives around routines that occur at predictable times. These set events provide a consistent structure and keep us grounded in a fast-moving world. We brush our teeth daily, take out the trash once a week, pay our bills once a month, change the air filters in our homes once a quarter, and celebrate holidays the same way each year. These moments occur at predictable times, on predictable days. This allows us to keep everything straight. Without this rhythm, we would struggle through our daily tasks and obligations, inevitably forgetting some of them.

In business, daily, weekly, monthly, quarterly, and annual routines can provide that same stability. And you can support your entire team by setting these events early and posting them clearly on a master company calendar. The regularity and clarity of such routines can get every part of the company into what I call "business rhythm."

Some departments in your company already understand this concept fully. Your accounting department, for example, would never be able to invoice all of your clients or get through their mountain of administrative tasks each month without an iron-clad schedule in place. They know precisely when to send those invoices, as well as when they have their quarterly financials and annual audits. Everything is clearly scheduled out so it gets done at the right time.

Considering how well this works in accounting, I am often surprised to see so many executive teams that fail to exercise the same discipline or rigor when it comes to running the rest of their company. While they almost always have an annual planning process and quarterly review meetings, they often lack a predictable and structured schedule for communicating and making decisions the rest of the year.

Everything from daily communication to your annual planning meetings and annual holiday parties should be on your master calendar, which should be shared across the organization. The big industry trade shows, the three-day weekends, your fun events, your board meetings and performance reviews: they should all be coordinated and laid out on the calendar before the year even begins, with the dates and times set aside for everyone to see.

HUDDLE UP

Once you recognize the importance of scheduling everything, a lot of opportunities present themselves, particularly when it comes to creating a business rhythm to your meetings. Organizing everyone's time often creates space for meetings that add value on a daily, weekly, monthly, and yearly basis.

DAILY HUDDLES

I strongly believe that executive teams should meet or at least communicate on a daily basis. I learned the value of these "daily huddles" from my very first coaching session with Verne Harnish. Verne explained that these huddles were meant to be short, quick opportunities to get everyone on the same page at the start of the day. I liked the idea so much, I immediately went back to my team at Catapult and told them I wanted to schedule it into our workdays.

My team looked at me like I was crazy. We were already so busy, how could we justify taking any time away from our daily tasks?

"Trust me," I told them. "If you still hate these meetings after six months, we'll remove them from the schedule."

Six months later, they would have called me crazy if I tried to get rid of them.

By then, the executive team had seen the value of daily huddles. We communicated more effectively, made important decisions more quickly, achieved better alignment, and navigated competitive threats more agilely. That was a lot of added efficiency for between fifteen and twenty minutes each morning. In fact, over time, we cut that time down even further. Eventually, we got our huddles down to about five to fifteen minutes.

Daily Huddle Agenda

- Day/Time: Daily at 8:30 a.m.
- Length: Five to fifteen minutes
- Agenda items:
    - Share noteworthy news.
    - Discuss roadblocks and bottlenecks.

I carefully moderated each meeting to make sure it always stayed on track. To make sure we made the most of our time, I tackled those agenda items by asking everyone in the meeting two questions:

- What's going on in your part of the business that we need to know about?
- What do you need help with?

Sometimes, the answer to both was "nothing." When someone did have a point to raise, though, it was my job as moderator to determine how to deal with it. For minor problems, I'd pair up those who needed help with those who could contribute. That way, they could take the issue offline and resolve it. Any topics that required a larger discussion were tabled and added to the agenda of our weekly tactical meeting.

WEEKLY TACTICAL MEETING

The weekly tactical meeting was longer than the daily huddle and allowed for a deeper discussion of the issues that arose during daily huddles or elsewhere in the business. These meetings were usually between sixty and ninety minutes, which allowed sufficient time to resolve most ongoing issues and left room for someone to present and get input on a project.

Weekly Tactical Meeting Agenda

- Day/Time: Tuesdays at 8:30 a.m.
- Length: Sixty to ninety minutes
- Agenda items:
  - Review weekly activities and key metrics.
  - Resolve tactical and resource issues.
  - Allow others to present or get input.

The aim was to keep everything very tactically focused. We'd check in on our quarterly initiatives (or as we called them, our "rocks") and attempt to resolve any issues slowing progress. Any major strategic discussions were postponed to the monthly or quarterly meetings when we'd have more time and scope to focus on them.

MONTHLY STRATEGIC MEETING

While we held the daily huddle and weekly tactical meetings over a conference line or Zoom, for the monthly strategic meeting, I flew in the leadership team. The meeting took up about half a day and included a working lunch. In total, leadership spent between four and six hours in person at headquarters.

Also unlike the daily and weekly meetings, the monthly strategic meeting required preparation. For a daily huddle, the only preparation was knowing if you needed to speak up with an update or a problem you'd encountered, and the weekly tactical meeting might require some input on the topic at hand, but I led the meeting and introduced those topics. For the monthly strategic meeting, I let others lead the conversation on each issue under discussion. And that meant they had to do some work ahead of time.

This was our time to really dig into critical issues that had come up over the past month that we couldn't resolve quickly and brainstorm about ongoing strategic topics.

Monthly Strategic Meeting Agenda

- Day/Time: Third Wednesday of each month at 9:00 a.m.
- Length: Four to six hours
- Agenda items:
  - Discuss, analyze, brainstorm, and resolve critical issues affecting long-term success. One to two major topics max.

By limiting the topics under discussion, we gave each as much time as possible, allowing everyone to contribute until we discovered the right solution.

QUARTERLY REVIEW MEETING

The quarterly review meeting was meaningfully different than the shorter, more regular meetings. It was more like a mini annual planning meeting. The main distinction between a quarterly and annual meeting, in fact, was the scope. In a quarterly meeting, we were focusing on progress over a single quarter instead of the entire year.

Quarterly Review Meeting Agenda

- Day: Third Wednesdays in January, April, and July
- Length: One to two day offsite meeting
- Agenda items:
  - Review quarterly objectives, competitive landscape, industry trends, key personnel, and team development.
  - Brainstorm on important issues.

This meeting was about tracking key performance indicators (KPIs) and making sure everyone was on the same page when it came to our priorities. There was still room, though, to work on those big problems that continued to hold our organization back. With the extra time, we would often bring in an outside facilitator and/or other team members to help move those issues forward.

ANNUAL EXECUTION PLANNING MEETING

This meeting is so important, I'm going to cover it in detail in the next chapter. For now, I'll simply include the basic agenda.

Annual Execution Planning Meeting Agenda

- Day: Thursday and Friday the week before Thanksgiving
- Length: Two to three days, offsite
- Agenda items:
  - Review financials, key metrics, major accomplishments, and failures for the year.
  - Develop theme, execution plan, strategic initiatives, and forecast for the following year.

MASTERING YOUR CALENDAR

Once this business rhythm is established for the executive team, it should trickle down to the rest of the organization. Every team in every department should have a daily huddle to share important information and help each other overcome obstacles. And as I've already mentioned, all of this should be on your company calendar months or even a year ahead of time. That calendar should be available on your intranet for every employee to see. This scheduling allows you to avoid conflicts and coordinate events to be most impactful.

Imagine, for instance, the relief your people will feel knowing months ahead of time when the office Christmas party is. With that date marked on their calendar from January, there's no risk they'll plan their own party on the same night or accept an invitation to a party that they then have to cancel. Your admin team will also have plenty of time to reserve a location and schedule catering for the event without having to worry about both already being booked.

Your executive team will appreciate knowing when your quarterly review meetings fall, so they can plan their vacation around those dates. And members of your board will appreciate it if you consistently schedule meetings the week before or after your quarterly strategy meetings.

When everyone's schedule is aligned, everyone knows what's expected, allowing the whole organization to run more smoothly.

KEY TAKEAWAYS

- Scheduling all key events, from meetings to holidays, provides a predictable structure that helps teams stay on the same page and reduces last-minute conflicts.
- Implementing a regular rhythm of daily huddles, weekly tactical meetings, monthly strategic meetings, quarterly reviews, and annual planning meetings ensures that the executive team stays aligned and addresses both short-term issues and long-term strategy.
- Make your master calendar available to everyone in your organization to avoid conflicts.

PRO TIPS

- You will get the most resistance from your team when first introducing the daily huddle. Push through anyway. It will transform your company, especially if you're growing and operating in a fast-moving environment.
- If your company has less than twenty-five employees, include everyone in your daily huddle. It will not only keep everyone aligned and informed but create a sense of energy and enthusiasm.
- If you have a healthy and disciplined daily huddle, weekly tactical, and quarterly review meeting rhythm, you might not need to hold monthly strategic meetings. I maintained our monthly meetings largely because my executive team lived in multiple cities.

FURTHER READING

Start to Scale: Secrets to Starting and Scaling Any Size Organization
by Verne Harnish

CASE STUDY

Charlie Pace: Leading with Predictability and Transparency

Charlie Pace's experience establishing a business rhythm began during his time at Deloitte Consulting, where he worked in their supply chain practice. His co-leader introduced a weekly stand-up meeting for the fifteen-member team, in which each person gave an update and asked for help when needed. Conducting these meetings standing up ensured they were kept short and to the point. This approach allowed the team to stay focused, address roadblocks quickly, and maintain progress toward their goals. As a result of that meeting cadence, their team became the most productive on that project.

Charlie brought the principles of regular, clear communication he learned from this experience to SiteStuff, an online procurement marketplace for commercial real estate, where he initially joined as director of operations and later became CEO. At SiteStuff, he established a structured communication cadence that included weekly executive team meetings, monthly town halls, quarterly board meetings, quarterly investor updates, and annual planning sessions. This discipline created an environment of proactive communication and transparency, enabling smoother operations and fewer surprises. Thanks to this consistent rhythm for strategic and operational matters, SiteStuff landed on both the Inc. 500 and Deloitte Fast 50 lists of fastest growing companies in the country. The company was successfully acquired by Yardi Systems in 2007.

During the transition period at Yardi, Charlie worked with a nutritionist and discovered that his body was not processing gluten or dairy effectively. He went through a month-long cleanse that resulted in significant health benefits, including losing thirty-five pounds. Inspired by this transformation, he decided to move into the gluten-free food industry, acquiring Smart Flour Foods. The company provides culinary-driven gluten-free products for the restaurant industry, including pizza crusts, breads, buns, and brownies.

At Smart Flour Foods, Charlie replicated the same level of predictability and transparency that had been successful at SiteStuff. He ensured that his teams—from employees to investors—were well-informed and aligned, using structured meeting cadences to communicate effectively. His commitment to consistent communication, the transparent sharing of information, and the establishment of meeting routines allowed Smart Flour Foods to stay organized, proactive, and engaged. Under Charlie's leadership, Smart Flour Foods has established itself as a recognized leader in the gluten-free food industry, whose products are known for their excellent taste and texture.

Chapter 22

Execution Planning

DIFFICULTY: 4/5

A week before recruits arrive at Isone for Mountain Grenadier basic training, the officers and senior noncommissioned officers get together on base to carefully plan the next five months. Their goal is straightforward, if far from simple: to ensure the upcoming boot camp is comprehensive, efficient, and effective.

This complex exercise is a combination of top-down and bottom-up planning. The base commandant, who is ultimately responsible for coordinating five companies and five hundred new recruits, sets high-level training objectives, schedules training grounds for each company, establishes safety protocols, and allocates his professional military instructors and staff to support the overall effort.

But it's up to each individual company, led by its captain, to figure out the rest. Each captain works closely with his lieutenants to outline daily activities, training modules, and physical fitness routines. This is also when lieutenants build the master schedule for the new recruits that I detailed in the previous chapter. At the same time, he works with his sergeant major and quartermaster sergeant to plan and allocate housing, meals, ammunition, transportation, and fuel.

This exercise can be tricky since every calculation has to take into account both the initial new recruit headcount and expected dropout rates. For those doing this for the first time, professional instructors often provide additional support because it is easy to get lost in the weeds. In the end, though, each company captain submits the equivalent of a "budget" to the base commandant, who in turn submits an overall combined budget to military command.

Thus, high-level priorities are set at the top, budgets are calculated bottom-up, and a complete picture for the next five months is formed. It's a very effective process, one that allows the army to plan not just for boot camps but for every eventuality, including war.

A DIFFICULT NEEDLE TO THREAD

In the last chapter, I mentioned the need for an annual planning meeting as a key event that should always be on your schedule. This meeting is so pivotal that it deserves its own chapter. This is the event that sets a company's strategic direction and operational priorities for the upcoming year. It's your chance to review past performance, identify areas for improvement, and set actionable objectives that drive the organization forward.

Crucially, it's also your best opportunity to take dedicated time away from the daily grind and have the deep, thorough discussions that need to happen if you want to keep pushing the company forward.

That's a lot of potential upside, but it's easy for these events to fall short of that promise. A well-planned and well-executed annual planning meeting has to thread the needle between consensus and debate. In the first place, it has to offer a collaborative environment where everyone feels safe to voice their perspective on the best solutions and strategies to employ in the coming year. Because you need to hear new ideas, it's important to leave room for some vigorous debate. Even if you find this somewhat uncomfortable, you need a passionate exchange of views from your best and brightest who all feel strongly about their vision for the future of the company. If everyone starts out agreeing on the same ideas, that's going to harm you in the long term. You want people to fight for new ideas that they truly believe in.

But you also need everyone to eventually rally around a common vision. A successful annual planning meeting has to end with everyone fully committed to the same goals for the next year. By the time everyone heads home, you need the entire senior leadership team to put their concerns and disagreements aside and align around the strategy you all believe in.

DO YOUR HOMEWORK

Because this is such an important meeting that can easily fail to achieve its goals, you can't just walk in and expect it to run smoothly. You need to prepare, and that preparation is significant. This begins with choosing an offsite location. Technically, you could hold this meeting in-office, but I recommend finding somewhere away from the daily routine. A new space removes distractions and provides a fresh perspective, encouraging creative thinking. You want that space to encourage discussion and collaboration, with room to relax enough to allow those innovative ideas to really come out.

Annual planning meetings should be scheduled to take place relatively late in the year. I always had ours the week before Thanksgiving, just ahead of the holiday season and the end of year rush.

With a location and time set, everyone attending should have homework assigned ahead of time so that the whole team can hit the ground running. You want to limit wasted time and maximize the effectiveness of every discussion. Homework for senior executives should include reviewing the company's financial performance, market trends, competitive landscape, and internal metrics. Each leader should also gather insights from their respective departments, identifying key challenges and opportunities.

Pre-meeting homework might also include a SWOT analysis—

covering your strengths, weaknesses, opportunities, and threats—and customer feedback to provide a comprehensive view of the current state of the business.

THE CATAPULT HOMEWORK ASSIGNMENTS

- For everyone:
  - Our ten biggest accomplishments during the previous year
  - Our five biggest failures during the previous year
  - What does our company do really well?
  - What do we not do well?
  - What are three things we should stop doing next year?
- For the CFO:
  - YTD financials and key performance metrics
  - Aged receivables, bad debt, write-offs, and refunds
  - Latest cash metrics
  - Top twenty customers by revenue
- For the VP of HR:
  - New employees hired this past year
  - Employee turnover this past year (and explanation)
- For the VP of Sales:
  - Revenue forecast by region/business unit for upcoming year
- For the VP of Marketing:
  - ROI of marketing initiatives from previous year
  - Marketing plan and budget for upcoming year
- For Business Unit Leaders:
  - Business unit performance metrics
- For the CTO/CIO:
  - Major technology trends impacting the business

The aim here is to have a complete overview of the company already prepared before anyone steps foot in the meeting. Financials, market trends, the state of your main competition, growth over the previous several quarters and years, customer feedback, it should all be at your fingertips before you arrive. That way, no time is wasted offsite and all decisions are based on real world data, not conjecture.

THE REVENUE FORECAST

One piece of homework is particularly important for the planning meeting ahead: the revenue forecast. This is so critical because everything has to flow from your revenue projections. Hiring, marketing, research and development (R&D): those topline priorities only matter in the context of revenue. After all, you can't spend money you don't make.

Since so much hinges on this forecast, you should make sure it is a realistic, bottom-up exercise, not a wishful top-down number imposed by the CEO. In the same way the Swiss Army planned for each boot camp budget by first building an understanding of how much food and gasoline each company needed, you build a revenue forecast using numbers from those who will have to produce that revenue. This exercise is usually led by the VP of Sales who creates the forecast by going salesperson by salesperson, customer by customer, and business unit by business unit—until they can add it all together into a number they are confident represents the company's likely revenue for the next year.

The exact forecasting process is different for each company. At Catapult and FlashParking, we had a "baseline" forecast that everyone committed to hitting no matter what and a "target" forecast that we believed was achievable but more of a stretch. Most years, we hit the target because it wasn't pie-in-the-sky. It was practical, with realistic goals we could attain.

If you're backed by venture capital (VC) funding, your forecast will include a combination of revenue and fundraising. The discussion focuses on "runway"—the amount of time you can run your business before your next round of funding. In the end, though, the same rule applies: you can't spend money you don't have. Either you're making that money through revenue, through fundraising, or a combination of both. But everything flows from the amount you'll have in the bank over the next year.

RUNNING THE MEETING

The key to running an annual planning meeting effectively is understanding that half the purpose of this meeting is to allow people to disagree. The other half is getting people to shake hands and fall in line behind the new consensus before they leave. For three days, everyone gets to fight for their vision of the company. Once those three days are up, though, it's too late to raise objections. Everyone has to be on the same page.

With those two goals in mind, I started every annual planning meeting with a quote from General Colin Powell, former US secretary of state and chairman of the joint chiefs of staff: "Loyalty means giving me your honest opinion, whether you think I'll like it or not. Disagreement, at this state, stimulates me. But once a decision is made, the debate ends." This was my way of reminding my executive team that I expected them to passionately argue their positions over the next few days before coming together to support and commit to the decisions we would make to move the company forward.

That point made, we moved into the meeting proper, which began with a look at the recent past. While most of an annual planning meeting should focus on the upcoming year, it's important to take a look back and spend about half a day reviewing the past year, including:

- Financial performance
- Key metrics
- Strategic initiatives
- Key wins and losses
- New hires and employee turnover
- Major accomplishments and failures
- Lessons learned

If you're blind to the past, you'll make the same mistakes in the future. This year in review is your opportunity to see what went right and what went wrong before engaging in discussions about what to do in the coming year. For that reason, this look back should be a really hard, honest examination of the company's performance. This is not a time for bravado. Your aim here is to accurately set the stage for the discussions over the next couple of days.

The review is when your homework really pays off. Instead of wasting time looking all this up on the fly, you can run through the information quickly and in an organized fashion.

The rest of the offsite meeting should concentrate on the year ahead. Discussions should include (but should not necessarily be limited to) a review of:

- Overall economic indicators
- Industry trends
- Competitive analysis
- Technology trends
- SWOT analysis
- Overall strategy
- Revenue forecast
- Hiring projections
- Market expansion
- Key positions to be filled
- Major marketing initiatives
- Strategic goals
- Strategic initiatives
- Key performance metrics

I liked to start the discussion with the SWOT analysis because each item here opens up topics of debate for everyone to hash out. What new markets should we be exploring? What key positions do we need to hire? What were our major operational issues?

Whatever order you make your way through this list, don't lose track of the fact that your revenue forecast should drive all budget decisions. All discussions should be anchored by those figures.

By the end of this multiday meeting, your aim should be to have a *draft* budget for the coming year, clear objectives and key performance indicators (KPIs) for each department, and an action plan with assigned responsibilities and timelines across the whole organization.

Importantly, the goal is not to *finalize* the upcoming year's budget during this meeting, only to get everyone's input on a *first draft*. The CEO and CFO will lead a smaller team through several more iterations of the budget until a final one is reached by early January—ahead of the annual all-hands kickoff meeting. At the annual planning meeting, your aim is simply to get extra insight that will allow the CEO and CFO to consider all opportunities and risks at play for the coming year.

The final item on my list at every planning meeting was setting an annual theme. This was something to rally the whole company around. It was a chance to land on a single idea everyone in the room—and then everyone in the company—could get behind. That was always a great exercise to help the team put disagreements aside and come together around the vision we'd all crafted for the coming year.

At Catapult, we summarized our entire plan for the upcoming year in a one-page strategic plan as described in the book *Scaling Up* by Verne Harnish. This one-page plan included all the most important information our employees needed to know for the upcoming year, such as our annual forecast, key initiatives, KPIs, and annual theme.

We shared this document with the whole organization following our annual kickoff meeting in January, and we continued to revise it as needed after each quarterly review meeting.

STRATEGY VS. EXECUTION PLANNING

Before moving on to our next topic, I want to take a moment to create some separation in your mind between two related but independent types of planning: strategy and execution. These terms are often used interchangeably—I've been guilty of it myself—but it's helpful to associate them with meetings that have similar but different aims.

Despite what you may hear at some companies, the type of meeting we've been covering in this chapter is an *execution* planning meeting. This type of meeting provides a roadmap for the company, guiding decision-making and ensuring all efforts are aligned around achieving the company's objectives.

Strategy planning, on the other hand—or as I prefer, *strategy development*—is episodic in nature. It doesn't just happen on a consistent quarterly or annual rhythm. The conversations that take place in strategy development meetings occur when they're necessary. The reason for this is that strategy planning is an iterative process designed to slowly consider an overhaul of key strategies at the heart of your company.

If a new AI product could potentially disrupt your company, there's no reason to delay discussions about it until you meet with the whole executive team in November. You should start working through your response as soon as you find out about it. Equally, with such a significant disruption, you don't want to make that decision in an hour. You need to give yourself a number of meetings scheduled over weeks or even months to come to the right conclusion.

The same is true if you are considering changing your entire marketing strategy or if you are mulling over acquiring a competitor. These conversations happen over time and on their own time scale.

That's not to say strategy planning and execution planning never overlap. It is good practice to set aside some time during your annual (and quarterly) planning meetings to discuss ongoing larger strategic topics with the entire executive team, such as those covered in Chapters 3, 5, and 6. I like to hold those higher-level conversations after dinner over a few cocktails each night for an hour or two. Everyone is a bit more relaxed and ready to noodle on an idea. Since we aren't looking to resolve anything immediately, everyone feels a little freer brainstorming and throwing out new suggestions. I've found that some of the biggest and best ideas surface in these more relaxed moments at offsite meetings.

The strategy/execution distinction may seem like a fine one, but I've seen it really muddy the purpose of meetings and disrupt progress. When my good friend and business partner, Dan Sharplin, agreed to come out of retirement and take over as CEO of FlashParking in 2020, he naturally took over our annual planning meeting process.

As the CEO, Dan ran the show, but after the first couple days, it became apparent that he and I had very different leadership styles. Dan is much more strategy focused—and if you couldn't tell by the entire theme of this book, I am more execution focused. Dan loves to hold as many decisions "up in the air" as possible, for as long as possible, so he can thoroughly think through all of the variables. Like a Chinese acrobat spinning multiple plates on bamboo poles, he'll keep turning ideas over in his mind until he's satisfied with the answer.

I'm not exaggerating here. He's been known to wait weeks before committing to a final decision. In fact, his previous company, Site Controls, coined a term for this phenomenon: "Danbiguity."

Danbiguity works very well in the strategy development meetings where you can iterate ideas over long periods, but it can cause real trouble in an execution meeting that requires landing on some clear deliverables. And that's just the trouble we had with Dan at our first planning meeting. By the end of day two, we had not made a single major operational decision. Every decision was being held up by larger strategic considerations that Dan wanted time to think about.

I knew I had to step in. The rest of the executive team needed clear marching orders for the coming year. They had to be able to get back to work the following week and go to their respective teams with instructions on what initiatives to start working on.

That evening, I took Dan aside and shared my concerns. After a heated debate, we agreed to a compromise. We'd take all open strategic topics off the table and iterate on them in a separate series of weekly meetings with Dan, Juan (the company cofounder), and me. For the rest of the annual planning meeting, though, we'd refocus on arriving at the clear objectives, timelines, and accountabilities the rest of the team needed.

Once we were back from the offsite, we set aside two hours each week for strategic discussion. To be honest, I wasn't looking forward to it. But over the next five weeks, Dan changed my mind. While I found the process maddening at first, we managed to unlock a brand-new strategy for the company.

In that fifth meeting, all three of us were looking up at a whiteboard full of ideas when Dan asked us, "Are you seeing what I'm seeing?"

We pulled out the calculators on our phones, put some numbers in Excel, and realized that we had just come up with a completely new industry-changing concept—which we eventually called Hardware-as-a-Service (HaaS). It was a strategic breakthrough, one that would make us more profitable than anyone else in our industry. And it would not have happened without all that strategic iteration.

--- **KEY TAKEAWAYS** ---

- Annual execution planning meetings are the cornerstone of a company's strategic direction and operational priorities for the following year. It's your chance to review past performance, identify areas for improvement, and set actionable objectives that drive the organization forward.
- Holding annual planning meetings offsite helps the team focus away from daily distractions.
- Before you arrive, assign everyone homework so all necessary information is readily available.
- Effective planning is a mix of high-level strategic goals and detailed bottom-up inputs. The annual meeting must incorporate contributions from each department to create a realistic and achievable execution plan.
- The meeting should provide space for debate, allowing team members to passionately voice differing perspectives on the company's direction. However, it must end with alignment, ensuring that

everyone is committed to the shared goals and priorities for the coming year.

- Have structured or unstructured discussions over lunch and dinner. I have seen great ideas emerge from that more relaxed time together.
- Establishing an annual theme helps align everyone around a single, motivating idea for the year.
- Execution planning meetings focus on establishing clear deliverables, timelines, and responsibilities, while strategy development is more iterative and involves longer, ongoing discussions. Keeping these distinct helps maintain focus and avoid confusion during execution meetings.

PRO TIPS

- Bring in internal or external subject matter experts to present as needed.
- Turn off your cellphones and close your laptops but plan regular breaks to check email.
- Build some time into your agenda to get out and do something fun together.
- Start the meeting with an ice breaker so everyone can get to know each other on a personal level. This is especially important if you've added a new member of the executive team.
- If you're new to this process, it can be helpful to bring in a professional business coach to facilitate your execution planning meeting.

FURTHER READING

Scaling Up: How a Few Companies Make It…and Why the Rest Don't by Verne Harnish

CASE STUDY

Execution Planning with FreeScale Coaching

Rich Manders was first introduced to the concept of the one-page strategic plan when he met Verne Harnish in 1997. Rich immediately began implementing this framework, conducting quarterly planning meetings with his executive team in order to produce a one-page strategic plan to get everyone at his company aligned behind a common set of priorities.

This practice proved instrumental in driving operational excellence and growing his business to over $100 million in sales and three times the industry's average profitability over the next twenty years.

After founding and running seven businesses, Rich decided to leverage his extensive experience to cofound FreeScale Coaching Systems in 2015, which focuses on helping scale middle market businesses. Rich and his cofounder, Wayne, work with CEOs and their leadership teams to drive their vision, raise their level of execution, and overcome impediments to growth.

As a coach, Rich believes that implementing a business management framework is crucial for running a successful high-growth company. He recommends popular frameworks like ScalingUp and the Entrepreneurial Operating System (EOS). He continues to advocate for quarterly planning meetings based on Agile principles borrowed from software development, where companies run in ninety-day sprints, setting clear objectives and metrics and reevaluating progress each quarter. This approach ensures that the company remains responsive to changes, maintaining a consistent cadence of evaluation and adjustment.

These meetings generate the kind of same one-page strategy plan that Rich used to build his own companies. This document aligns the team around common goals and priorities. According to Rich, quarterly planning sessions combined with that one-page strategy plan are vital for driving execution and ensuring that everyone in the company is focused on the most critical objectives.

Rich organizes his two-day planning meetings around six fundamental questions that he believes everyone in the company should be able to answer consistently.

1. Who are we?

Review the company's core values and core purpose.

Evaluate every employee for performance, alignment with core values, capacity to do their job, and desire to be in their role.

2. Where are we now?

Review the state of metrics and strategic initiatives.

Assess executive team health using Pat Lencioni's *The Five Dysfunctions of a Team*.

Reevaluate the company's market position using Alexander Osterwalder's *Business Model Canvas*.

3. Where are we going?

Adjust strategic direction as needed, with a focus on one, three, and ten-year goals.

4. How are we going to get there?

Define key metrics and strategic initiatives for the next quarter and year.

5. Who is going to do what?

Assign specific projects and responsibilities to individuals with clear timelines.

6. What is the most important thing right now?

Establish a quarterly theme and priority, incorporating a contest to drive engagement.

FreeScale has facilitated over six hundred planning meetings. Rich recommends holding these planning meetings offsite to remove distractions and allow for frank and open dialogue through dinner and after. Between planning meetings, the executive team should check in weekly to maintain accountability and address issues proactively.

1. How did we prepare for this?

2. Who is going to do what?

3. What else do I need to know right now?

Chapter 23

Keep Good Records

DIFFICULTY: 4/5

Like all large, well-organized bureaucracies, the Swiss Army is a meticulous record keeper. This practice is fundamental to operational efficiency and strategic planning. It's also crucial for establishing historical accountability. These impeccable records covered everything you can imagine. We had operational records documenting training mission details, logistics, and outcomes. Our financial records accounted for budget allocations, expenditures, and resource management.

We also kept equipment maintenance logs and inventory lists. These records allowed us to manage the Swiss Army's extensive array of military assets effectively, minimizing downtime and optimizing readiness. They also ensured every weapon and every explosive was accounted for every single day.

As a lieutenant, it was my job to carefully track the ammunition my platoon used. Every morning, on our way to our training grounds, we picked up bullets, grenades, mortars, anti-tank rockets, and other explosives from the ammunition depot, overseen by our company's sergeant major. While it was impossible to track every shot fired, I was personally responsible for accounting for every explosive detonation involving grenades, mortars, rockets, and demolition explosives.

The number of detonations and the amount of ammunition returned at the end of the day had to reconcile with the sergeant major's records. Any inconsistencies had to be resolved before the day was over. Luckily, my numbers always added up. If they hadn't, my platoon would have had to stay out for as long as it took to find the missing munitions.

That meant, if an explosive failed to detonate, we had to wait fifteen minutes and then go find it and explode it. We couldn't leave any unexploded munitions in the field. The risk to other soldiers would be immense.

You might assume this was a rare occurrence, but explosives fail to detonate for all sorts of reasons all the time. Someone might forget to pull the safety pin from a grenade in the heat of the moment. A detonator might not be inserted all the way into an explosive charge. And it's not unheard of for some soldier to try to pocket a grenade as a memento from his time in the service.

No matter what the reason, if the munitions didn't match what was in the log, we had to find whatever was missing and return it. The numbers had to balance, no matter what.

DON'T ASSUME YOU'RE A GREAT RECORD KEEPER

Steve Mariotti, founder of Network for Teaching Entrepreneurship, says: "At their core, companies only do three things. They make or buy stuff. They sell stuff. And they keep records."

Despite recordkeeping being one of the three things a company must do, most entrepreneurs don't really pay much attention to that part of their business. Because it isn't sexy and doesn't add any immediate value, many do the bare minimum and assume that's good enough. They tend to do just enough to keep revenue coming in and keep the accounts accurate for tax purposes. Anything more feels like a waste of resources.

That practice can work for a while—until it comes time to sell their business. That's when most business owners realize what good record-keeping actually looks like and just how important that process is.

I'm not pointing any fingers here. I'm as guilty of these assumptions as anyone. I have sold two companies in my lifetime: Inquisite in 2007 and Catapult Systems in 2013. In both cases, my records were not up to the high standards of the process. I didn't learn this lesson in 2007 because my friend and business partner, Jim Martin, had stepped into the role of president and oversaw the due diligence process when we sold Inquisite to Allegiance. I was busy running Catapult at the time and only witnessed the process at a distance.

It wasn't until my CFO and I oversaw the process while selling Catapult to Chinasoft that I truly understood the value of great recordkeeping. Over the four-month due diligence process, I was shocked by how detailed and invasive it was. Before the process began, I had thought we were pretty good at keeping records at Catapult. In fact, I prided myself on how well organized we were.

But for all that attention to recordkeeping—far more than most entrepreneurs put into the effort—I wasn't prepared for the level of scrutiny we underwent. I spent those four months chasing down files and records that covered the entire twenty-year span I'd spent running my company. I had to find documents I never thought I'd need. In some cases, I even had to re-create documents that were either lost forever or never existed in the first place. Twenty years is a long time for things to fall through the cracks. Somehow, an employee or two failed to sign their employee agreement. A few client contracts went missing, as did a few board meeting minutes.

I had failed to appreciate that every single misplaced document or missing signature could hold up our entire mergers and acquisitions (M&A) transaction. The gaps in our records created additional risk for the buyer, which would invariably get passed down to us in the form of a price cut or the requirement of additional representations and warranties.

In the end, I saw us through the whole process, and we negotiated the sale at an excellent price, but the difficulties of those months stayed with me. So when I was tasked with running M&A at Flash-Parking after transitioning from president to chief strategy officer, I knew exactly what I was looking for.

I ran M&A my last three years with the company, and during my time in the role, I oversaw the acquisition of ten companies. I quickly discovered that being on the buyer side of the table was a lot more fun. The role came naturally to me. As an entrepreneur and founder myself, I could uniquely relate to each seller as a peer and help them navigate the whole process.

For each transaction, once we agreed on a deal price and structure and signed a letter of intent, I worked with a law firm and an accounting firm to go through confirmatory due diligence with the seller. Our document request list had over 250 items on it—that's types of documents, not number of documents. That may seem absurd, but it's fairly standard. I recommend you look up one of these M&A due diligence lists online and use it for reference in your own company. They're easy to find and a great goalpost to measure your own recordkeeping by.

None of the ten companies we acquired had records as organized as Catapult, but some were close. The difference between those companies who consistently kept good records and those who didn't was stark. For the former, like Catapult, the due diligence process, while tedious and time-consuming, was manageable. There were no surprises, no price reduction, no onerous reps and warranties in the final purchase agreement.

For the latter…let's just say the opposite was the case.

PULLING TEETH FOR BETTER RECORDS

Whether you plan on selling your company one day or not, maintaining good records is a foundational element of any well-run business. Beyond the benefits reaped during the acquisition process that I've already outlined, quality recordkeeping provides a clear and accurate picture of your financial health, operational efficiency, and compliance with regulations. It enables better decision-making and allows leaders to track performance, identify trends, and hold people accountable. It also serves as a safeguard during audits, legal disputes, or tax filings, ensuring transparency and accountability.

Luckily, there are some parts of your company you don't have to worry about too much. Accounting, HR, and legal are inherently good at keeping records. It's in their DNA. Therefore, your attention should turn to those who really struggle in this area, and none struggle more than sales.

Getting sales to organize their records is like pulling teeth. If it was up to them, they would store all customer files on their individual laptops—if that. Salespeople maintain records everywhere, including just in their own heads.

To change this dynamic, you have to get a little creative, and a little tough. At Catapult, we wouldn't start an engagement or pay any sales commission until all signed agreements and statements of work were uploaded to the appropriate customer folder. Sales balked at first, but the policy change was simple and effective.

Improving recordkeeping isn't just about getting tough with those functions that create the most problems, it's also about giving more power to those who have the expertise to maintain this practice. For that reason, I believe accounting should own recordkeeping. They should have ultimate authority and be held accountable for all record maintenance efforts.

To help them succeed, make sure you standardize where you store your records, using one central cloud-based repository with granular permission-based access. It doesn't matter what system you use—SharePoint, OneDrive, Google Drive, Dropbox—they are all pretty much equivalent. Along with setting a single location for your documents, think carefully about access. Obviously, not everyone in your organization should have permission to view everything. As you improve record organization, you can take the opportunity to consider what roles should have access to what folders.

ORDERING YOUR RECORDS

The best way to organize your records is to structure your corporate files as if you intend to share that information in a data room during M&A due diligence.

As I mentioned above, there are extensive lists of document requests available online to get an even deeper sense of the level of maintenance and organization you should aim for. But the following list gives you a straightforward, relatively simple organizational structure you can implement across your company.

M&A DUE DILIGENCE FILE DIRECTORY STRUCTURE

1. **Corporate Documents**
   - Articles of Incorporation
   - Bylaws and Amendments
   - Shareholder Agreements
   - Capitalization Table
   - Board Meeting Minutes
2. **Financial Information**
   - Financial Statements
   - Tax Returns and Filings
   - Budget and Forecast Reports
   - Audit Reports
   - Accounts Receivable and Payable
3. **Legal Documents**
   - Litigation and Dispute Files
   - Intellectual Property Documentation
     - Patents and Trademarks
     - IP Agreements and Licenses
   - Regulatory Compliance Documents
   - Contracts and Agreements
     - Vendor Contracts
     - Bank Agreements
4. **Operational Information**

- Business Plans and Strategies
- Operating Units and Organizational Chart
- Product and Service Descriptions
- Inventory Lists
- Supply Chain Documentation
- Production Schedules and Reports

5. **Human Resources**
   - Employee Contracts
   - Salary and Compensation Plans
   - Benefits Plans
   - Employee Handbook
   - Organization Chart

6. **Sales and Marketing**
   - Customer Lists and Relationships
   - Customer Agreements
   - Sales Reports and Analytics
   - Marketing Strategies and Plans
   - Market Research Reports
   - Branding and Advertising Materials
   - Press Releases and Public Announcements

7. **IT and Systems**
   - IT Infrastructure Documentation
   - Software Licenses and Agreements
   - Commercial Software Packages in Use
   - Data Security Policies
   - System Architecture Diagrams

8. **Technology**
   - Technology Overview and Software Architecture
   - Technical Architecture Diagrams
   - Security Audits and Certifications
   - Third-Party Systems and Open-Source Code in Use

9. **Real Estate**
   - Property Deeds and Titles
   - Lease Agreements

- ○ Zoning and Environmental Reports
- ○ Facility Management Plans
10. **Risk Management**
    - ○ Insurance Policies and Claims
    - ○ Risk Assessment Reports
    - ○ Business Continuity Plans
11. **Environmental and Health & Safety**
    - ○ Environmental Compliance Reports
    - ○ Health and Safety Policies
    - ○ Incident Reports and Records
12. **Strategic Partnerships**
    - ○ Joint Venture Agreements
    - ○ Partnership Contracts
    - ○ Collaboration Agreements

This list can feel a little intimidating at first. But if you approach it systematically now, it's relatively easy to maintain this structure moving forward—preparing you for any future need for your records.

KEY TAKEAWAYS

- Keeping detailed records is essential for operational efficiency, financial accuracy, and strategic planning.
- Good recordkeeping is crucial if you ever want to sell your business. Poor documentation can create additional risks for buyers, resulting in lower valuations, delays, or a more onerous purchase agreement.
- Even if you're not currently planning on selling your business, structuring records as if they will be used in M&A due diligence is a great way to organize your corporate documents.
- Accounting, HR, and legal are typically good at keeping records, while sales and other departments may struggle. Policies to enforce better documentation are necessary to maintain consistency.
- Assign ultimate responsibility for company records to the

accounting department, given their natural inclination for accuracy and organization. Provide them with the tools and authority to ensure good record maintenance.

- Using a centralized cloud-based repository with defined permissions ensures easy access to necessary documents while maintaining security.

PRO TIPS

- Conduct regular internal audits of company records to ensure they are complete and organized. This reduces the risk of missing documents or inconsistent records during critical times.
- Go completely paperless—don't keep any physical files. Even if some customers, vendors, or partners send you paper documents, invest in a few good scanners and digitize them.
- When you set up permissions for your central cloud-based corporate document repository, make sure only a few select people have "delete" permissions on anything. While most of these systems have decent "recycle bins," you might not even notice if someone accidentally deletes a file or an entire folder.

CASE STUDY

Dan Sharplin and the Sale of Site Controls

Dan Sharplin knows a thing or two about mergers and acquisitions. Having overseen over fifty transactions during his tenure at Lone Star Technologies and Tanknology, he's gained a deep understanding of the M&A process including buy-side, sell-side, and joint ventures. It's no surprise, then, that when he founded his own company, Site Controls, he built it from the ground up to be acquired someday.

The inspiration for his company came from the convergence of three trends in the early 2000s: the emergence of cheaper sensor technology, widespread internet connectivity in commercial buildings, and a willingness for companies to outsource non-core functions. Dan started the business in 2002. He spent the first eighteen months conducting market validation and product testing, releasing his first product in 2003. Site Controls quickly became a leader in energy management solutions for multisite commercial businesses, specializing in providing comprehensive systems that helped companies monitor, control, and reduce energy consumption across multiple locations.

Starting Site Controls with a clear plan to sell the company someday guided every decision Dan made. He and his team constantly analyzed a list of potential acquirers, tracking what those companies were looking for and how Site Controls could fit into their strategies. Despite this focus and preparation, when Enernoc—a clean tech company poised to go public—approached them with an acquisition offer in 2006, the company wasn't ready.

Site Controls would have been an ideal "tuck-in" acquisition for Enernoc and would have benefited significantly from the public offering. However, because Site Controls lacked the necessary artifacts, processes, and compliance measures to be part of a public company, Dan had to pass on the deal. After this missed opportunity, Dan vowed that his company would always be ready for an acquisition in the future, with all necessary audits, records, and documentation in place.

Dan put his CFO, Dave Osowski, in charge of ensuring that all record-keeping and financial artifacts would be meticulously maintained from then on. They focused on establishing proper corporate hygiene, audit trails, and comprehensive documentation to ensure they were always prepared for due diligence. In 2010, when the transaction window opened again, Site Controls, with the help of an investment banker, executed a disciplined M&A process.

Leveraging his extensive M&A experience, Dan knew exactly what potential buyers would be looking for and ensured the process was smooth and efficient. Site Controls held potential buyers to a strict calendar of deliverables, gave them access to a fully organized data room containing all corporate documents and artifacts up front, and even supplied buyers with their own purchase agreement, expecting a redlined version to be returned with the buyers' initial offer.

Chapter 24

The 80/20 Rule

DIFFICULTY: 3/5

In officer candidate school, we spent about a third of our time in a classroom studying a wide range of military topics—everything from leadership to infantry tactics, rules of engagement, military ethics, weapon systems, logistics, mission planning, and communications.

One of our lectures introduced us to the Pareto Principle. More commonly known as the 80/20 rule, it asserts that 80 percent of outcomes can be attributed to 20 percent of causes. According to this principle, 80 percent of battlefield success comes from 20 percent of combat skills; 80 percent of equipment failures can be traced back to 20 percent of components; and 80 percent of the success in military operations can be attributed to 20 percent of the actions taken during the mission.

The main point of this lecture was to discuss the strategic allocation of combat resources, both defensive and offensive. The key word for the lesson was "leverage." In every military campaign, each side is looking to leverage an advantage using this math. If 80 percent of your strategic objectives can be achieved by focusing on 20 percent of your key targets, your best strategy is almost always to leverage that 20 percent.

For example, in the face of an advancing enemy, if there is a natural bottleneck like a bridge or mountain pass, it's wise to concentrate the majority of your forces (the 80 percent) on that smaller area (the 20 percent) rather than spreading them evenly across the entire front line. Equally, instead of blowing up a thousand enemy fuel trucks, you can achieve the same results by sabotaging a single refinery plant at a lower military cost.

While not always expressed so mathematically, this idea has been central to military planning since the beginning of military conflict. From the battles of ancient Greece to today, identifying high-value targets where you can apply the most leverage has been crucial for effective military engagement.

MY BILLION-DOLLAR MISTAKE

While academically interesting, at the time, I felt the 80/20 rule was a little obvious and self-evident. It was not until years later that I realized that the obvious can still elude you. But by then, I'd already found myself on the wrong side of a particularly costly 80/20 equation.

Perhaps I shouldn't be so hard on myself. After all, while the 80/20 rule is clear in most military strategies, it's not always so obvious in business. Many entrepreneurs fail to appreciate that 80 percent of their profits come from 20 percent of their customers, or that 80 percent of their sales are made by 20 percent of their salespeople. You can go years without noticing that 80 percent of your support calls come from 20 percent of your users. These rules can be hard to observe because in the real world, they aren't quite as mathematically perfect as they appear on paper. The percentages vary quite a bit in reality, but as unscientific as that might sound, most 80/20 rules still hold true in some sense.

My own 80/20 troubles came out of a well-known example of the principle in the IT industry. Ask any tech entrepreneur, and they'll tell you that 80 percent of their users leverage only 20 percent of the functionality of their systems. In my experience, it's closer to 90/10 or even 95/5. Think of how few features you use in Microsoft Word or Excel. How many buttons have you actually clicked in your email program or CRM system? Most of us use the same few features over and over again. The rest are there for the minority of specialists who have very specific needs.

In 1997, I got this equation completely backward. That was the year we launched Inquisite, one of the very first web-based survey tools on the market. Our strategy was to develop a sophisticated and feature-rich application in order to penetrate the high end of the market first—in this case market research firms—and then expand into other, broader market segments like marketing and HR departments.

Our rationale was simple: if we could satisfy the complex functionality needs of our most demanding users, then we could easily meet everyone else's needs. At first, this approach seemed to work perfectly. Our customers appreciated our software's advanced capabilities, our competitors struggled to keep up with our rich feature set, and we commanded a premium price. Inquisite grew rapidly and became cash flow positive within a couple of years.

Then a new breed of competitor emerged. Companies like Zoomerang and SurveyMonkey started targeting the lower end of the market. They leveraged the 80/20 rule and decided to develop only 20 percent of the functionality so they could better cater to 80 percent of the market—or more accurately, they developed 5 percent of the functionality to service 95 percent of the market.

They didn't have a sales force. They offered no support, training, or service level agreement of any kind. Their features were minimal. All they had going for them was a "freemium" version of their product that allowed users to survey a number of respondents for free. Customers would only start paying after exceeding a certain volume.

At first, we didn't feel threatened by these tiny competitors. Frankly, we would make fun of them internally. After all, what respectable corporate customer would use an online survey tool with the word "monkey" in it? We continued adding features and signing high-end clients. We were so set on our strategy, we refused to develop an entry-level, lower-cost version of our product for fear of cannibalizing the rest of our business.

As everyone knows now, SurveyMonkey got their strategy right, and we got ours wrong. All of those perceived weaknesses in our competitors were in fact strengths they leveraged to their advantage. Their limited feature set allowed them to get to market quickly. Because their software was so simple, anyone could use it without training or customer support. By not having a sales force or support staff, they were able to keep their overhead low and increase their margins. Finally, their freemium business model encouraged people to try out their product and allowed them to rapidly capture market share.

By the time we sold Inquisite to Allegiance in 2007, our growth had plateaued, and our premium pricing was under pressure. Survey-Monkey, on the other hand, acquired Zoomerang and raised capital from a private equity firm at the unbelievable valuation of $1 billion.

While we were pleased with the valuation and outcome of Inquisite's sale, I can safely say without violating any confidentiality agreement that it wasn't anywhere near $1 billion.

With our head start in the market, we could easily have beaten all new competitors if we'd pivoted right away. By staying on the wrong side of the 80/20 rule, we threw away all our advantages—and all the potential financial reward that would have come with them.

DO THE MATH

Once you really absorb this principle, you see 80/20 opportunities everywhere. And once you identify the 80/20 scenarios that are critical to your company's success, you should give those factors the most focus.

At Catapult, we used this philosophy to adjust how we dealt with clients. Instead of eagerly suggesting more features to them, we would try to convince them they were being overly ambitious. We steered them toward a pared-down system that could deliver 80 percent of the value they were seeking by only implementing 20 percent of their initial requirements. This was far cheaper, and we could get it done in a fraction of the time.

From there, we could add more functionality to the system as needed, based on the feedback they received from their users. We rarely ended up building as large a system as they had initially envisioned.

You might think we'd lose money with this strategy, but the opposite was true. We completed these initial projects more quickly and converted more one-time customers into long-term partners. There was always another project they needed help with, another program they needed developed. We might have lost some revenue on that first project, but we were able to leverage the good will and freed up time to move onto the next project together.

KEY TAKEAWAYS

- The 80/20 rule applies to many aspects of business where 80 percent of outcomes result from 20 percent of efforts. Regularly analyze your business to identify the critical 20 percent of actions, customers, or products that yield the most results.
- Apply the 80/20 rule to client projects by focusing on delivering 80 percent of the value by implementing just 20 percent of the requirements. This approach not only saves time and cost but also builds trust, leading to additional future projects.
- Beware of competitors leveraging the 80/20 rule against you.

PRO TIPS

- Eighty percent of complaints and support issues often come from 20 percent of clients. If that's the case in your business, consider firing those clients.
- When developing new products or systems, either for your

customers or internal use, focus on simplicity. Start with the essential features that meet the needs of the majority of users before expanding to advanced capabilities.

CASE STUDY

Leveraging the 80/20 Rule with Koverroos

Mark Jansen transitioned from a career in the chemical industry to entrepreneurship after experiencing limited recognition for his contributions in the corporate world. His journey into business ownership began when he acquired Responsible Consumer Products, also known as Koverroos, a company that manufactured and sold high-end covers for outdoor furniture and barbecue grills. Before Mark took over, Koverroos operated a small factory in Connecticut, where they manufactured and sold their products—primarily to retail stores and manufacturers on an OEM basis. The company had also recently begun selling directly to consumers through a rudimentary website, though this channel accounted for only a small fraction of their overall sales.

Upon acquiring the company, Mark quickly identified significant inefficiencies in the existing business model. In particular, he focused on the manufacturing process, which was seasonal and costly, resulting in minimal profit margins. Recognizing the potential of the nascent direct-to-consumer channel, Mark saw an opportunity to outsource manufacturing to a more efficient third-party provider and focus his efforts on improving the company's online presence. By partnering with a manufacturer whose busy season was counter to Koverroos', Mark was able to streamline production, reduce costs, and eliminate the overhead associated with running a factory. He then invested in revamping the company's website, which led to a fivefold increase in direct-to-consumer sales in just one year at margins approaching 85 percent.

Mark's decision to restructure Koverroos by outsourcing manufacturing and focusing on the company's website is a textbook example of the 80/20 rule in business. Initially, the direct-to-consumer channel represented only a small portion of Koverroos' sales, but it had the highest profit potential. By dedicating the majority of his efforts to growing this high-margin direct-to-customer channel, Mark was able to significantly increase the company's profitability. At the same time, he minimized his focus on the low-margin, resource-intensive manufacturing operations, which had previously consumed the bulk of the company's time and energy with little return. This strategic shift transformed Koverroos into a more profitable business by concentrating on the areas that truly drove value.

On the heels of this initial success, Mark founded a private equity fund to acquire other inefficiently run businesses and apply these same principles. To date, Mark has acquired and successfully transformed twelve other companies.

Chapter 25

It's All About Who You Know

DIFFICULTY: 3/5

Switzerland has two infantry officer candidate schools: a German-speaking school in Bern, and a French-speaking school in Chamblon. Growing up in the French-speaking part of the country, my preference was obvious. While I did learn German as a second language in school, it was "high German," the standard form spoken in Germany. In Switzerland, most people speak Swiss German, a dialect that is so different from high German, most non-native speakers find it difficult to understand.

Considering this limitation, you can imagine my reaction when I received my orders to report to Bern. I tried every avenue to get transferred to Chamblon. I wrote letters, filed petitions, and spoke with as many administrative officers as I could. I explained to everyone who would listen how weak my Swiss German was. Despite my efforts, every person gave me the same answer: the Chamblon school was full, and my only option was Bern.

I eventually accepted my fate and decided to make the best of it. After all, I reasoned, the experience would at least improve my Swiss German. And that might offer some longer-term benefits in my career.

During my first week in Bern, I did my very best to adjust, but the language barrier quickly proved to be as big an issue as I'd feared—particularly in the classroom. Out in the field, it wasn't so bad. It doesn't take much to translate the commands being barked at you, no matter the language. But in the classroom, I really struggled to follow along with the lessons. The instructors spoke in Swiss German to a classroom full of Swiss German speakers. Their annoyance every time I raised my hand to ask them to switch over to high German required no translation. Begrudgingly, they'd oblige, but before long, they'd inevitably revert back to Swiss German.

This tedious back-and-forth lasted five days. On the sixth day, I was summoned to the office of the school commandant. After a customary salute, he asked me to sit down. Once I was settled, he pointed to his Mountain Grenadier insignia on the collar of his dress uniform—a connection we shared. After a brief conversation in German, he switched to French and asked me about my experience at the school so far. I explained my language difficulties, and my failed attempts at transferring over to Chamblon. But I assured him that I could handle it. I had all the textbooks in French. I knew the situation was frustrating for all parties, but I'd find a way forward.

He nodded along. When I'd finished, he leaned over and asked, "How would you feel about attending officer candidate school in Chamblon instead?"

"I'd love to, sir, but as I just said, I was told there was no room there this year."

He asked me to wait outside and made a single phone call to his counterpart in Chamblon. When he hung up, he summoned me back into his office and told me to pack my gear. The very next morning, I was heading to Chamblon.

WHO CAN IMPACT YOUR SUCCESS?

Sometimes, big, seemingly impossible things really just come down to knowing the right person to get on the phone. A single call changed my entire officer candidate school experience. And leveraging a few relationships changed the fate of my company.

As I mentioned in Chapter 5, Catapult Systems landed on our unfair advantage over our competitors in 2002. Our *Microsoft Manifesto* outlined our strategy to focus all of our company's efforts on selling and delivering Microsoft solutions. Our strategy was fairly detailed and included items such as exiting all non-Microsoft business within a year, only pursuing customers who had already made an investment in Microsoft tech, and only hiring Microsoft consultants. But it lacked one critical strategic component: we needed to build much deeper relationships within Microsoft.

I didn't realize that shortcoming in our plan until a few years later when I was introduced to David Fuess. In his own way, David was the right person for the moment. I met him through Microsoft. I'd let them know that I was interested in expanding into the Dallas market. David lived in Dallas and had recently retired from another IT consulting firm after it had been acquired. He was looking for his next opportunity, so Microsoft made the introduction.

We clicked immediately. Not only was David an amazing sales leader, he had mastered and perfected the art of leveraging the Microsoft channel. Under his leadership, we developed the cornerstone of our Microsoft strategy. The idea was as simple as it was bold: identify the top one hundred people at Microsoft who could impact our business and establish a relationship with each one of them.

Despite the simplicity of the idea, it was not easy to implement. First of all, it was not immediately clear *who* should even be on the list. The first twenty to thirty people were pretty obvious—and we already knew most of them. After that, though, it got harder. The obvious answers were often the wrong ones. For instance, neither Bill Gates nor Steve Ballmer were ever on the list. Those high-level executives were not involved in the decisions that affected an organization of our size. We did have a handful of VPs and EVPs on the list, but most of our Microsoft influencers were folks in sales, marketing, product groups, technology centers, and their consulting organization.

In order to create meaningful connections with everyone on that list, we had to divide and conquer. Everyone on our executive team—except those in accounting and HR—had a role to play. So did people throughout the company. We carefully and deliberately divided up the list across multiple layers of our organization, including sales and marketing people, solutions architects, and principal consultants.

We tried to pick the most logical person for each relationship. If I already knew one of the VPs at Microsoft, then I was assigned to that person. If someone on our sales team lived in the same city as a critical member of Microsoft's marketing team, they were told to make contact. Technical architects were often paired with Microsoft peers.

These relationships didn't necessarily have to go very deep. It might be no more than the occasional conversation when both parties attended the same conference. It might be as minor as following the Microsoft team member's blog and reaching out online with some positive feedback. We coached everyone on being authentic and authentically curious, seeking to add value to the relationship long before we ever thought to make an "ask."

Our influencer list never remained static. We updated it every quarter to account for people changing roles and moving to new companies. Whenever a new person moved into a key position, we assigned someone at Catapult to build a relationship with them.

This might seem like a lot of work, and it was. But those relationships played a crucial role in our success with Microsoft. Ultimately, it was part of what led to Catapult Systems being recognized repeatedly by Microsoft as their Worldwide Partner of the Year. We were simply always top of mind whenever a Catapult-type project came across one of our influencer's desks.

Meanwhile David continued to be a valuable member of our team. Not only did he open our Dallas office, he'd go on to open our Denver and Phoenix offices too. He eventually became our EVP of Sales and then president, before replacing me as CEO (as we'll discuss in Chapter 27) after I sold Catapult Systems in 2013.

Talk about leveraging a great relationship.

RESOLVING CONFLICTS WITH A PHONE CALL

Knowing the right person isn't just important when trying to get into the right school or scale your business, it can also help you avoid expensive misunderstandings. This is particularly true when it comes to lawsuits. So often, lawsuits and other misunderstandings are best resolved not by lawyers or other go-betweens but through direct conversation with a person who is empowered to de-escalate the situation.

That said, before we go further, I want to make clear that I'm not offering legal advice in this section, only detailing my own experiences with lawsuits in business (my publisher made me add this sentence). That experience has taught me that there's almost always someone on the other side of a lawsuit who can work with you to get a deal done. The trick is finding the right person.

I've followed this advice multiple times in my business career, but one time in particular comes to mind when I think of this topic. Two years into my time on the FlashParking executive team, we were gaining significant traction in the industry. We had grown tenfold in that period and were beginning to get noticed by customers and competitors alike. I knew we needed to bring on more senior talent to help us scale the company even further, and I started looking for someone with significant experience within the parking industry.

I asked Juan Rodriguez, the company's cofounder, who he would bring in if he could hire anyone in the industry.

Without hesitation, he replied, "That's easy: Alan Poulton. He's the best in the business. But we're never going to get him."

To which I responded, "Why don't we find out?"

At the next industry trade show, we set up a casual meeting with Alan, and sure enough, he was interested. The only problem was the noncompete agreement he'd signed with his current employer. But after our employment attorney reviewed the document carefully, we believed it wasn't enforceable. We made Alan an offer, and he joined FlashParking as our EVP of Sales.

The following week, both Alan and FlashParking were sued by his former employer.

As you might expect, our attorneys wanted to dig in for a fight. At that point in my career, I'd learned two valuable lessons when it comes to lawsuits. First, litigation always takes longer and costs more than you think. It's not just the legal fees. Lawsuits are also a huge distraction to the rest of the business. In the end, the only real "winners" are the attorneys.

Second, litigation is often a posture for companies that feel wronged or threatened. When they feel mistreated, their first instinct is to have their attorneys contact you or just go straight to a lawsuit. This sets off your attorney's natural instinct to respond with their own show of force, usually in the form of a countersuit.

In other words, both parties can end up in an expensive lawsuit over relatively minor misunderstandings because no one is willing to de-escalate.

With those lessons in mind, I decided to do everything in my power to resolve the dispute amicably before turning it over to the attorneys. I knew that my best option was to reach out to the highest-ranking businessperson I could find on the other side and see if we could come to an understanding. In my experience, most businesspeople, especially senior executives, are quite reasonable and don't want to litigate any more than you do. If you can remove the emotion from the situation and talk through the issues, there's often a deal to be made.

I reached out directly to the president of Alan's former company. It took a few weeks, but we negotiated a mutually agreeable compromise. FlashParking made a few minor concessions, and we got to keep Alan. The lawsuit was over.

I don't want to imply this strategy works 100 percent of the time. But if you are willing to put your lawyers on pause for a minute and if you can reach the right person on the other side, you may find there's a compromise that both sides can live with.

- Building strong relationships can create unexpected opportunities. Knowing the right person to call can open a new door or solve a seemingly insurmountable problem.
- Create a list of influential people who can help your business grow, whether they are partners, potential clients, or thought leaders.
- Establishing relationships with key industry players requires a coordinated effort. Encourage everyone in the organization, not just sales or leadership, to participate in strategic networking.
- When faced with legal disputes, direct conversations with senior decision-makers on the other side can often lead to a faster, mutually beneficial resolution than involving lawyers.

PRO TIPS

- Some people are naturally good at networking and maintaining relationships. I am not one of those people. I've had to be intentional in this area of my life and put systems in place to "force" myself to maintain both personal and professional relationships.
- One of the easiest systems you can put in place is setting up recurring appointments on your calendar to reach out to people in your life.
- Provide training to your employees on authentic networking— how to show genuine interest, add value before asking for anything, and maintain a relationship over time.

FURTHER READING

Never Eat Alone: And Other Secrets to Success, One Relationship at a Time by Keith Ferrazzi

CASE STUDY

Amy Jo Martin and Digital Royalty

Amy Jo Martin, a small-town girl from Wyoming, moved around a lot as a kid and learned early the importance of building new relationships—a skill that would become invaluable in her career. After earning a degree in marketing from Arizona State University, Amy began her professional journey working with large corporate clients before being recruited by the NBA to work with the Phoenix Suns as their director of new media. Amy quickly became known for her ability to leverage emerging technologies, particularly social media, which was still in its infancy at that time. Her pioneering work led to Shaquille O'Neal asking her for help developing his own social media presence.

During a team plane ride to play the Lakers, Shaq was promoting Amy's social media expertise to his teammates when he suggested she start her own business. A few weeks later, Amy founded Digital Royalty. Digital Royalty specialized in humanizing brands and helping them monetize their influence online. The company's clientele included high-profile brands such as Fox Sports, Dwayne "The Rock" Johnson, Nike, and Motorola.

One of Amy's significant breakthroughs came from an online relationship she developed with Virginia, an executive at Hilton Worldwide. Initially just trading travel stories online, that relationship deepened over time and eventually led to a $4 million account with the company.

Amy's relationship-building skills were further exemplified when she connected with Tony Hsieh, the founder of Zappos. Their connection started organically when Amy reached out to Tony to inquire into Zappos' social media policies. Tony responded two weeks later with a simple, "Be real and use your best judgment." What began as a professional exchange on social media evolved into a deep and organic relationship, with Tony becoming one of Amy's first investors. Tony's advice to "productize" her intellectual property led to the creation of Digital Royalty University, a move that significantly scaled her business. This relationship not only provided Amy with capital but also invaluable mentorship that guided her through the challenges of entrepreneurship.

By being genuinely curious and adding value to others, Amy has demonstrated how powerful relationships can be in achieving business goals. Today, with her new company, Renegade Global, Amy coaches clients on how to build and nurture connections online. These connections often lead to new leadership positions, speaking engagements, or board seats. Her philosophy emphasizes that it's not just about who you know, but how you get to know them.

Chapter 26

Leave Nothing to Chance

DIFFICULTY: 2/5

Once a year or so, our Mountain Grenadier base hosts a military delegation from another country. This is standard practice for most militaries to foster cooperation, exchange knowledge, and assess combat readiness.

These delegations—which usually include a range of high-ranking officers and specialists, from generals and chiefs of staff to military attachés and intelligence officers—tour multiple bases across the hosting country. When they come to Switzerland, they always make time to see the capabilities of our special forces. And we are always happy to put on a show for them.

When I was a lieutenant in Isone, we hosted a delegation from the United States. Hosting leaders from the largest, most powerful military on the planet, we knew we really had to pull out all the stops and do something special to impress our guests. After a short reception with our base commandant in the mess hall, we drove them in all-terrain vehicles to a set of bleachers we had installed on top of a hill.

Below, they could see one of our training grounds, laid out carefully for the demonstration. In the days ahead of their visit, we'd set up four large armored vehicle targets and thirty human targets to simulate an enemy mechanized platoon. On the other side of the delegation was our urban combat training facility made up of reinforced concrete buildings.

As soon as everyone was seated, our delegation liaison handed them safety earmuffs and binoculars to better view the training ground below. Then he gave the signal for the demonstration to begin.

Two Mountain Grenadier units stealthily crawled through the grass into position directly below the bleachers. In the blink of an eye, the units quietly loaded their anti-tank rocket launchers, took aim, and opened fire simultaneously, hitting the first two armored vehicles. Within seconds, they had reloaded and fired again, hitting the remaining two. This would have been impressive on its own, but we added a little Hollywood flair to the proceedings. While we were setting up the scene for the attack, we'd placed gasoline tanks behind the targets. The resulting explosions were massive. You could feel the concussion and the heat in the visitor stands.

Even as the resulting blaze continued to rise skyward, the rest of the Grenadier platoon, which had remained completely camouflaged in flanking positions until that moment, opened fire on the human targets while simultaneously launching a barrage of mortars. The whole action took no more than a few seconds. When the dust cleared, the enemy platoon had been completely obliterated. There wasn't a single target left standing.

We weren't done yet. While the vehicles continued to smolder, our liaison directed the delegation's attention to concrete buildings on their left. He explained that the enemy had taken a defensive position in four of the buildings and that our mission was to overtake them.

We began our assault with heavy cover fire while three Grenadiers threw live grenades into the windows of the building on the far left. Each throw, including one into a tiny window on the third floor, was performed flawlessly. The acoustics of the concrete building amplified the three detonations, which once again could be felt all the way in the stands.

A small unit then stormed the building, taking one floor at a time with more grenades and gunfire. That unit then provided cover fire for another team, who climbed up the backside of a neighboring four-story building. That unit then rappelled down the front of the building under attack, breaching one floor at a time through the windows. All four enemy buildings were secured in a matter of minutes.

Without a single shot misfired, our demonstration was over.

If all of this seems like something you have seen before in a movie, your instincts are right. This sequence of events would never happen in a real combat situation, but that wasn't the point. Our objective was to showcase as many of our capabilities as possible while impressing the visiting dignitaries. It was meant to look real, feel real, and come across as perfectly orchestrated, just like you see in an action movie.

And just like an action movie, what felt improvised was actually carefully planned and drilled over and over again. Everything was tightly choreographed. We knew exactly where to go, where to shoot, and how far away each target was so we could range our sights. We had practiced every grenade throw dozens of times beforehand so we wouldn't miss.

It took real skills, real discipline, real practice—but nothing about it was unexpected. *We left absolutely nothing to chance*, and we performed our tasks perfectly.

PREPARATION OVER IMPROVISATION

The best performances look effortless and spontaneous, but almost always, that perception is inaccurate. Whether it's a military drill, an alley-oop in the NBA, or an engrossing scene in a film, it's far less off-the-cuff than the audience assumes. And the same should go for any "performance" you give to an important client or investor. It should look natural, but you should leave nothing to chance.

When I first joined FlashParking, one of the biggest concerns

I heard over and over again from potential customers was that our system ran in the cloud. Our entrenched parking technology competitors, all of whom required a rack of computer servers onsite to run their antiquated systems, had successfully convinced most parking operators and asset owners that it was simply impossible to run a garage or a surface lot from the cloud. On call after call, in meeting after meeting, I heard about how the transaction speed required to process a credit card and open a gate was simply too high for the cloud.

Nothing could be further from the truth, of course. Far larger companies with higher transaction volume and faster speed requirements had been successfully running their systems in the cloud for over a decade. But our competitors were doing a good job convincing everyone in the parking industry it was still the 1990s.

In order to address this misperception, we devised a program we referred to internally as "cloud therapy." The idea was to invite key customers to come spend half a day with us in Austin so we could showcase the reliability and speed of our products. A lot hinged on the success of these demonstrations, so everything was tightly scripted and choreographed from the moment we picked our customers up from the airport to the moment they departed again.

Juan Rodriguez and I handled the pick up personally. Our guests would ride into the city in my Tesla Model X. The car itself served multiple purposes. First, it immediately got our guests' attention. This was back when many people had never ridden in an electric car, let alone seen one with "falcon wing" doors that opened like the DeLorean in *Back to the Future*. More importantly, though, the car allowed me to immediately direct the conversation to the cloud. My Tesla was connected to the cloud, allowing it to receive regular software updates "over the air" to fix problems and add new functionality without ever having to bring it into the shop—a feature shared by our FlashParking equipment.

The drive from the airport to our offices took us through downtown Austin, at which point I would naturally point out that most of the garages in the city ran our parking equipment. I would then casually ask our guests if they wanted to see our equipment in action before heading to our research and development (R&D) lab. They always said yes. Again, this was no accident. They'd flown in to learn about our tech; they were as likely to say no to visiting our garages as those military delegations were to say no to seeing the Grenadiers storm those buildings.

Their interest secured, I drove in and out of several carefully selected (but seemingly random) garages, each featuring different capabilities of our product. At one garage, I prepaid with a mobile app and entered with a QR code; another garage read my car's license plate and automatically opened the gate on the way out once I had paid. Of course, I always made a point of demonstrating our credit card processing speed, whether it was at the kiosk or on my phone.

Not only were these locations chosen deliberately ahead of time, the entire experience was carefully prepared for. Before our guests' arrival, a member of our team would do a complete run-through of every garage, making sure everything worked perfectly. They would even pick up trash if they saw any. Keep in mind, we didn't own or operate any of these facilities—they just used our equipment. But we left nothing to chance.

After driving in and out of multiple garages, we would head over to our R&D lab, which was set up with every possible garage and surface lot configuration you can imagine. There, we showcased some of our more unique capabilities, like the ability to swap out any parking kiosk component by removing four screws and unplugging a USB cable. This revolutionary architecture allowed our customers to replace any defective or damaged component themselves without having to wait hours or days for a technician to show up. No longer would gum stuck in a credit card reader cause long, costly delays.

The technology spoke for itself, but we still made sure our lab looked immaculate and every piece of equipment worked perfectly. The presenter for the demonstration, Carlos Hernandez, our VP of Product, was also thoughtfully chosen. He had a gift for making our visitors feel comfortable with our products, and he was a master at fielding even the hardest questions.

After the lab, we transitioned our guests over to a large conference room where lunch was waiting. We always catered from Rudy's BBQ, a meal everyone would love—again leaving nothing to chance. Not wasting a moment, we continued our demonstration over brisket, showcasing our dashboard and data analytics on the big screen and explaining how our customers could see in real time the performance of all of their facilities—something no one else in the industry could do. As everyone finished their meal, we brought in our head of AI to discuss some of the futuristic capabilities we were working on.

To wrap up the day, we drove out to our thirty-thousand-square-foot manufacturing facility in Dripping Springs. I'm sure you can guess the state of our facility on those tour days: spotless. There wasn't a speck of dust to be found anywhere. Every assembly line was humming, every inventory rack was full, and every station was manned. Our VP of Manufacturing, Kevin Rose, led the tour, explaining along the way how we performed quality checks at every stage of the manufacturing process, where we sourced our components, and the redundancy of our supply chain.

By the time our visitors got back to the Austin airport, their heads were spinning. Considering their previous assumptions about the industry, it must have felt like they had just come back from a visit to the future. It would have been hard not to be impressed. After all, we'd curated the entire experience to produce that reaction, and we'd left nothing to chance.

And that effort produced the desired effect. To my knowledge, every parking operator and asset owner who came through Austin for cloud therapy eventually became a FlashParking customer.

EVERY DETAIL MATTERS

From the perspective of our visitors, everything they saw on their tour just happened to go perfectly. But that effortless perfection required a lot of care and attention to detail.

I want to be clear, though, that just like the Mountain Grenadiers, we never deceived anyone about our capabilities. We didn't exaggerate our potential or our quality. Every garage we visited was a real garage that worked just as successfully every other day of the year. All we did was eliminate any potential negative contingencies.

When presenting to an important customer or investor, that sort of care can make all the difference. Every detail can impact the outcome. In those moments, you can't afford to leave anything to chance; the stakes are simply too high.

A meticulously planned and rehearsed presentation ensures that your message is clear, concise, and aligned with your goals. It allows you to anticipate and manage potential questions or concerns, minimizing the likelihood of unwanted surprises that could derail the conversation.

When your aim is to build trust and demonstrate competence, any deviation harms your credibility. From that perspective, thorough preparation should be the bare minimum you expect from your team. It's a show of respect for your audience's time. And it positions you as a reliable, professional partner or investment opportunity.

KEY TAKEAWAYS

- The best performances often appear spontaneous but are the result of meticulous planning and repeated rehearsal. Success comes from leaving nothing to chance.
- Whenever showcasing your product or service, plan every step of the experience. Think about transportation, setting, and presentation to ensure every interaction is memorable and builds confidence.
- From ensuring equipment works perfectly to choosing the right food, every detail in the customer experience—even seemingly small aspects like cleanliness—contributes to the overall impression.
- Choose team members who excel at both presenting and answering challenging questions to be part of key customer and investor presentations.

- Rehearsing presentations or demonstrations helps ensure everything goes smoothly. Have team members practice with real equipment in the real environment whenever possible. Use a timer to make sure you can get through your entire presentation in the allotted time.
- For your most important presentations, video record your rehearsals to perfect your delivery, timing, and transitions.
- Identify potential doubts or objections customers might have and address them proactively during demonstrations.

CASE STUDY

Mastering the Art of Preparation: Lessons from Jason Parrish

Jason Parrish's journey as an entrepreneur began with a passion for magic as a child. Starting at the age of twelve, he performed magic shows at birthday parties, captivating audiences with his cape, wand, and well-rehearsed sleight-of-hand. These performances were more than just a hobby; they taught him the importance of preparation and attention to detail. Jason understood that to impress his audience, he needed to leave nothing to chance, practicing each routine until it became second nature.

Years later, Jason dropped out of the University of Texas to cofound SMART Technologies with Jeff DeCoux in 1994. Together, they sought to solve a complex problem in the emerging digital world—enabling customers to access their accounts online. At a time when the internet was still in its infancy, this was a groundbreaking idea. They began networking in Austin, drawing interest from angel investors, one of whom funded their attendance at Networld, an industry trade show. There, they met an executive from Ziff Davis Publishing who was keen to modernize operations at *Computer Shopper* magazine. Impressed by Jason and Jeff's vision, the executive scheduled a site visit to Austin to see their operation firsthand.

SMART Technologies had a problem, however: they had neither a physical office nor a fully developed product. In fact, they only had three employees at the time. Faced with this predicament, Jason and Jeff turned to Bill Hayden, a business connection in Austin, who offered them the use of his company's training room for their demonstration. With only a few weeks before the presentation, Jason prepared for his biggest magic trick yet. He and Jeff meticulously set up the space to resemble a professional office. They placed a SMART Technologies sign on the door, recruited thirty clean-cut friends to sit at desks and pretend to work on their computers, and had Jason's girlfriend pose as a receptionist to complete the illusion. They even borrowed some plants to make the entrance appear more welcoming. Leaving nothing to chance, Jason and Jeff spent countless hours building a clickable demo and practicing their presentation, ensuring every detail was flawless.

On the day of the visit, the three Ziff Davis executives, including their president, found a seemingly bustling company. The staged office and polished demo left a lasting impression, and SMART Technologies won the contract. Six months later, Ziff Davis launched Computer Shopper NetBuyer, which quickly became one of the largest e-commerce platforms of the era. This success put SMART Technologies on the map, leading to contracts with industry giants like Apple and Minolta, and ultimately culminating in the company's acquisition by i2 in 1999.

Jason went on to become a successful serial entrepreneur, bringing his discipline of meticulous preparation to every company he founded. This standard has become central to his latest venture, Altus Nova Technologies, a digital transformation company. At Altus Nova, the principle of leaving nothing to chance is embedded in their innovative approach to requirements gathering, which has led to an impeccable track record with clients. By ensuring that every project detail is anticipated and addressed, Jason has continued to build a legacy of reliability and excellence across all his ventures.

Chapter 27

Look for Your Next Leaders

DIFFICULTY: 3/5

In the military, succession planning and promotion from within are critical components of leadership continuity and organizational stability. Without them, any military would quickly fail to function. After all, you can't just go out and hire a general from a rival country or advertise for a captain who can run a special forces unit. All promotions, by nature of the institution, come from within.

This approach guarantees that as individuals move up through the ranks, they have been tested at each level and are fully prepared to take on greater responsibilities. A key aspect of this system is the principle that each commander has a designated second-in-command who is ready to step into the commander's role at a moment's notice. In the US, this is called an executive officer (XO), although we don't use that term in Switzerland. The appointment of an XO ensures that leadership is never compromised and there are no gaps in command.

To prepare them for their potential future responsibility, the second-in-command is actively groomed for leadership through mentorship, shadowing, and hands-on experience. Sometimes, this includes stepping into the commander's role for a meeting or for certain prescribed tasks.

When I was a lieutenant in Isone, for instance, I regularly stepped in for my captain and took over as company commander when he was pulled away for various duties. In turn, I selected one of my corporals to lead my platoon while I oversaw the company. I wasn't the only lieutenant in this position. My captain did this with all his lieutenants, giving each valuable experience while also seeing who had the right skills for further advancement.

That way, whether it was a routine promotion or a field promotion in case of emergency, the military always knew who to thrust into leadership, confident they were adequately prepared for the increased responsibility.

PREPARE FOR THE EXPECTED AND UNEXPECTED

Because of the exceptional nature of its mission, military leaders always have to think about the worst-case scenario. Who takes over if I'm incapacitated or killed? It's a real, live question that has to be answered. In most businesses, though, this is a question we can delay answering for long periods, and since no one likes to dwell on sickness, retirement, or death, many leave it permanently unanswered.

However, unless you want to put the long-term success of your company at risk, you—and every other leader in your organization—has to think about who is next in line to take over. After all, it may not be as likely as it is in the military, but leaders get sick all the time. They need time off for family or to avoid burning out. They get hit by buses the same as everyone else. They also get promoted or leave to start a new company. In each of these scenarios, someone has to step in and provide continuity of leadership.

To prepare for the inevitable and the unexpected requires

consideration of three separate but related topics: professional mentorship, promotion from within, and succession planning.

In my experience, few companies do any of these systematically. But if you do, you'll find that, like the military, you have people ready to rise up and step in at every level and in every situation.

PROFESSIONAL MENTORSHIP

When I joined Dell Computer Corporation as a programmer in 1992, our team was tasked with rewriting Dell's order entry system using a new development environment called PowerBuilder. I had never even heard of it.

As I started reading the manual and fumbling my way through my assignments, I quickly discovered the available materials were inadequate for the task. In many companies, the next obvious step would be to reach out to a designated member of the team with more experience and a deeper understanding of the technology, but Dell didn't have an official mentoring program. So I decided to create my own.

I found the best PowerBuilder developer in our department, an outside contractor named Joe Horecny, and I asked to shadow him as much as I could. Joe didn't have to say yes, but he proved a willing and truly fantastic mentor.

When Joe stayed late, I stayed late—often working eighty hours a week right alongside him. After six months, he had helped transform me into an expert PowerBuilder developer. I went on to write two PowerBuilder training manuals, develop a set of commercial PowerBuilder libraries, and leverage that platform heavily to launch Catapult Systems. In fact, my PowerBuilder libraries and training materials provided some of the core products we used to set ourselves apart when we launched in 1993.

I'm grateful to Joe and my time learning from him, but I shouldn't have had to find a mentor on my own. Every successful organization should already have a mentorship program in place. These programs offer substantial benefits for both employees and the organization as a whole. Pairing less experienced employees with seasoned professionals provides an opportunity for accelerated learning and development, allowing junior employees not just to develop important skills but to gain valuable insights into the company's processes, industry standards, and leadership methods. These relationships also foster a culture of knowledge-sharing and promote greater job satisfaction by showing employees that the company is invested in their personal and professional growth.

I realize that setting up mentoring programs isn't feasible for every job. You can't justify double billing a client or losing out on a thousand billable hours just so a young lawyer or consultant can do six months of on-the-job-training. At the same time, some senior employees have no interest in or talent for mentorship. The last thing you want is to pair a junior member of your team with an unwilling mentor.

However, when such programs are feasible, one-on-one mentoring is a game changer. I saw it all the time at Catapult. Robyn Hutton is an excellent example. She was our first senior software developer dedicated to building and maintaining our internal applications. She was our sixth-ever hire and a prized member of the team. As our company grew, though, demand exceeded her capacity. At that point, we brought on a junior developer right out of school, Rachel Switzer. To ease the transition, we had Robyn mentor her. This worked out so well that, when Rachel went on to become a successful billable consultant at Catapult a few years later, we brought in another junior programmer for Robyn to mentor, Mohammod Rahman, who also went on to be a success at the company.

It ended up being an ongoing, never-ending cycle. And everyone benefited from it.

PROMOTION FROM WITHIN

Within the concept of mentorship lies implicitly the second key to developing new leaders: promoting from within. Many organizations fail to realize that the most important source of future leaders is the team they already have in place. Internal candidates have a lot of advantages over external hires. They already have a deep understanding of the company's culture, values, and processes, reducing their learning curve and allowing them to contribute more quickly in their new role. They also bring with them institutional knowledge and established relationships that can enhance team cohesion. Additionally, the very process of promoting from within helps retain top talent, as employees are more likely to stay with a company that offers clear career advancement opportunities.

Finally, when you do this right, you can actually seamlessly promote multiple positions at once. If everyone in a leadership or management position knows who should replace them, one promotion can lead directly to another. When I promoted Mike Able from controller to CFO at Catapult, he had already spent several years training Melanie Zoerner to take over as controller. Both moved into their new roles at the same time.

None of this means that internal promotion is always the right call. Sometimes, you have to fill a specialized position, and there are no good options inside the company. When you need a certified architect and you don't have anyone on staff with the right knowledge and experience, your best option is to go to the market. And sometimes, you need someone to come in with some outside perspective to disrupt how you do things, or someone with specific industry experience.

These are legitimate reasons to hire outside, but they should be the exception. Wherever possible, it's almost always better to promote from within.

SUCCESSION PLANNING

Even before her move, everyone knew that Melanie had been marked for promotion. She was very clearly Mike's protégé, so everyone treated her as the future controller. That kind of clarity in succession is very helpful to organization efficiency and cohesion. Everyone knew the plan, so everyone could plan for that future.

Despite this fact, most companies—especially smaller ones—don't even think about succession, let alone plan for it. They remain so preoccupied with immediate business challenges and short-term objectives, they don't think about the inevitable need for new people in vacated positions.

Even if it feels like a distant concern, though, it's worth putting time and effort into succession planning for all leadership positions in your organization. Succession planning should include both of the concepts we've already covered. For those who show promise in your company, there should be a clear path they can follow to top leadership positions. That path should include established leaders mentoring those they see as their successors. Like my captain in the Mountain Grenadiers, those in leadership positions should aim to pass down crucial knowledge and strategies that ensure continuity in leadership when they move on to their next role or retire.

When I codified this policy at Catapult, I strongly encouraged everyone in leadership to prepare someone else to take over their role. It was a prerequisite for promotion. I demonstrated this principle in my own position. As I mentioned in Chapter 25, I trained and promoted David Fuess to be my eventual successor over an eight-year period. By the time I sold the company, he had become president. When I exited, he became CEO. He would go on to use those same skills to become CEO of another company some years later.

A REWARDING PART OF LEADERSHIP

When I bring this topic up, any pushback I get often comes in the form of a question: "What if I train them and they leave?" To which I respond, "What if you don't train them and they stay?"

Inevitably, some people—including your most highly qualified people—will leave your company. They'll accept the training, the mentorship, and the promotions, and then they'll find a position elsewhere. However, this is no reason to avoid preparing them for leadership.

After all, what's the alternative? Good people want upward

mobility, and if you don't give it to them, the possibility they leave will turn into a certainty. Succession planning reinforces your company's culture of growth, demonstrating to employees that the organization is invested in them and their career progression. That improves retention and morale across the company.

Besides, if you do this right, even those who do leave will exit grateful for all the work you put into them. They may pay that investment back by becoming clients or vendors. They may send other great leaders and specialists who are looking for a new challenge your way. And who knows, perhaps they become one of those outside people you end up hiring when you need some fresh perspective.

Mentorship and succession planning is about more than filling spots in your org chart. It's rewarding in its own right. It allows you to share what you know, build up those you believe in, and display the kind of leader you want to be. Leadership can be a lonely place; why not create a peer to share the burden and responsibility with?

KEY TAKEAWAYS

- Create formal mentorship programs where experienced employees can provide guidance to newer or junior team members. This accelerates the development of junior employees, enhances job satisfaction, and fosters a culture of growth within the organization.
- Promoting from within helps retain top talent, provides career advancement opportunities, and maintains institutional knowledge. Internal candidates are often better equipped for new roles due to their familiarity with company culture and operations.
- Create clear paths for career advancement and communicate these opportunities to employees. This transparency encourages engagement and loyalty, as people are more likely to stay with a company that supports their growth.
- Business leaders must ensure continuity through effective succession planning. Designating a second-in-command and grooming

them to step into a leadership role helps maintain stability during transitions.

- You can never guarantee your top talent will remain with the company, but mentorship and succession planning remains rewarding in its own right.

―――――――――――――― **PRO TIPS** ――――――――――――――

- Not every employee wants to be a mentor, and that's okay. Don't force someone into the role if they don't want it.

CASE STUDY

Towne Park: The Power of Mentorship, Culture, and Ownership

Jerry South's entrepreneurial journey began after completing three years of service in the army, which he joined right after high school to fund his college education. Later, while attending college, Jerry took a job as a valet at a local Marriott, where he realized that the most exciting part of his day was interacting with people and parking cars. Recognizing the lack of employee focus and customer care at the valet company he worked for, Jerry saw an opportunity to create a better, more customer-focused and employee-friendly business.

In 1987, he cofounded Towne Crier Valet with his best friend, Sam Medile. A year later, they incorporated the company as Towne Park. Jerry was determined to revolutionize the valet parking industry by focusing on high-quality service in the hospitality market. His first business plan, written in 1990, laid out a strategy for capturing the entire parking market in Annapolis, Maryland, which he achieved three years later. Jerry's military background gave him a disciplined, structured approach to business, emphasizing attention to detail and professionalism. His team adopted these values, and Towne Park became known for its sharp appearance and hustle, qualities that resonated particularly well with hotel clients who valued excellent service and employee reliability.

One of the core principles that drove Towne Park's success was Jerry's belief in professional mentorship and promotion from within. He understood that a company's growth depends not just on its leaders, but on empowering every employee to rise within the ranks. This philosophy was embedded in the company's culture from the beginning. Those employees who demonstrated initiative, loyalty, and the ability to train others were the ones who advanced quickly.

Towne Park's culture was built on the idea that no employee could receive a promotion until they had successfully trained their replacement. This not only ensured continuity in service quality but also created a pipeline of future leaders within the company. Promotions were often tied to new market opportunities. As Towne Park expanded into cities, employees were given the chance to lead these new territories, ensuring that Towne Park's values and operational excellence were maintained as the company grew. In return, those employees not only earned promotions but also a share in the profits from these new markets.

Jerry offered more than a path to promotion and financial success. The mentorship he provided extended far beyond operational training. He ensured that employees understood the financial metrics driving the business and taught them the importance of profitability, efficiency, and maintaining margins. As a result, employees at all levels became invested in the company's success, both figuratively and literally.

Jerry introduced the company's first employee stock plan in 1999, a move that gave employees a tangible stake in the business. This culture of ownership was Towne Park's "secret sauce"—the key differentiator that allowed Towne Park to achieve success at a level that other companies simply could not replicate. Anyone could hire valets, source uniforms, or create training programs, but it was Towne Park's culture that provided its marketplace advantage. Employees knew that by contributing to Towne Park's growth, they were not only securing their own future but also working toward earning a place within the company's ownership structure.

By the time Jerry sold Towne Park to a private equity firm in 2014, the company had grown to thirteen thousand employees operating in fifty-three markets, with some of the highest margins in the industry. Thanks to Jerry's mentorship and the promotion-from-within culture, twenty-four teammates became millionaires, and thirty-five others received checks of $600,000 or more. Jerry's approach to leadership—fostering an environment of growth, mentorship, and shared success—created a legacy where employees weren't just workers, they were partners in the company's achievements.

Chapter 28

Trial and Error

DIFFICULTY: 4/5

The Mountain Grenadiers operate in environments where speed, agility, and efficiency are critical to mission success. As a result, we constantly try to eliminate any nonessential equipment or process that could slow us down. Depending on the nature and duration of a training mission, we would optimize for weaponry, ammunition, explosives, climbing gear, food, and water to improve mobility, endurance, and our ability to adapt swiftly to changing conditions.

But there was always a fine line we had to tread between minimizing our load and not having enough materials to get the job done. All that speed and stealth didn't matter much if we couldn't complete the mission.

When we prepared for a demolition or sabotage mission, for example, we had to strike the right balance between firepower and mobility. We had very precise tables in our instruction books that told us how much explosive material we needed to blow a hole in six inches of wood or three inches of concrete or an inch of steel, but you don't usually get the chance to measure the thickness of the concrete for a bridge you have to destroy. Often, we only saw the target through binoculars. Sometimes, all we had was a map and the location of the target. We also had to adjust for time constraints. It makes a huge difference if you have hours to set up your explosives in broad daylight or thirty seconds in the middle of the night.

The only way to get the numbers right on these missions was practice. Since we weren't going to blow up actual civilian infrastructure during our training missions, we conducted regular exercises at Isone's explosives training ground. Built into the side of an old quarry, it provided the perfect location to build all kinds of targets and blow them up. We would remotely analyze wooden poles, metal beams, or reinforced concrete pillars of various thickness, prepare our charges, set them in place, and detonate them. After the smoke cleared, we would examine the results, make adjustments, and repeat the exercise over and over again.

We got the balance wrong plenty of times. Sometimes, we'd walk over to find the structure still standing. Other times, we'd send telephone poles flying in the wrong direction. If we really went overboard with the explosives, we might blow the object clear to the other side of the quarry. But through repeated trial and error, we honed our demolition skills. And because we got all that practice, we were ready to optimize our load and be as lean and mean as possible when missions really counted.

EFFICIENCY REQUIRES MISTAKES

"Lean" has become one of the most popular terms among startup entrepreneurs. Introduced by Eric Ries in his book *The Lean Startup*, the approach recommends businesses engage in hypothesis-driven experimentation over elaborate planning, continuous customer feedback over extensive market research, and iterative development over traditional up-front design.

In some ways, though, lean has been boxed in by the nature of that book—because these ideas are just as valuable for established organizations as they are for startups. It's an odd assumption because lean was originally inspired by the streamlined production method developed by Japanese automakers in the 1980s. From the beginning, this philosophy sought to eliminate wasteful practices and increase value-producing ones in the most cost-effective way possible in large, mature businesses as much as recently founded upstarts.

At its core, lean has nothing to do with size. It's about process, specifically the power of embracing trial and error. Rather than spending months researching, planning, and developing a comprehensive business plan, lean is about making a series of educated guesses—a business hypothesis, as Ries refers to it. Once you develop a reasonable hypothesis, you go test it quickly with real customers, partners, and vendors. Then you gather as much feedback as possible and make adjustments. Once you've revised your initial assumptions, the cycle starts all over again, making more adjustments along the way.

The emphasis is on nimbleness, speed, and agility across the organization.

At Catapult, we crystallized our commitment to experimentation in the saying, "Try lots of stuff, keep what works." Though *The Lean Startup* came out decades after we were actually a startup, we used similar concepts in our approach to creating two divisions of our company: managed services and cloud services. Both offerings were radically different from anything we'd done previously. In both cases, we went from initial concept to commercial launch in less than three weeks.

In order to formulate our initial business hypothesis, we developed several "business model canvases" for each offering using the approach described in *Business Model Generation* by Alexander Osterwalder and Yves Pigneur. A business model canvas is a one-page strategic management template. It's a high-level visual diagram that describes a company's value proposition, infrastructure, customers, and finances, and it helps to align critical activities and illustrate potential trade-offs.

Once we had a business model canvas in place for each project, we skipped over the traditional path of doing market research asking potential customers whether they would hypothetically purchase our new services and instead immediately developed a minimum viable product (MVP). We took our best guess at pricing and started selling the new solutions to real clients right away. Since we had not yet developed any meaningful IP and only had a skeleton crew to deliver it, we carefully selected a few manageable target markets for the initial rollout. That allowed us to control demand.

Streamlining and moving at speed could be hectic. Each time we closed a deal with a new client, for instance, we had to scramble to pull together a delivery team. But we found a way to make it work. And with each new engagement, we listened carefully to our client's feedback, adjusted our thinking, and further developed and refined our offering.

A year after the initial launch, we had completely overhauled the two offerings based on the feedback we had received. Some of our initial assumptions turned out to be accurate; most of them didn't. But both projects had become highly profitable, multimillion-dollar business units.

STOP DOING IT

Aside from managed services and cloud services, we tried a number of other initiatives over the years using similar techniques. Many of them failed. I remember one I was quite fond of at its inception. As I related in Chapter 26, early on at Catapult, we'd leveraged my knowledge of PowerBuilder to bring in clients. One way we did this was by offering an intro and advanced training class on the development environment.

At the time, there was a void in training for PowerBuilder, so this training component, though a loss leader, brought in some of our first customers. Years later, I resurfaced the idea of reestablishing a training element to our offerings for some of the newer tools in use. We quickly spun up some training programs to see if it would have the same impact.

What I had failed to realize when I recommended this idea was that in the intervening years many companies had sprung up whose sole purpose was training on Microsoft products. Facing steep odds, we still committed to the project. We got people certified, we pivoted multiple times based on feedback, and we tried everything we could think of to get some traction in that space.

None of it made much difference. The initiative was a dud. So I made the tough call and killed it.

Killing a project you believe in is, in some ways, the hardest part of absorbing a lean mindset. A lot of time, effort, and ego gets invested into these projects, and often, it's easier to keep going, keep tinkering, and keep putting off a final decision a little longer.

Because this is so hard, you have to build into your culture an understanding that a failed project does not represent a personal or business failure. It's always better to have had the courage to try something than to try nothing.

If you work hard, invest enough, iterate and pivot, and six months later, the initiative still isn't working, there's no shame in cutting your losses.

And those losses, with a little distance, often turn into wins anyway. Our failed training programs turned into partnerships with established organizations in that space. And every time we failed to blow something up in the Mountain Grenadiers, we learned something. The next time, we avoided those same mistakes, which made success all that much more likely.

KEY TAKEAWAYS

- The lean methodology, involving hypothesis-driven experimentation, quick iterations, and customer feedback, can be effectively applied in both startups and established businesses.
- Embracing trial and error is a key driver of progress. Testing ideas, assessing the results, and iterating based on feedback help refine strategies and lead to optimized solutions.

- When developing a minimum viable product, focus on simplicity and target a small, manageable segment of the market. This allows you to test hypotheses and gather valuable feedback without overwhelming resources.
- Ending a project that isn't yielding results is crucial to the lean philosophy. If an initiative is still failing after six months, kill it.

PRO TIPS

- For each new experiment or project, define clear success metrics from the outset. This will help in determining early on whether the initiative is working or should be terminated.
- Keep a list of all the initiatives you've tried over the years—as well as information on which ones succeeded, which ones failed, and why. Include your initial assumptions and which ones proved incorrect. This will help you get better over time.
- Be transparent and acknowledge the initiatives that have failed and that you have shut down during company meetings. This will help reinforce a culture of risk-taking where trial and error is encouraged and failure is not punished.

FURTHER READING

Business Model Generation: A Handbook for Visionaries, Game Changers, and Challengers by Alexander Osterwalder and Yves Pigneur

The Lean Startup: How Today's Entrepreneurs Use Continuous Innovation to Create Radically Successful Businesses by Eric Ries

CASE STUDY

Autumn Manning's Lean Approach at YouEarnedIt

Autumn Manning's journey toward embracing lean startup principles began long before her business career. In fact, it was shaped by a childhood marked by agility and adaptability. Growing up in California and Arkansas, frequently moving between homes, she developed an ability to adjust quickly to new environments and challenges. Autumn's academic pursuit of behavioral psychology at the University of Arkansas also provided her with a unique perspective on understanding human behavior, which would later serve her well in her career.

Upon graduation, Autumn took her first role as director of research and development at SVI, a tech-enabled consulting and services firm specializing in organizational development. This role involved designing leadership and culture-driven tools, further sharpening her skills in measuring and influencing behavior.

In 2013, Autumn was recruited by Kenny Tomlin, the founder and CEO of Rockfish, to join YouEarnedIt, a fledgling software startup. At first glance, YouEarnedIt appeared to be a simple employee recognition and rewards system. However, Autumn's behavioral psychology background gave her the insight to see its true potential: a platform that could deeply impact employee engagement and even change their behavior. She believed that recognition alone wouldn't create long-term engagement but saw an opportunity to design a platform that would fundamentally change how employees interacted with their company's culture and performance metrics. To achieve this vision, Autumn would have to rely on her ability to measure and understand what truly motivates behavior, the driving force behind YouEarnedIt's unique approach.

The bulk of YouEarnedIt's success came from Autumn's implementation of lean startup principles. From the outset, she focused on building a minimum viable product (MVP) to validate the platform's concept. This initial version of YouEarnedIt was a simple front-end website with a working prototype that showcased a rewards catalog, but it wasn't yet fully functional. Autumn immersed herself in the market, spending most of her time engaging directly with HR leaders, CEOs, and employees to understand their needs and validate her assumptions about the product. She recognized the importance of gathering real customer feedback before scaling. This early validation allowed her to fine-tune the platform and build only the necessary features, preventing wasteful spending and development. For the first year, YouEarnedIt's lean approach was driven by this ongoing cycle of testing, learning, and iterating.

Autumn also applied lean principles to how she scaled the company's operations and team. Instead of hiring ahead of demand, she adopted a strategy of hiring behind the need, ensuring the company remained lean and agile. She focused on optimizing the sales funnel and only brought on new talent once customer demand clearly outpaced the current team's capacity. This approach extended to YouEarnedIt's company culture, where the emphasis was on performance, agility, and ownership.

Through her disciplined use of lean startup principles, Autumn successfully grew YouEarnedIt from an MVP to a highly regarded platform that transformed employee engagement and performance. Thanks to this approach, YouEarnedIt not only survived in a crowded HR tech space but thrived, eventually achieving market penetration that attracted acquisition interest.

Chapter 29

Give Back

DIFFICULTY: 2/5

Since Switzerland's military is structured as a militia force, a significant portion of the population is trained as reservists. This allows the government to rapidly mobilize military resources for noncombat situations, much as the US would deploy the national guard for disaster relief, public safety, or infrastructure support when necessary. When the country experiences floods, avalanches, or forest fires, the military's logistical capabilities, equipment, and trained personnel can be crucial in delivering aid, coordinating evacuations, and rebuilding damaged infrastructure.

Before calling up inactive reservists for these needs, though, the Swiss military will usually draw upon active-duty personnel already training at a boot camp or a repetition course. If you're currently in uniform, geared up, and away from family and work, it's simply faster and more efficient to send you out to secure a public event or handle a public health crisis.

I experienced just this when I was in the middle of basic training. Some heavy thunderstorms had caused flash flooding in a nearby valley, leading to landslides that blocked access to mountain pastures. These pastures were essential to the local farmers, as their cows were still grazing up there and needed to be tended to.

Our entire Mountain Grenadier company, over 120 men, was dispatched to help repair the trails and restore access. We left behind all of our combat gear, put on our work fatigues, grabbed shovels, picks, saws, and mallets, and boarded military trucks heading straight for the village. The trucks drove us as far up the valley as they could. From there, we hiked another couple hours to reach the landslide site. What followed was days of hard, backbreaking labor digging the trails out. The terrain was too steep and narrow for any vehicles, so everything had to be done manually.

We worked from dawn until dusk every day. The farmers worked side by side with us to secure every inch of land. By the end of our third day, we had repaired the trails and restored the farmers' access to their cattle.

Our job done, we headed back down the mountain. That's when something wonderful happened. The local villagers greeted us with applause. We received hugs from grandmothers who expressed their deep gratitude. The entire community turned out to show how appreciative they were of our efforts.

Despite the exhaustion, it felt incredibly rewarding to have given back to that little community in such a tangible way. We had made a real difference.

THE DREAM MACHINE

At some point in the evolution of most companies, leadership develops a desire to become a better member of their community. Often, before this point, companies are too small to do much beyond sell their products or services. They don't have the money, the time, or the focus to do anything but grow. Once they have more resources, though, many leaders cast around for the opportunity to do *something*.

That's definitely what happened at Catapult. We reached a point where we wanted to contribute to our community. We started by donating to a couple charities. After a few years, though, this began to feel like just another financial transaction, one that didn't really involve the team at all. So we changed tactics and tried volunteering at Habitat for Humanity. That was more hands-on and something the team could do together. If you've never taken a Saturday to help build someone a home, I highly recommend it. It was a rewarding experience.

Since that went so well, we looked for more ways to give back. We adopted a highway, cleaning up trash on the side of the road. We organized a 5K race and used the proceeds to sponsor the oldest theaters in Texas, the Paramount and State Theatres. Because it was for the arts, everyone ran it in costume.

We also instituted a policy allowing every employee to take one day a year off to volunteer for an organization of their choosing, and we encouraged team members to coordinate and take that time together.

All of these activities had merit. They were all for a good cause, and they all brought the team together. Still, we felt something was missing, we just couldn't quite say what. Then, in between presentations at a Verne Harnish Scaling Up conference, John Ratliff, the CEO of Appletree Answers, shared with us how his company gave back. Essentially, he'd adapted the Make-a-Wish® foundation for his company.

The executive team and I looked at each other and immediately said, "We have to do something like this."

We came up with the Catapult Dream Machine. The rules were simple: any Catapult employee could submit a "dream" for themselves, a family member, or a fellow employee. There were no restrictions on the type of dream they could submit, although the focus needed to be outside standard workplace desires. This wasn't a place to ask for a promotion or a raise. Otherwise, all dreams were welcome. Our executive team reviewed each dream request and decided whether or not to grant it.

The day after we launched the program, we got our very first dream request. It came from one of our San Antonio employees. His wife had been deployed overseas with the Air Force for almost a year and was coming home in a couple of weeks. They had a two-year-old daughter, whom she hadn't seen in over a year. His request was that some of his San Antonio colleagues be given the time off to come to the airport with him. He wanted to have a big crowd there to welcome her home.

We decided we could do better than that. Several dozen employees from both our Austin and San Antonio offices were there with him that day, as requested, but we also had a huge "welcome home" banner printed by BuildASign.com. We weren't done either. After a year apart, we thought our employee and his wife might enjoy a few days to get to know one another again before jumping back into everyday life. So we hired a limo to pick them up from the airport and take them to a local resort for an all-expenses-paid three-day romantic getaway while the grandparents took care of their daughter.

The dream was a huge success, and the cost of granting it was surprisingly low. BuildASign printed our banner for free. We were able to use points to cover the resort. But the bill wasn't what mattered. The fact that all our employees were there to support one of their own—that was impactful. To say that the whole team was profoundly emotionally touched would be an understatement.

That first dream proved we'd found the right program for our company. And we kept going from there. In the years that followed, we fulfilled many dreams. We flew one of our employees to England to be with her dying mother. We bought an electric scooter for a disabled Marine. When one of our employees told us about the school district where her daughter taught—how few resources they had and how few kids had decent shoes—we bought new shoes for every single kid in that class. The pictures we got in return with the kids holding up those shoes along with some handwritten notes left us speechless.

Some dreams cost money; others just a little time and imagination. But each one meant the world to the whole company. We came together to take care of one another. That was our community. That was our way of truly giving back to the people who mattered to us. And that, in and of itself, was a dream come true.

THIS IS NOT PR

Before moving on, I want to share one last dream with you. It involved the eight-year-old nephew of one of our employees who had been diagnosed with an incurable disease. Despite living in Dallas, he was a diehard Denver Nuggets fan, and our employee's dream was to take him to the next game they played against the Mavericks.

We immediately granted the dream. Unfortunately, though, the Nuggets weren't coming to Dallas that year. Undeterred, we called in a few favors and found someone inside the Nuggets' organization who was willing to help. We flew our employee and his nephew to Denver, where they were picked up in a limo by the Nuggets and taken to the team's private practice. The nephew even got to play a little one-on-one with his idol, Carmelo Anthony.

That evening the Nuggets provided them with floor seats to the game and a signed jersey by Carmelo. They spent the night at a nearby hotel and flew back to Dallas the next morning. The total cost for that dream: $175. But the return on investment was priceless.

It's an incredible story, one that still brings tears to my eyes every time I think about it. It would have been easy to get some positive PR from a story like that. But we never tried to cash in on these priceless dreams. We never used them for marketing. In fact, these stories were never shared outside the company.

Despite being perhaps the most impactful program we ever implemented in Catapult's more than twenty-year history, you never found information about it on our webpage. For a long time, I even hesitated to write about it. The reason is simple: cashing in on doing good undoes much of the positive feeling around the project. Giving back should be authentic—it has to come from a genuine place—that's the only way it has real value for your employees. If you make this about publicity, your employees will see through it.

Of course, we continued to cut checks, build homes with Habitat for Humanity, run our 5K for the local theaters, and give time off for volunteering. All of that was shared with the public, but the Catapult Dream Machine, that was just for us. It was a chance for leadership and employees to come together and do something truly special for *our* community. And it was always meant to remain within that community.

- Companies often start giving back through simple charitable donations. As they grow, these efforts should evolve into more meaningful, team-oriented programs.
- Giving back as a team, rather than through purely financial transactions, creates a stronger sense of community within the company.
- Offer employees a day off to volunteer, either individually or as a group. Coordinated group efforts not only make an impact but also strengthen team bonds.
- If you struggle to find the right programs or causes for your company, create your own ways to give back within the organization.
- True giving must come from a desire to make a difference, not from a desire for recognition. Employees can sense when initiatives are genuine, which makes the impact much more profound and meaningful.

───────── **PRO TIPS** ─────────

- When considering causes, ask yourself: What is different about your company, your team, and your products or your services that would allow you to give back to your community in a unique way?
- Let employees suggest or vote on causes or charity projects. This ensures that giving initiatives resonate with your workforce and helps create personal connections to the projects.

FURTHER READING

The Soul of Money: Reclaiming the Wealth of Our Inner Resources by Lynne Twist

CASE STUDY

BuildASign and the Power of Community Giving

Founded in 2005 by Dan Graham and his three partners, BuildASign started with a simple idea: to provide an online platform for customers to design and order custom signs without needing to visit a print shop. The team, originally formed to provide custom web development, had pitched the idea to over one hundred sign shops across Austin. They were rejected by all of them. Undeterred, they decided to launch an online prototype, driving traffic through Google Ads. After refining their search strategy, the orders began to flow, and BuildASign rapidly expanded, growing from a small startup outsourcing print jobs to a company with its own manufacturing and shipping capabilities.

By 2011, BuildASign had expanded its product offerings to include items like yard signs, car magnets, banners, bumper stickers, and T-shirts. The company now had several hundred employees, many of whom were veterans and military family members. These employees noticed an increasing number of "welcome home" banners being ordered by families of military personnel returning from overseas. Wanting to do something more meaningful for the community than their existing nonprofit discount program, the team decided to offer ten thousand free "welcome home" banners to military families. This initiative was promoted through military spouse blogs and quickly gained momentum, reaching the ten-thousand-banner threshold in just over a week and a half.

Recognizing the impact of the program, Dan and his executive team decided to make it permanent. The initiative became a central part of BuildASign's culture.

Military families often responded with heartfelt thank-you cards, photos, and even challenge coins to show their appreciation. Many families who ordered free banners also became dedicated customers, purchasing additional items like signs and T-shirts. Those additional purchases helped subsidize the program. Some military families even advocated for the company in online forums, defending it against negative reviews and sharing stories of their positive experiences.

A particularly moving element of the program came from BuildASign's veteran employees, who created a special ritual to honor fallen service members. Banner orders were often placed months in advance of the homecoming date. Sadly, a military family would occasionally contact BuildASign to cancel their order after losing a loved one in service. Rather than simply canceling the order, the veteran staff members took it upon themselves to create a personalized memorial banner. They would hand-roll the banner, write a heartfelt message, and send it to the grieving family along with flowers. This act of compassion was done privately, with the veteran employees coming together to ensure each banner was treated with the utmost respect and care. What began as a simple gesture of support for military families had evolved into a deeply personal tradition for BuildASign's veteran team.

By 2017, BuildASign had produced over five hundred thousand free banners for military families, solidifying its reputation as a company that gave back to the community. However, this wasn't just a corporate initiative; it had become a source of pride and purpose for the employees, particularly the veterans, who found a meaningful way to support families in their most difficult moments. This culture of empathy and service continues to define BuildASign's approach to business and community engagement, showcasing the powerful ripple effect that giving back can have on both a company and the people it touches.

Chapter 30

The Compound Effect

DIFFICULTY: 3/5

At some point in the final two weeks of basic training, every Mountain Grenadier platoon goes through a completely unsanctioned, officially prohibited ritual. Each lieutenant is free to design this induction ceremony as he sees fit. For my platoon, I ensured it would be a night my cadets would never forget.

Our ceremony began on the last Tuesday of boot camp. At 1:00 a.m., I stormed into my platoon's barracks, waking them up with the bang of a practice grenade. This sound, like a loud firecracker, would, in the past, have left them completely discombobulated. Indeed, in their first week of training, when we woke them up in the middle of the night, they couldn't help tripping over themselves and struggling into their pants. This time, they were unrattled, jumping to their feet immediately.

I ordered them to put on their work fatigues, bring their harnesses and helmets, and line up outside, where a long climbing rope with preset knots every three feet awaited them. Fastening themselves to the rope, they formed up in single file. We then started running straight up the mountain along an old gravel road, singing cadence songs the entire way. Again, I found their progress striking. The first week, they wouldn't have been able to make it even five minutes doing this. Now, my men weren't even breathing heavily after thirty minutes.

That was enough time to reach our first destination: a gun range, where empty sandbags awaited them. Each man had to fill his sandbag with gravel and carry it on his shoulder up and down a brutal set of stairs for the next sixty minutes. My platoon smiled the entire way.

Next, we ran to a nearby retention pond filled with murky water. Where once they would have hesitated, they all dove in, despite still being tied together. With their fatigues soaked and heavy, they emerged on the other side, and they resumed running up the mountain, still smiling.

After another thirty minutes, we arrived at an old monument dedicated to Grenadiers of the past. For a moment, we all took a knee and bowed our heads. Before they could even fully catch their breath, though, they were back on their feet and running fifteen more minutes to an old bridge over a deep ravine, where my corporals had anchored four ropes. My men instinctively checked each other's harnesses and, without missing a beat, four at a time, leaped backward into the darkness below.

At the bottom of the ravine, they were directed to climb into a pitch-black water drainage pipe and start crawling. Once again, no one hesitated. They crawled on their hands and knees for more than two hundred yards, until they reached an underground water tank made of thick concrete walls that we had illuminated with a few flashlights.

When the last man arrived, we started the final phase of our induction ceremony. Behind me, my corporals held our platoon flag. The first recruit stepped forward, saluted me with a crisp hand motion and introduced himself as "Cadet Dafflon." I saluted back and then struck him across the face with my open hand as hard as I could. His head snapped back but returned immediately to its rigid position, his unflinching eyes locked on mine. I extended a "brother's handshake," responding with his new title: "Grenadier Dafflon." We repeated this until every cadet had been inducted into the brotherhood of Mountain Grenadiers.

As their lieutenant, I couldn't have been prouder. We had started with thirty-nine recruits in my platoon five months earlier; of the twenty-seven who remained, all made it through the ritual. These young boys, fresh out of high school, had become hardened men. Their hands were leathered from gun grease, their feet calloused from countless blisters, and each had developed an intense, focused gaze in their eyes. They were soldiers now, and I would not hesitate to go into battle with any one of them.

This transformation didn't happen overnight. It was the result of incremental, deliberate training. Each week, the challenges grew. Every march was longer, every pack heavier, and every obstacle more demanding. Every combat skill they learned, from marksmanship and map reading to hand-to-hand combat and situational decision-making, was meticulously layered, one on top of the other. These skills interconnected and reinforced one another, ensuring that each enhanced the effectiveness of the others.

The compounding nature of that training resulted in the well-rounded and proficient warriors I greeted that night as brothers in arms. We capped the night by filling our muddy, sweaty helmets with beer and drinking, singing, and hugging each other like Vikings celebrating a victory until the sun rose.

THE OVERNIGHT MYTH

I hate the term "overnight success." The only concept I hate more is the idea that entrepreneurs get "lucky" when things go their way. In my experience, there is no such thing as an overnight success or luck. There is only opportunity. Some companies are disciplined and prepared enough to take advantage of it, while others have to sit on the sidelines and watch the opportunity pass them by.

The thesis of this book is that the discipline and preparation required to take advantage of the right moment are forged in a company's daily habits, decisions, and actions, however small they might appear on the surface. The way you set up your employee onboarding, the structure of your organization, the quality of your checklists and communication with frontline workers: all those little things add up over time and allow you to build momentum. If you keep doing the right little things long enough, then that momentum can reach critical velocity, and you become an "overnight success."

In his book *The Compound Effect*, Darren Hardy defines the concept he titled his book after as "the principle of reaping huge rewards from a series of small, smart choices." Most of us understand this principle on a financial level. The obvious example is how we save and the power of compound interest.

Hardy suggests that the same principle applies to every aspect of our lives, including our health and relationships. For example, taking the stairs each day will have little or no impact on your overall health tomorrow, next month, or even next year. But compounded over several years, those stairs can have a profoundly positive impact on your health. As Hardy explains, "Even though the results are massive, the steps, in the moment, don't feel significant."

I believe this same compound effect applies to running a business. In fact, the compound effect is central to getting the heavy-metal flywheel that Jim Collins describes in *Good to Great* spinning for you. Collins describes how pushing the flywheel takes great effort in the beginning, but once you achieve sufficient momentum, it starts working in your favor. As Collins puts it, "You're pushing no harder than during the first rotation, but the flywheel goes faster and faster. Each turn of the flywheel builds upon work done earlier, compounding your investment of effort."

To achieve that momentum, little improvements in process and execution make it ever easier to keep pushing until the wheel really gets moving.

Unfortunately, the compound effect applies to your bad habits as well. Hardy references the habit of eating fast food once a week, which produces no immediate consequences, but may potentially have a huge impact down the road. In business, the lack of a well-structured company calendar, poor meeting structure and cadence, a lack of measurable goals or an unfair advantage: all of these little things slow down your momentum over time until it takes monumental effort to get that flywheel spinning again.

COMPOUNDING BUSINESS SUCCESS

No single idea in this book is going to transform your business overnight. In the twenty-nine chapters before this one, I've presented plenty of advice on execution, but none of it is going to immediately take you to the top of your industry. There are no golden tickets here. The day after you codify your best practices or institute better training programs, your business might run a little better—if you squint—but it won't magically revolutionize the entire organization.

However, if you implement any of these ideas and give it time, it will eventually produce a measurable positive impact. And if you add another, you'll see even more impact.

To quote James Clear in *Atomic Habits*:

Too often, we convince ourselves that massive success requires massive action. Whether it is losing weight, building a business, writing a book, winning a championship, or achieving any other goal, we put pressure on ourselves to make some earth-shattering improvement that everyone will talk about. Meanwhile, improving by 1 percent isn't particularly notable—sometimes it isn't even noticeable—but it can be far more meaningful, especially in the long run. The difference a tiny improvement can make over time is astounding. (Page 15)

The key to making significant progress in your execution, then, is patience. It takes time for each change to show its full value. And it takes time to fully implement each concept. You can't integrate every idea in this book all at once. If you love all the recommendations you've read, you can't just go in tomorrow and rewrite every policy. You have to choose a few suggestions—no more than four or five—and focus on those *across an entire year*. Half-hearted or rushed implementation isn't going to lead to the results you're looking for. Each change should be a priority that you integrate and track over several months.

That means you have to use some discretion here. Choose the ideas you feel will make the most impact on your organization and concentrate on those first. Ideally, you want a variety of difficulty ratings in each set of priorities. Bundling a few relatively easy changes with a few complex tasks can earn you some quick wins and allow you to focus on the truly difficult stuff.

Remember, the military can't turn anyone into a special forces soldier in a week. It requires deliberately designed programs that incrementally build on each new skill to slowly turn a civilian into an elite fighter.

The same is true for your business. Let the compound effect work for you, and with a little patience, you can build a company that will stand the test of time.

KEY TAKEAWAYS

- "Overnight success" is a myth. Businesses that appear to succeed overnight are usually built on a foundation of disciplined habits, processes, and consistent efforts that compound over time.
- The recipe for growth is small, deliberate actions that build upon each other over time.
- The positive effects of change take time to become evident. Implementing business improvements requires patience, careful prioritization, and a long-term commitment to allow changes to compound into significant results.
- Just as positive habits can build momentum, negative habits, like disorganized meetings or poor organizational structure, can have a devastating impact over time.

- Choose a few ideas from this book at a time and concentrate on implementing them over a year. This allows for thorough, well-executed changes that are more likely to have a lasting positive impact.

PRO TIPS

- Each idea you implement from this book at your company needs a budget and an executive sponsor to be successful.
- Measure the impact of implemented changes over several months to gauge effectiveness.

FURTHER READING

Atomic Habits: An Easy & Proven Way to Build Good Habits & Break Bad Ones by James Clear

Good to Great: Why Some Companies Make the Leap and Others Don't by Jim Collins

The Compound Effect: Jumpstart Your Income, Your Life, Your Success by Darren Hardy

CASE STUDY

Amy Jo Martin and the Compounding Power of Your Personal Brand

After successfully exiting Digital Royalty—her first company, which was dedicated to establishing and monetizing personal brands online—Amy Jo Martin often found herself approached by individuals eager to learn how she built not only her own brand but also some of the world's most humanized corporate brands. Hesitant to become a consultant, Amy decided to try a different approach: she organized a two-day workshop for a small group of ten individuals. This experiment was intended to test whether she would enjoy coaching others in a more structured environment—and she did. The overwhelmingly positive feedback from her initial group led her to launch Renegade Global in 2021, which teaches individuals how to amplify and leverage their thought leadership through technology, storytelling, and personal branding.

At Renegade Global, Amy teaches her clients, known as "renegades," how to harness the power of personal branding in the digital age. Amy's approach centers around three core reasons for building a personal brand. First, she emphasizes that "humans connect with humans, not logos." By creating an authentic personal brand, individuals can foster genuine relationships that ultimately lead to business opportunities. Second, she highlights the value of scalability—an online presence works tirelessly even when you are not physically present, allowing you to extend your influence far beyond the limits of a single day. Third, she underlines that investing in one's personal brand is an investment in oneself—an investment that grows, compounds, and remains transferable across all stages of one's career or personal journey.

Amy's journey with Renegade Global is rooted in the concept of the compound effect—the idea that small, consistent actions can accumulate into significant, transformative results over time. She encourages her students to distribute content across various platforms and in a multitude of ways, knowing that the longevity of each piece of content can lead to compounding returns. Each blog post, video, or article can work as an advocate for an individual's brand, compounding in value as it reaches more people. By being deliberate about the value they deliver and consistent in their messaging, Amy's renegades are equipped to harness the power of compounding to grow their brands exponentially.

A central part of Amy's strategy is the importance of consistency. She stresses to her students that building a personal brand is not a one-time effort but a series of continuous, small actions that ultimately build powerful momentum. She often shares her own experience of documenting her journey—day after day, for seventeen years. This relentless consistency allowed her to foster relationships and build an audience that eventually unlocked opportunities she could never have foreseen. Like compounding interest in finance, each meaningful connection or piece of shared content adds to an individual's brand equity, which ultimately pays dividends in the form of career opportunities, partnerships, and influence.

By focusing on authentic connection, consistent effort, and long-term value, Amy has transformed a simple idea into a movement that helps others unlock their own potential. Amy's story is a testament to how the compound effect, when applied with intention and authenticity, can create a brand—and a life—that grows exponentially, reaching new heights and helping others do the same.

Conclusion

I generally skip the conclusions of the business books I read. So I made a point of putting all of my best ideas into the book itself.

All I really have left to say is that I'm grateful you've made it all the way to the end. I hope these ideas prove useful to you in your business.

Remember, this book is designed to allow you to dive in anywhere at any time. Whether you've read it straight through or jumped in only for the chapters that immediately interested you, the book is designed to be read and reread in any order. Feel free to come back for that one big idea you need or even just skip to the Key Takeaways and Pro Tips to remind yourself of what we've covered. Ultimately, this is meant to be an easy (and hopefully enjoyable) resource for you for years to come.

All that's left to do, then, is to get to work. Read what you need, implement what will make a difference, and execute across your organization. These ideas have been central in making the Swiss Mountain Grenadiers into the elite military force it is today. I've lived by them in the Grenadiers, in business, and in life.

For that reason, I'm confident they can transform your business and have your organization running like clockwork.

SamGoodner.com

Catapult's Golden Rules of Customer Service

Below, I've included all sixty golden rules we shared with new hires at Catapult.

THE BASICS

1. We sell a service, not a product. Products are tangible; they can be touched, tested, and returned if necessary; they have features and benefits. Services do not. While we seek to produce tangible deliverables through our services, what we are really selling is a "promise" and a "relationship." This requires an impartment of trust from the client.

2. Our services are used to provide solutions to our clients. We want to be remembered by the solutions that we make possible.

3. We expect everyone at Catapult Systems to make critical business decisions without having to ask for management approval. If you have an idea to improve a work process or need to make an on-the-spot decision, ask yourself:

A. Is it right for the customer?

B. Is it right for Catapult Systems?

C. Is it ethical?

D. Is it in line with Catapult's Core Values?

E. Are you willing to be held personally accountable for your decision?

If the answer to all five questions is "yes," don't ask, just do it.

4. When in doubt, always fall back on our Core Values:

ACCOUNTABILITY

Accept responsibility and ownership. Do what you say you're going to do.

PASSION

Love what you do. Show enthusiasm in the work you do.

INITIATIVE

Be proactive. Make it happen. Innovate.

TEAMWORK

Work together. Assist others. Share information.

AGILITY

Adapt and respond quickly. Embrace change.

FUN

Maintain a positive attitude. Contribute to a fun work environment.

5. Our minimum standards of professional conduct at Catapult Systems are:

A. Show up on time.

B. Say "please" and "thank you."

C. Do what you say you're going to do.

D. Finish what you start.

6. Companies are not our clients. People in companies are our clients.

7. Clients are nervous. They may not have done anything similar to what they're doing with us. They have committed to an expensive proposition, and their own personal or professional success may be on the line. It's your responsibility to make them feel at ease.

8. Clients retain us to help them reach their objectives not solely because of our technical prowess but also because they expect us to be in the same boat with them. Act as a partner, not as a contractor.

9. There is no school for clients to learn how to act as clients, whereas we are trained professionals in what we do. It's our job to make the client-consultant relationship work, not the other way around.

10. With projects, the process is as important, if not more important, than the results.

11. Clients who are treated well will overlook minor errors or short-comings on the part of service providers. Those who are not treated well will accept no errors. They will, in fact, hunt for errors to find fault with you or your work.

12. Surprises are for Valentine's Day. If there is one thing our clients hate, it's being surprised. Share all you know about the present and future with your client, both good news and especially bad news. There is practically no bad news that a project cannot recover from other than surprising bad news.

13. IT consultants' costs appear extremely expensive, so act expensive. Do not waste time. Do not nickel and dime your client. Dress in a style commensurate to your billing rate and appropriate to the environment.

14. We do not usually compete for business with other consulting firms. Most of the time we compete with our client's ability to do the job themselves.

15. As professional consultants, it is assumed, actually expected, that we are familiar with our client's business, their challenges, their industry, where the project fits within their overall plans, and our role in the project. The last thing you want to ask your client during your first visit is: "What would you like me to do?" Always show confidence. Remember you have the whole Catapult team behind you if you need help.

16. When stuck, always ask for help.

17. True negotiating is finding a successful outcome for both sides. Trying to persuade or convince the client that your position is the "only one" that makes sense is a losing proposition.

18. Every interaction you have with someone has two consequences: the issue at hand and your relationship with that person. As a result, you must always ask yourself: "Where did I come out on the issue, and what did I just do to my relationship with that person?" Winning only one of these is completely useless; you've got to learn to win on both.

19. The three pillars of influence for consultants are Likeability, Explanation, and Trust. If they dislike you, if you don't explain things in ways they can understand, or if they don't trust you, then your chances of success are greatly reduced.

20. Trust has to be earned. You always start with a zero balance in your "trust account" with a new client. Trust is deposited in small drops and withdrawn in buckets. What's worse, they won't tell you when you've lost their trust, and they don't care what made you do what you did to lose their trust.

21. Don't criticize our competition. They are professionals just like we are. Let them do the negative campaigning. Stick to what you have to offer rather than what the others lack.

22. First impressions count. Your first meeting, the first hours, and the first day are what form the client's first impression of you. Believe it or not, it sticks. Be on your best behavior, dress well, act prepared, and project professionalism in those first encounters.

23. Acquiring additional business while in your current assignment (cross-selling) is a very attractive method of rounding out your project and increasing revenue. A consultant's role in this is critical, as you are closest to the issues your client is facing and can recognize many ways you can serve them that they have not thought of or stated yet.

SMART ESTIMATING

24. Never give an estimate to a client on the spot. The first number out of your mouth, regardless of disclaimers, will be the number they remember forever.

25. Never submit an estimate for work without the underlying assumptions. If it's a verbal statement, start with the assumptions and follow with your estimate. If it's written, make sure the numbers and the assumptions are as close as possible. Regardless of what you're told, an estimate creates a form of commitment.

26. Try to submit estimates as a pair of numbers—an upper and lower estimate. As you find out more about the task you're estimating, the range should become narrower.

27. Estimates should always be for a list of tangible deliverables. These should be things that are clearly identified. Help the client understand that as deliverables change, the price may change as well.

MANAGING EXPECTATIONS

28. We're in the business of managing customer expectations.

29. The client's perception of reality is reality. No matter how successful we may think a project is, if the client doesn't think it's successful, then it's not.

30. The most effective way to meet expectations is to understand them and then to (1) act so you can satisfy them or (2) reset them to ensure the ultimate success of your project.

31. We have a tendency to blame others for setting expectations too high. Could it be you who set those expectations by what you said or did or the way you said it? Avoid making statements in which you unintentionally commit others or that are too broad (allowing the client to interpret them in many different ways). And it's always better to underpromise and overdeliver.

32. The key to resetting expectations is communicating that what you plan to deliver (or the way in which you will be delivering it) will meet their real needs, even if different from their stated wishes.

The key point to make is that you will still get them to the target, but over a different route.

GETTING REQUIREMENTS

33. The last words of a failed consultant are, "They never said they needed that!" It's not the client's job to tell us what they want or what they need; it's our job to help them define what they need.

34. Searching for requirements is like trawling: cast a wide net, collect as much information as possible, and use what's of value. Do not limit yourself to using one technique alone, such as interviewing. Collect data, watch business processes at work, talk to users.

35. Good listening takes effort. It's more than eye contact, nodding your head, and asking follow-up questions. It takes allowing for silences. It takes courage to listen as though we're trying to memorize what's being said, then spending time to think of an answer. Formulating an answer while we're listening—it can't be done.

36. Always end a "conversation" by (1) thanking your client for their time, (2) asking if you can contact them if you have any further questions, and (3) asking your client if there were questions you should have asked that you did not.

37. When a client asks for a drill bit, what they're really asking for is a hole. Don't look for specifications of the tool; look for a description of the underlying problem.

GETTING WORK DONE

38. The most common cause of decision-making problems in a project is asking the wrong people to decide: those who think they are empowered to make a decision and are later overruled, or those who know they are not empowered and avoid making decisions. Pick your decision-makers carefully and know who they are.

39. A common explanation (a.k.a. excuse) for delays is external dependencies: "But I was expecting it from Joe and never got it."

Experienced consultants know their dependencies and watch them carefully. Don't be afraid to follow up before the due date. Escalate quickly if a reliable commitment cannot be obtained.

40. Known slippage is good. All projects have slippage (delays). The sign of a healthy project is when all delays are known and actions can be taken to remedy them. Projects fail when delays are not known or ignored. So instead of hiding delays in your work (and secretly hoping to catch up), let your project manager, your team members, and your client know. Slack is built into every one of our efforts, but it should not be wasted.

41. It's not how you fail but how you recover. We all make mistakes. Clients judge us by how we handle the error. The key is avoiding excuses and finger-pointing. Instead, concentrate on how to make it right.

42. The best way to share bad news with your client is to present it along with a plan of attack to remedy the situation. Never give bad news without a plan.

43. We should not judge the significance of a problem by the level of intervention it requires from us. What you may think is a minor technical problem may be what bothers your clients most.

44. Your time is their money—don't waste it. Making travel arrangements, negotiating your next assignment, reserving seats for your own training, and managing your investments are not billable activities. That is not where our clients want to spend their money. There are reasonable exceptions for missing work on a project: medical or family emergencies or a true emergency at a prior client—both of which need to be communicated to the client promptly.

MANAGING YOUR SCOPE OF WORK

45. You cannot manage what you can't specify. One key to managing scope is knowing what your scope of work is. This is not an area to go on gut feelings or assumptions. Look for documented sources

of scope definition: the RFP, the contract, the project plan, your deliverables list, and so on. If you can't find it, develop a draft on your own and get your client's approval.

46. Better than simply knowing your scope, try to get at the rationale behind it: the business challenges you're trying to solve, the thinking behind your scope, and the measures of success.

47. Scope changes can come from any direction: from your client, from your project manager, from you team members, and even from yourself, as in when you decide on your own that a certain approach would be "better" or an added feature would be "cool." So keep an eye out in all directions.

48. The slow but steady increase in the budget in "small" amounts is similar to how our scope of work increases unless it's managed. Even the smallest scope changes should be acknowledged. The larger ones should be documented and approved, the smaller ones less so, and the smallest ones recorded and filed, but not formally.

49. It's not a scope change until all parties agree.

50. Think—is it really scope change or just an inconvenience? Can I justify my position if I have to? What's the basis? A document? Meeting notes? Or just an assumption on my part?

51. Significant scope change attempts can't be resolved on the spot. Acknowledge the attempt by working up a response that includes a clear description of the change, suggested alternatives, the impact on the schedule and/or cost of the project, the associated risks, and a clearly defined path for the evaluation and approval of the alternatives.

52. Not all scope changes are bad. If it makes sense for the client's business, does not derail your project, and your client is willing to accept changes in timing or compensation, what's to complain about? Remember, some scope increases are a sign of the client's trust in us and a source of additional business.

53. The best way to keep people from changing their minds is not to wait until the change occurs but to get them to agree to the implications of making a change before they make the original

decision. Airlines do it by warning you of penalties when you change the dates on an advance purchase ticket. You could tell your client that the decision they are about to make will commit you and your team members to perform something that will be wasted if they change their mind. Remember to relate change to the agreed upon deliverables.

DEVELOPING CLIENT RELATIONSHIPS

54. The key to good communication with clients is to have frequent contact, preferably face-to-face and one-on-one. Artificial communications such as email, voicemail, and PowerPoint presentations are not nearly as effective. "Face time" requires considerable effort, but it's the most effective way to understand each other. And when one understands, one listens, adapts, and becomes a partner.

55. Whether you like it or not, life is a popularity contest. Be professional, but more importantly, be personable. Clients want to work with people they like.

56. One way to improve work relationships is to strengthen your personal relationships. This means getting to know your counterpart's personal history, their interests, their family, their hobbies or pets, and letting them see into your life so you both understand each other's concerns and preoccupations.

57. Time spent in personal exchanges with client counterparts is rarely a waste of time, whether it's just prior to or after a meeting, an informal drop-in, lunch, or dinner. The cost in time or money is miniscule compared to the benefits gained. Do not, however, take this as freedom to toss your professionalism aside.

58. It's not practical, in fact it's sometimes impossible, to have "face time" when you are at a physical distance from your client, such as when you're working offsite. One way to make up for that (serious) disadvantage is to create opportunities to meet with your client. If that's not possible, check in by phone as often as you can without seeming nosy.

59. Politics in the workplace? We are consultants, advisors, and problem solvers but not in the corporate politics arena. There is not much you can do to remove or avoid the politicking. Do not take sides. Work only with facts.
60. Humor does have a place in your relationship with clients if used properly and if the client appreciates it. Pick the subject matter and timing carefully. Avoid risky subjects like politics, religion, and your former clients.

Appendix 2

Recommended Reading

Blanchard, Ken, and Spencer Johnson. *The One Minute Manager.* William Morrow, 2015.

Buckingham, Marcus, and Curt Coffman. *First, Break All the Rules: What the World's Greatest Managers Do Differently.* Gallup Press, 1999.

Clear, James. *Atomic Habits: An Easy & Proven Way to Build Good Habits & Break Bad Ones.* Avery, 2018.

Collins, Jim. *Good to Great: Why Some Companies Make the Leap and Others Don't.* Harper Business, 2001.

Collins, Jim, and Jerry I. Porras. "Building Your Company's Vision." *Harvard Business Review,* September–October 1996. https://hbr.org/1996/09/building-your-companys-vision.

Collins, Jim, and Jerry I. Porras. *Built to Last: Successful Habits of Visionary Companies.* Harper Business, 1994.

Daly, Jack. *Hyper Sales Growth: Street-Proven Systems & Processes. How to Grow Quickly & Profitably*. Forbes Books, 2014.

Daly, Jack, and Dan Larson. *The Sales Playbook for Hyper Sales Growth*. Advantage Media Group, 2016.

Daniels, Aubrey C. *Bringing Out the Best in People: How to Apply the Astonishing Power of Positive Reinforcement*. McGraw Hill, 2016.

Doerr, John. *Measure What Matters: How Google, Bono, and the Gates Foundation Rock the World with OKRs*. Portfolio, 2018.

Ferrazzi, Keith. *Never Eat Alone: And Other Secrets to Success, One Relationship at a Time*. Crown Business, 2005.

Gawande, Atul. *The Checklist Manifesto: How to Get Things Right*. Metropolitan Books, 2011.

Gladwell, Malcolm. *Blink: The Power of Thinking without Thinking*. Back Bay Books, 2007.

Hamel, Gary, and Michele Zanini. *Humanocracy: Creating Organizations as Amazing as the People Inside Them*. Harvard Business Review Press, 2020.

Hardy, Darren. *The Compound Effect: Jumpstart Your Income, Your Life, Your Success*. Balance, 2020.

Harnish, Verne. *Scaling Up: How a Few Companies Make It…and Why the Rest Don't*. Gazelles, Inc., 2014.

Harnish, Verne. *Start to Scale: Secrets to Starting and Scaling Any Size Organization*. Forbes Books, 2024.

Lovett, Ron. *Outrageous Empowerment: The Incredible Story of Giving Employees Their Brains Back.* Advantage Media Group, 2018.

Mauborgne, Renée, and W. Chan Kim. *Blue Ocean Strategy: How to Create Uncontested Market Space and Make Competition Irrelevant.* Harvard Business Review Press, 2005.

Moore, Geoffrey A. *Crossing the Chasm: Marketing and Selling Disruptive Products to Mainstream Customers.* Harper Business, 2014.

Murphy, James D. *Flawless Execution: Use the Techniques and Systems of America's Fighter Pilots to Perform at Your Peak and Win the Battles of the Business World.* Harper Business, 2006.

Osterwalder, Alexander, and Yves Pigneur. *Business Model Generation: A Handbook for Visionaries, Game Changers, and Challengers.* John Wiley and Sons, 2010.

Ries, Eric. *The Lean Startup: How Today's Entrepreneurs Use Continuous Innovation to Create Radically Successful Businesses.* Crown Currency, 2011.

Rumelt, Richard. *Good Strategy, Bad Strategy: The Difference and Why It Matters.* Crown Currency, 2011.

Smart, Brad, and Chris Mursau. *Foolproof Hiring: Powerful, Proven Keys to Hiring HIGH Performers.* Forbes Books, 2023.

Smart, Brad, and Geoff Smart. *Topgrading: How to Hire, Coach and Keep A Players.* Pritchett LP, 2005.

Smart, Geoff, and Randy Street. *Who: The A Method for Hiring*. Ballantine Books, 2008.

Stewart, Thomas A. "How to Think with Your Gut: How the Geniuses behind the Osbournes, the Mini, Federal Express, and Starbucks Followed Their Instincts and Reached Success." *Business 2.0*, November 2002. http://www.marketfocusing.com/b20_1.html.

Twist, Lynne. *The Soul of Money: Reclaiming the Wealth of Our Inner Resources*. W. W. Norton & Company, 2006.

Case Study Index

- Chapter 1. Randy Cohen—TicketCity
- Chapter 2. Doug Harrison—Scooter Store
- Chapter 3. Stephen Shang—Falcon Storage
- Chapter 4. Clayton Christopher—Deep Eddy
- Chapter 5. Caroline Goodner—OrganiCare
- Chapter 6. Tom Rhodes—Sente Mortgage
- Chapter 7. Tom Moran—Addison Group
- Chapter 8. Holly Turner—Stampede America
- Chapter 9. Rob Lynch—Oliva Gibbs LLP
- Chapter 10. Todd Bartee—Aquasana
- Chapter 11. Julio Torres—Tordec
- Chapter 12. Jeff Everage—Trident Proposal Management
- Chapter 13. Cyrill Eltschinger—I.T. UNITED
- Chapter 14. Randy Murphy—Mama Fu's
- Chapter 15. Zeynep Young—Double Line Partners
- Chapter 16. Willo Crenshaw—Austin Outhouse and The Modern Group
- Chapter 17. Rebecca Wayland—Trident Proposal Management
- Chapter 18. David Kirchhoff—WeightWatchers.com Inc.

Appendix 4

Reading Guide

LEVELS OF DIFFICULTY

1. **Easiest**—you implement this principle in your company within **1–4 weeks**.
2. **Easy**—you can implement this principle within **1–3 months**.
3. **Moderately Difficult**—it should take you no more than **3–6 months** to implement this principle.
4. **Difficult**—it will take you **6–12 months** to implement this principle.
5. **Most Difficult**—it will probably take you **12–18 months** to fully implement this principle.

RECOMMENDED CHAPTERS TO READ BASED ON YOUR CURRENT BUSINESS CHALLENGE(S)

BUSINESS CHALLENGE	CHAPTERS
High Employee Turnover Struggling to retain top talent and reduce costly turnover.	1, 2, 3, 13, 16, 17, 18, 20, 27, 29
Lack of Employee Engagement Employees lack motivation, commitment, or alignment with company goals.	2, 3, 4, 9, 12, 13, 16, 18, 20, 27
Delivery or Quality Issues Inconsistent product or service delivery and quality standards are damaging customer trust and satisfaction.	4, 8, 9, 10, 11, 12, 13, 15, 23
Plateaued Growth The company has stopped growing despite efforts to expand.	5, 10, 12, 14, 18, 21, 24, 28, 30
Sales Challenges Struggling to close deals, meet quotas, or grow revenue streams.	4, 7, 10, 13, 19, 25, 26
Poor Communication Across the Company Inefficient communication leading to misunderstandings and poor collaboration.	8, 12, 20, 21
Accountability Gaps Team members are not taking ownership or responsibility for their roles.	8, 9, 13, 21, 27
Lack of Innovation The company struggles to innovate and stay ahead of competitors.	5, 18, 24, 28
Weak Company Culture Difficulty creating a cohesive, value-driven workplace culture.	1, 2, 3, 7, 14, 16, 17, 20, 29, 30
Unclear Business Strategy A lack of clear direction in the company's overall strategy.	5, 6, 22, 24, 28
Struggling with Change Management Difficulty implementing changes and getting team buy-in for new initiatives.	9, 18, 20, 21
Underperforming Financially The business is struggling to meet financial targets and has shrinking profit margins.	4, 5, 9, 12, 15, 23

BUSINESS CHALLENGE	CHAPTERS
Lack of Team Alignment	2, 3, 8, 9, 10, 13, 20, 22
Teams are not aligned with the company's vision, goals, or priorities.	
Overreliance on Key Individuals	7, 12, 27
Certain team members are overly critical to operations, causing risks if they leave.	
Overcoming Founder Dependency	4, 8, 12, 23, 27
The business is too reliant on the founder or senior leadership for day-to-day operations.	
Everything Is Going Well	6
Everything is running smoothly, employee morale is high, and the business is doing great financially.	

About the Author

SAM GOODNER is a serial entrepreneur, angel investor, and mentor with a passion for solving business problems through the innovative use of technology. A dual citizen of Switzerland and the United States, Sam has experienced a diverse journey from serving as a mountain infantry officer in the Swiss Army to being recognized as an *Inc.* 500 CEO and Ernst & Young Entrepreneur of the Year.

In 1993, Sam founded Catapult Systems, which grew into the world's leading Microsoft Systems Integrator before being acquired in 2013. During this same period, he also founded and sold two software product companies (PowerDOC and Inquisite), started a mobile application development firm (Mobile Alchemy), and launched a digital agency (Slingrock).

A global traveler and lifelong learner, Sam took his family on a year-long journey around the world in 2014, homeschooling his two children while embracing education and exploration.

In 2016, Sam invested in FlashParking, a small technology startup. As president and later chief strategy officer, he helped guide the company to becoming the largest parking technology company in the world with over $100 million in revenue and a valuation of $1 billion.

Now retired from running companies, Sam focuses on sharing his insights with entrepreneurs and business leaders.

SamGoodner.com